D0844949

DISCARD

GEORGIAN COLLEGE LIBRARY #??

71.45
2501-01

END-TO-END
LEAN
MANAGEMENT

A Guide to
Complete Supply Chain
Improvement

Library Commons
Georgian College
Barrie, ON
L4M 3X9

by Robert J. Trent, Ph.D.

J.ROSS
PUBLISHING

HD38.5 .T738 2008
0134 111 529 613
Trent, Robert J.

End-to-end lean
  management : a guide to
    c2008.

2009 02 23

Copyright ©2008 by Robert J. Trent

ISBN-13: 978-1-932159-92-9

Printed and bound in the U.S.A. Printed on acid-free paper
10987654321

Library of Congress Cataloging-in-Publication Data

Trent, Robert J.
End-to-end lean management: a guide to complete supply chain improvement /
by Robert J. Trent.
  p. cm.
Includes index.
ISBN 978-1-932159-92-9 (hardcover : alk. paper)
  1. Business logistics. I. Title.
  HD38.5.T738 2008

658.7—dc22   2008023458

This publication contains information obtained from authentic and highly regarded sources. Reprinted material is used with permission, and sources are indicated. Reasonable effort has been made to publish reliable data and information, but the author and the publisher cannot assume responsibility for the validity of all materials or for the consequences of their use.

All rights reserved. Neither this publication nor any part thereof may be reproduced, stored in a retrieval system, or transmitted in any form or by any means, electronic, mechanical, photocopying, recording or otherwise, without the prior written permission of the publisher.

The copyright owner's consent does not extend to copying for general distribution for promotion, for creating new works, or for resale. Specific permission must be obtained from J. Ross Publishing for such purposes.

Direct all inquiries to J. Ross Publishing, Inc., 5765 N. Andrews Way, Fort Lauderdale, FL 33309.

Phone: (954) 727-9333
Fax: (561) 892-0700
Web: www.jrosspub.com

This book is dedicated to some very special people—

my wife Jan,

my daughter Ellen,

my son Jack,

our daughter-in-law Natalie,

and our new granddaughter Sophia.

CONTENTS

Join a volunteer candle-making group as they apply the theory of constraints to remove bottlenecks, improve flow, and increase productivity by almost 200 percent per hour.

Pick up some valuable lessons from NASCAR pit crews and see how different organizations are applying those lessons.

PREFACE

Too many firms today look for quick and easy solutions when they search for cost savings and performance improvements. It seems that hardly a day goes by when there is not an announcement that some company is cutting thousands of jobs through downsizing, a process that moves right to an end state without really understanding how to get there. Or how about the companies that beat their suppliers up year after year for ever lower purchase prices, a noncooperative cost-management technique that can eventually lead to a supplier's demise? One only has to look to the U.S. auto industry to see this approach in action.

It is also hard to ignore the mad stampede to China and other parts of Asia as companies continuously search for lower price goods. Unfortunately, longer supply chains that make planning difficult, along with congested ports, airports, and roads, combined with some well-publicized quality lapses that can tarnish a brand in the blink of an eye raise questions about whether there might be a better way to manage a business. Respected lean experts have commented that much of what companies do to improve today is closer to mean than lean. The way that many firms perform cost cutting today is far different than actually removing waste from a supply chain. Cost cutting and lean are not interchangeable concepts.

Each of these conditions—downsizing, forcing suppliers to provide continuous price reductions, and outsourcing to China—has something in common. They usually do not remove any real waste from the supply chain, and, in fact, they are often temporary measures. These approaches simply cover waste with coercive behavior, ridiculously low labor costs that will change over time, or artificially maintained currency values. *Business Week* recently reported that over half the international companies responding to a survey conducted by the American Chamber of Commerce in Shanghai and Booz Allen Hamilton said that China is already losing its allure as a manufacturing hub.[1] Some companies are looking to shift production elsewhere in their continuous quest for lower labor costs.

---

1. "Roadblocks in China," Business Week 4075 (March 17, 2008):8.

WANTED—A BETTER WAY

What we need today, and what some have been saying for some time, is a better and perhaps more permanent way to structure and manage supply chains. For many, that better way can be found in lean. In theory, lean promotes a relentless attack on waste wherever it occurs. Unfortunately, most of what has been published about lean focuses on internal operations, particularly at manufacturing firms. The fact that most firms operate in tightly linked supply chains rather than their own little world has not yet had a major influence on lean research and proponents.

A strict focus on manufacturing firms and internal production is shortsighted, to say the least. Shouldn't every organization, including service providers, government agencies, universities, and hospitals be declaring war on waste? And can't waste present itself anywhere within a supply chain? An analogy here is to say that only manufacturing firms can benefit from a commitment to total quality. Anyone who makes a statement like that should not be taken seriously.

When discussing lean we also tend to get inundated with what the Japanese are doing, particularly Toyota and the Toyota Production System (TPS). Some books about lean are so laden with Japanese words and phrases that some readers might feel they could pass a Japanese proficiency test when they are through reading. Throughout this book the reader will see some references to Japanese terms. However, every attempt is made to avoid making this book a study in the Japanese language or Japanese production techniques. While the roots of lean are arguably in Japan (some maintain the roots of lean date back to Henry Ford and his River Rouge complex south of Detroit), this book will take a broader view of lean than what is typically associated with Japanese industry.

While still recognizing that operations are an integral part of a lean system, this book takes an end-to-end perspective of lean by looking across the entire supply chain. The rationale for this book is that few sources take an end-to-end view, a subject that Chapter 1 will address in more depth. Few, if any sources deal specifically with lean supply, lean transportation, lean operations, and lean distribution. Some will talk in a cursory way about the need to apply lean principles across the supply chain. Others will ignore these topics completely and stick with a narrow, internal perspective that focuses on operations and manufacturing. But is that enough today? In an era when supply chains compete directly against supply chains, hasn't the time come to move the application of lean way beyond our own four walls? It is time for a new lean paradigm.

STRUCTURE OF THE BOOK

This book is divided into two parts. The first seven chapters address the topics that fall under the domain of the lean supply chain. Each chapter will present ways to pursue lean across a specific part of the supply chain, and each approach or technique presented will promote some important lean objectives, including flow, pull, striving for excellence, standardization, simplification, and optimization. Each chapter will also include real-world examples that support the points being made.

Chapter 1 sets the stage by defining the concept of lean as well as its underlying objectives and principles. This chapter also addresses different types of supply chain waste, defines supply chains and supply chain management, and dispels certain myths about lean. The chapter also addresses the important issue of how organizations coordinate, integrate, and align their lean initiatives across the supply chain.

Chapters 2 through 5 systematically move across the supply chain from upstream suppliers through downstream customers. These chapters describe what the various parts of a supply chain must do to support a lean vision. While each chapter presents different ways to support lean, the participants across a supply chain must work together to eliminate waste, in whatever form that waste takes, from their respective areas without conflicting with the efforts of others. Each chapter also includes a model which shows the part of the supply chain that chapter addresses.

Chapter 2 presents lean supply, a topic that appears infrequently during lean discussions. Lean supply is not only about doing business with a set of suppliers that can ship on a just-in-time (JIT) basis. In fact, for various reasons most supply chains do not and should not feature JIT delivery systems. In reality, lean supply is much more than JIT delivery systems with suppliers. This part of lean includes selecting and then developing suppliers that practice lean principles; creating, where feasible, a physical supply network that features fewer suppliers providing more frequent deliveries of smaller quantities; and creating a supply organization that removes redundancy and waste from the supply management process.

Chapter 3 focuses primarily on lean transportation for the inbound side of the supply chain, although transportation occurs all across a supply chain. Featured here is a discussion about transportation deregulation and its effect on lean, along with the key elements, such as returnable containers and closed-loop delivery systems that are part of lean transportation.

Chapter 4 presents the essential elements of lean operations, perhaps the most widely analyzed part of lean. These elements include setup time reductions, facility layout changes, pull systems, uniform loading, level scheduling, and total quality systems. This is usually the place where companies start their lean journey simply because internal operations are the easiest part of the supply chain to manage and control.

Chapter 5 is our final stop along the lean supply chain. This chapter presents ways to ensure that lean distribution channels are an integral part of a lean supply chain. Topics presented here include demand estimation, record integrity, postponement, cross docking, make-to-order production strategies, information technology applications, optimized delivery networks, and network modeling and optimization. It will become evident that there is more to lean distribution than what meets the eye.

Chapter 6 stresses the important role that measurement plays within lean. Included here is a comprehensive set of lean performance measures, including measures that require support from participants across the supply chain. The chapter also addresses the dark side of measurement, a side that can be a major source of supply chain waste. Chapter 7 presents a set of tools and approaches that support lean supply chain initiatives. Some of these approaches, such as kaizen events and value stream mapping, are associated by almost everyone with lean. Other approaches, such as customer and supplier suggestion programs, are not associated with lean nearly as often.

The second part of this book, Chapters 8 through 16, presents a set of comprehensive lean applications. Each application highlights some aspect of lean that was presented in the first seven chapters. The lean application *What Goes Around Comes Around*, for example, expands on the value of returnable containers within a closed-loop transportation system. The application *Going with the Flow* shows the impact that bottlenecks have on productivity. A third application, *Beam Me Up, Scotty*, shows how the use of information technology helps a company manage customer inventory and optimize daily deliveries.

Only some of the applications in Chapters 8 through 16 feature a manufacturing environment; most of the other applications are outside the normal realm of lean. Even the several manufacturing companies featured are pursuing lean in places that are hard to imagine. Using a broad range of settings is done purposely to demonstrate that lean principles can be applied almost anywhere, a belief that permeates this book. Perhaps the title of this book really should be *Lean for Everyone*. The following lean applications make up the second part of this book:

- **Going with the Flow**. Join a volunteer candle-making group as they apply the theory of constraints to remove bottlenecks, improve flow, and increase productivity by almost 200 percent per hour (Chapter 8).
- **Lean Is the Pits**. Pick up some valuable lessons from NASCAR pit crews and see how different organizations are applying those lessons (Chapter 9).

- **What Goes Around Comes Around.** Appreciate how returnable containers in a closed-loop system drive out waste and reduce costs (Chapter 10).
- **Why Push When You Can Pull?** Learn how a packaging facility in a classic push environment moved toward a demand-driven, pull operation (Chapter 11).
- **Why Push When You Can Pull—The Lessons Learned.** Discover why the transformation from a push to pull environment is not always quick and easy (Chapter 12).
- **Lean Takes to the Skies.** Feel the "wow" factor as the world's leading aerospace company takes lean to entirely new levels (Chapter 13).
- **Beam Me Up, Scotty.** See how a leading company relies on remote sensing technology to manage customer inventory and optimize its product delivery network (Chapter 14).
- **Lean Is Electrifying.** Be shocked by what a major electric utility does that no other utility can do—and see the lean benefits that result from that capability (Chapter 15).
- **You're Choking Me.** Understand why a bottlenecked receiving process in a national distribution center is choking the flow of material across an entire distribution network—and what to do about it (Chapter 16).

As a philosophy, lean is extremely robust, which means it can perform without failure under a wide range of conditions. It is this robustness that makes lean so remarkable. Like Total Quality Management, managers can apply lean principles just about anywhere and at anytime. The concept is so much more than a set of tools or techniques, and to think otherwise fails to recognize the significance of this simple word. Let the lean journey begin!

ABOUT THE AUTHOR

Robert Trent is the supply chain management program director and George N. Beckwith professor of management at Lehigh University, where he teaches at the undergraduate and graduate levels. He holds a B.S. degree in materials logistics management from Michigan State University, an M.B.A. degree from Wayne State University, and a Ph.D. degree in purchasing/operations management from Michigan State University.

Prior to his return to academia, Bob worked for Chrysler Corporation. His industrial experience includes assignments in production scheduling, package engineering with responsibility for new part packaging setup and the purchase of nonproductive materials, distribution planning, and operations management at the Boston regional parts distribution center. He has also worked on numerous special projects.

He has authored or coauthored articles appearing in the *International Journal of Purchasing and Materials Management*, the *Journal of Supply Chain Management*, the *International Journal of Physical Distribution and Logistics Management*, *Total Quality Management*, *Supply Chain Management Review*, *Inside Supply Management*, *The Purchasing Handbook*, *Academy of Management Executive*, *Business Horizons*, *Team Performance Management*, *Supply Chain Forum: An International Journal*, and *Sloan Management Review*. His coauthored study on cross-functional sourcing team effectiveness was published through the *Center for Advanced Purchasing Studies* (CAPS) in 1993. A research report on purchasing/sourcing trends was published through CAPS in 1995. He completed a third CAPS project in 1999 that investigated how organizations reduce the effort and transactions required to purchase low value goods and services. A fourth CAPS project on global sourcing was published in 2006. He is also the coauthor of a textbook titled *Purchasing and Supply Chain Management*, now in its third edition. His book, *Strategic Supply Management—Creating the Next Source of Competitive Advantage*, was published in 2007.

Bob is a recipient of a National Association of Purchasing Management (now ISM) research grant for the study of cross-functional sourcing team effectiveness. He has also been awarded the *Class of 1961 Professorship* and the *Eugene Mercy Professorship* at Lehigh University. Bob is also active with the ISM, serving for many years as the Professional Development Director of the NAPM of the Lehigh Valley and, at the national level, as a member of the *ISM Educational Resources Committee*. He and his family reside in Lopatcong, New Jersey. He can be reached at rjt2@lehigh.edu.

Web
Added
Value™

Free value-added materials available from
the Download Resource Center at www.jrosspub.com

At J. Ross Publishing we are committed to providing today's professional with practical, hands-on tools that enhance the learning experience and give readers an opportunity to apply what they have learned. That is why we offer free ancillary materials available for download on this book and all participating Web Added Value™ publications. These online resources may include interactive versions of material that appears in the book or supplemental templates, worksheets, models, plans, case studies, proposals, spreadsheets, and assessment tools, among other things. Whenever you see the WAV™ symbol in any of our publications, it means bonus materials accompany the book and are available from the Web Added Value™ Download Resource Center at www.jrosspub.com.

Downloads for *End-to-End Lean Management: A Guide to Complete Supply Chain Improvement* consist of a presentation covering process modeling for the lean supply chain, a presentation outlining steps to conducting a value-analysis workshop for lean improvement, value stream mapping symbols and descriptions, a creative thinking techniques presentation, a continuum of supply chain relationships model, a group problem-solving aid, and a listing of websites offering free lean resources.

PART I: UNDERSTANDING THE LEAN SUPPLY CHAIN

UNDERSTANDING LEAN

Throughout industrial history few words have become as powerful as the word *lean*. Today almost everyone has heard this word used in some sort of context. Many of us probably have a book or two that explains this very simple word in excruciating detail. But what we may not appreciate is that this word, which at its core deals with the relentless pursuit and removal of waste, is really a powerful *business* philosophy and mindset that can mean the difference between success and failure in today's hypercompetitive world.

The reality of lean is that while most managers likely have a basic understanding of the concept, few organizations have truly achieved lean, partly because the pursuit of lean is a never-ending journey. Furthermore, lean adopters, as well as the research and writing that support the intellectual domain of lean, often focus narrowly on the internal operations of manufacturers. We conveniently ignore the hundreds of thousands of service and nonprofit organizations that just might benefit from the application of lean principles. And the idea that lean is an end-to-end concept where everyone along a supply chain has a role to play also gets lost too frequently in the shuffle.

This chapter begins our journey into the world of the lean supply chain. We begin by defining the concept of lean and presenting some important lean objectives. The second section elaborates on the important topic of waste, the archenemy of lean. The need to view lean from a supply chain perspective appears next, followed by the ongoing debate between some important philosophies. The chapter concludes with some myths and realities surrounding lean.

Table 1.1 Different perspectives of lean

Lean thinking James Womack and Daniel Jones	Lean thinking seeks to eliminate waste, specify value, line up value-creating actions in the best sequence, conduct those activities without interruption whenever someone requests them, and perform them more and more effectively.
Lean John Shook	A philosophy that seeks to shorten the time between the customer order and the shipment to the customer by eliminating waste.
Lean manufacturing www.isixsigma.com dictionary	Initiatives focused on eliminating all waste in manufacturing processes.
Lean John Kerr	Lean is essentially a business discipline that is built around obeying only the customer's demand signals and getting rid of waste everywhere in the supply chain.
Lean Lean Advisors, Inc.	Lean is simply a thought process, not a tool, used to look at your business, whether it is manufacturing, service, or any other activity where you have a supplier and a customer/receiver. The thought processes within lean are identifying waste from the customer perspective and then determining how to eliminate it.
Lean National Institute of Standards and Technology	A systematic approach to identifying and eliminating waste through continuous improvement, flowing the product at the pull of the customer in pursuit of perfection.
Lean Anonymous	Lean is a set of tools to reduce waste, where waste is defined as any nonvalue-added process for which the customer is not willing to pay.

WHAT IS LEAN?

A logical place to begin our discussion involves the definition of lean. Much like Total Quality Management, the perspective taken throughout this book is that lean is a business philosophy rather than a set of tools and techniques. At a very high level lean is the *relentless pursuit of eliminating waste across an extended supply chain.* Over the years many observers have offered their opinion on this topic, which Table 1.1 summarizes. One thing that readers should notice is that most of these viewpoints at least include the subject of waste, something that will be elaborated upon shortly. The reader should also realize that 100 people might give 100 different perspectives of lean.

Most of what we hear about lean is manufacturing oriented, which is not unusual since lean's early pioneers were largely manufacturing firms. Take a look at Table 1.2 to get a feel for how skewed the history of lean is toward manufacturing and production. This table presents the results of Google searches at a specific point in time. The table also presents the number of articles appearing in the ABI/INFORM Global database for the various terms. ABI/INFORM Global is one

Table 1.2 Lean terms search "hits"

Search term	Google results	ABI/INFORM articles
Lean manufacturing	2,500,000	1,455
Lean production	728,000	164
Lean operations	56,400	118
Lean procurement	28,300	6
Lean supply management	16,800	2
Lean purchasing	1,400	1
Lean logistics	31,800	21
Lean transportation	2,140	0
Lean distribution	9,340	11
Lean supply chain	74,800	49

of the most comprehensive databases for scholarly and business publications. At the push of a button this database can retrieve articles from over 1800 worldwide business periodicals. As both searches reveal, most of what is out there is about lean manufacturing or production.

The time has come to take a broader view of lean. The relentless pursuit of waste applies to any organization in any industry—profit or nonprofit, industrial or nonindustrial, service or manufacturing. Furthermore, the domain of activities that fall under the lean umbrella is broad. Virtually any activity that eliminates waste anywhere across the supply chain is a legitimate part of lean.

While the primary objective of lean is a relentless attack on waste, another way to approach the subject is to think about the principles that underlie this philosophy. James Womack and Daniel Jones, two scholars known for their work in lean, maintain that five principles underlie lean thinking: (1) specify value as defined by the ultimate customer; (2) identify the value stream that creates and delivers that value; (3) work to ensure information, materials, and product flow to the customer; (4) respond to demand only when there are clear signals to do so; and (5) relentlessly pursue perfection.

This chapter looks more closely at three of the more recognized principles of lean: flow, pull, and striving for excellence. Moving away from tradition, three other principles are discussed that go a long way toward eliminating waste: optimization, standardization, and simplification.

Keep It Flowing

Few would argue against the notion that better flow across the supply chain is, on balance, a good thing. Flow essentially means keeping the right material continuously moving toward a downstream entity that requires that material. While material flow receives the bulk of the attention, the truth is there are a variety of flows across a supply chain. In addition to material flow, we can have payment flows, information flows, ownerships flows, vehicle and equipment flows, people flows, and reverse logistics flows. There are two important points here: (1) interruption to the flow of any of these areas can be wasteful, and (2) every organization has flows of some kind.

From the perspective of the entire supply chain, it simply makes sense to organize activities so that work flows from step to step in an uninterrupted flow and at a rate that matches the demand pull from the customer.[1] The constant stopping and starting of flows adds little value that customers appreciate. Disruptions also affect supply chain throughput, supply chain capacity, and cycle time. The following examples show that flow is important at some lofty levels.

Improving flow can be a costly objective when a process features structural bottlenecks. Think about the perennial Rodney Dangerfield (i.e., I get no respect) of the transportation world—Amtrak.[2] In its efforts to capitalize on the decline in on-time air travel and rising fuel costs, Amtrak has invested heavily in its Acela high-speed trains to serve the crowded Northeast corridor. Unfortunately, the routes that the trains serve face so many constraints, such as curvy tracks and tracks that are shared with freight and commuter trains, that the trains rarely get to turn on the juice. Compounding these problems are multiple tracks that must squeeze into two tracks before entering a tunnel below the Hudson River. Upgrades costing $625 million for equipment, tracks, signals, and electrical power systems would only reduce the expected travel time between New York and Washington by 15 minutes. Shortening the trip by another 10 minutes would require new tunnels, bridges, and track around New York and Baltimore at an estimated cost of $7 *billion*. Going with the flow can be an expensive proposition.

Continuous flow can also save lives. Emergency hospital room personnel understand the importance of flow supported by efficient communication linkages and planning and staging. (Planning and staging is discussed in Chapter 5.) Paramedics working in ambulances must communicate with emergency room personnel about the status of patients being transported to an emergency room. Emergency room personnel must ensure that a room, medical personnel, and proper equipment and supplies are ready and waiting for incoming patients. Then, emergency room personnel must communicate early and often with operating room personnel if a patient requires emergency surgery. Any delay in the human flow can have tragic consequences.

The need for flow is not only on the ground. Most of us have probably taxied around a tarmac or circled the sky aimlessly as our flight waited its turn to move onto crowded runways or into congested airspace. Too many scheduled flights, especially around holidays, an antiquated and inefficient system for managing U.S. airspace, an increase in private jet travel that further clogs air routes, air traffic control technology that needs updating, labor tensions among air traffic controllers, restrictions about how many planes can take off and land in a particular time, and an occasional dose of bad weather have all combined to create a system that just doesn't flow like it should.[3] In fact, the summer of 2007 was one of the worst on record with less than 70 percent of commercial flights arriving on time. In previous years the summer average hovered closer to 80 percent of flights arriving on time.

The federal route map that planes follow is largely unchanged from the 1950s. Consider the airspace around Washington, D.C., which is one of the worst air bottlenecks in the United States. It is not uncommon there for east-west flights to merge into flight lanes with north-south flights. Furthermore, much of the airspace around this area, as well as north-south routes over the Atlantic Ocean, is assigned to the military, making it off limits to commercial aviation. With so many planes in the sky, and inaccuracies in radar that forces generous spacing between routes and planes, air traffic controllers often lack the flexibility to move planes around to facilitate flow. Any hiccup in the system soon reverberates across the entire network. A flight that has clear weather across its entire route can still get caught up in the clogged arteries in the sky, particularly if air traffic is being diverted into this airspace from areas that are experiencing bad weather. While planes obviously can't stop moving while in the air, their flow pattern often resembles a lazy circle that gently lulls passengers to sleep instead of a fairly straight line between two points.

Why did these three examples feature service providers? This was done purposely to show that lean principles apply to any organization in any industry. A myopic view that lean applies primarily to manufacturers is outdated and extremely boring. Later chapters will present ways to attack the constraints (i.e., the bottlenecks) that limit flow across all kinds of settings.

Pull, Don't Push

A fundamental feature of a lean supply chain is a focus on pull rather than push systems. It is amazing how two simple words, pull versus push, can have such a tremendous impact on how supply chains operate. What, then, is the difference between the two? Pull systems relay information or a signal from a downstream entity, such as a work center or customer, to an upstream operation about what material, part, or service is required, the desired quantity, and where and when something is needed. The concept of pull is integral to lean because no upstream activity or production occurs unless requested by a downstream entity. In a pull system action is taken in direct response to a request rather than in anticipation of a need or request that may never occur. In a push environment action is taken in anticipation of a request.

The reality is that few firms operate in a purely pull environment. Across the supply chain there are usually boundaries that separate push processes from pull processes. A company may have pull systems within their internal operations, for example, but suppliers still build to their own internally-derived forecasts and schedules. Internal production is based on a pull system, but material replenishment with suppliers still occurs on a push basis.

One company that effectively uses pull signals across its supply chain is Eastman Chemical. To maintain a total view of inventory, the company has developed a process called stream inventory management to balance material inflows and finished goods outflows. An information technology system receives all customer orders and then applies algorithms to translate finished-goods requirements into material replenishment requirements. As finished goods move out of the system to satisfy customer orders, the system triggers replenishment requests for raw materials. Customer orders pull raw material replenishment from suppliers. The push/pull boundary here is clearly upstream.

Most pull systems are at the operational level rather than the tactical or strategic level. This means they support *here and now* requirements rather than being overly concerned about what will happen in six months to two years. Pull systems are usually about execution rather than planning. Most supply chains, even those that are considered lean, feature a mix of push and pull planning and execution systems. Chapter 4 addresses pull systems in greater detail.

Make It as Perfect as Possible

The notion that poor quality creates waste should not even be in question. Quality gurus have long argued that any deviation from a desired target or state carries with it an associated loss. Table 1.3 highlights some of the wastes that result from Type I and Type II quality control errors. Type I errors occur when a decision is made to reject something as non-conforming when in fact it should have been accepted, while Type II errors occur when a decision is made to accept something that should have been rejected. In a lean supply chain there simply is little to fall back upon when quality errors occur, making the pursuit of zero defects critical to lean. Striving for excellence is an essential part of a lean supply chain.

Any defects that work their way through a supply chain should be considered a Type II error. The challenge with any quality problem is to identify the root cause of an error, which at times could simply be due to poor measurement, eliminate the root cause, and then prevent future problems from occurring. As Table 1.3 reveals, quality errors have earned their seat at the waste table. Not a single item on this list creates any value that customers appreciate.

Table 1.3 Type I and Type II quality errors and supply chain waste

Supply chain waste from Type I and Type II quality errors

- Searching for quality problems that do not exist
- Delivery delays
- Scheduling delays for subsequent customer orders
- Loss of productivity
- Return logistics cost
- Expediting costs
- Scrap and write-off costs
- Rework costs
- Loss of customer goodwill
- Liabilities and lawsuits
- Brand erosion
- Disruptions to schedules
- Material reordering costs
- Premium transportation costs
- Additional equipment and setup costs to rerun an order
- Performance penalties from customers
- Administrative costs of quality review boards
- Increased inspection and testing costs
- Additional material, packaging, labor, and handling costs
- Human stress
- Interruption to material flow

Those who expect to make lean a major part of their firm's strategic plans are urged to become well versed in the philosophy and techniques of Total Quality Management, a subject that is outside the scope of this book. This means becoming familiar with the work of W. Edwards Deming, Joseph Juran, and Philip Crosby, the three most prominent names in quality management, who are now deceased. The late Philip Crosby, a recognized authority on quality management, included waste in his famous *price of nonconformance* calculation. Joseph Juran was also well aware of the costs of poor quality in his *total cost of quality* calculation, something that Chapter 6 will present in more detail. After reaching a comfort level with these three individuals, feel free to progress to Six Sigma, today's version of Total Quality Management. Never underestimate the interrelationship between lean and Total Quality Management. Lean organizations have committed themselves to the pursuit of perfection.

Optimize across the Supply Chain

Optimization is a topic that is not often presented within lean discussions, which is a mistake. The desire for optimization can be pursued in many areas, and the result of something that is optimized is usually a reduction in waste. To *optimize* is to make something as perfect, effective, or functional as possible. While many observers will equate optimization with reduction, less of something does not have to be the case. The following are some areas that should benefit from optimization:

- Size of the supply base
- Number of transportation carriers
- Design of products and physical processes
- Number, size, and location of distribution, retail, and dealer outlets
- Number of customers within the customer base
- Number of component parts and stockkeeping units
- Number, size, and location of production facilities
- Type of information systems used and their features
- Order delivery network
- Any major process, such as new product development, supplier selection, demand estimation, and customer order fulfillment

Each of these areas should be made as perfect, effective, and functional as possible.

Establish the Standard

Standardization means to conform to something that is established as a model or ideal example (i.e., the standard). Too many firms fail to standardize their common parts, processes, practices, documents, contracts, measurements, policies, and procedures across their business units when opportunities for standardization exist. A failure to standardize usually leads to wasteful duplication of effort that fails to promote best practices. During product design, for example, the extensive use of custom designed components when standard or previously designed components are available can be wasteful.

Let's illustrate the standardization concept with an example that many readers have experienced firsthand. An area where a standardized approach should be in place involves matching lost items with their rightful owners at airports. Each day passengers leave behind thousand of often valuable items at security checkpoints. At the Newark Liberty Airport, for example, more than 1000 items are left behind each month. If not coordinated at a centrally led level, each airport will naturally develop its own internal process for handling these items, a clearly redundant effort. But does it have to be that way?

The Transportation Safety Administration (TSA) at Newark has created a database tracking system designed to reunite passengers with lost belongings.[4] Workers log each call about lost items and then cross-reference that call with the database of lost items. One passenger who was reunited with his $30,000 Rolex watch that he left behind said, "Those people (the TSA staff at Newark) were the most honest and most efficient people I can ever describe." The TSA at Newark airport has also prepared an operating guide that has been distributed to airport customer service managers across the country. This system is so successful that it was recognized as a national model by TSA officials in Washington, D.C. The challenge now becomes one of taking this best-practice system and making it the standard process that other airports will follow. To not make the best system the standard system is wasteful. Why continuously reinvent the wheel?

Make Life Simpler

Simplification, another powerful principle supporting lean, seeks to diminish the scope or complexity of something without diminishing its effectiveness. Two areas that often benefit from simplification include process design and product design. As used throughout this book, a process is a set of interrelated tasks designed to achieve a specific outcome. Virtually any work that is meaningful has a process underlying it. Processes do not relate only to physical production processes.

When simplifying our most important processes, such as customer order fulfillment, supplier evaluation and selection, or new product development, nonvalue-adding and wasteful activities will be targeted for improvement or elimination. Process improvement teams will search for creative new ways to perform necessary tasks, which should logically lead to shorter cycle times and cost reductions. Chapter 7 will present process mapping, value stream mapping, and value analysis as ways to support process improvement and simplification.

Simplification is an especially worthwhile endeavor during product development. When McDonnell Douglas (now part of Boeing) introduced a new version of its F/A-18, the company stated the jet was capable of carrying greater payloads with 33 percent fewer parts than its predecessor. In the late 1990s, Toyota announced that its new Camry was being delivered to showrooms with 25 percent fewer parts than the model it replaced.

Why be concerned with simplifying product designs? A simplified product almost always requires fewer part numbers, resulting in fewer suppliers, fewer material releases, less transportation, less inventory, and lower inventory management costs. Eliminating unnecessary components also reduces a product's cost, which reduces the value of the inventory required to support customer demand and service requirements. It can also be shown mathematically that fewer components support higher product reliability, thereby reducing the cost of poor quality. An objective at the start of any product development project should be to simplify product designs. Simplification is a good friend of lean.

ZEROING IN ON WASTE

At the heart of a lean supply chain is a relentless battle against waste. Broadly speaking, waste is any activity that adds no value from the customer's perspective, or an activity for which the customer would not willingly pay for as part of a product or service package. Waste can lead to three very visible outcomes: too much time to perform an activity or process, too much inventory spread across the supply chain, and costs that are too high compared with best-in-class competitors.

Supply chains consist of three kinds of broad activities: value-adding activities, nonvalue-adding activities, and wasteful activities. A value-added activity is one that transforms material or information into what a customer requests and is willing to pay. The objective here is to constantly improve these activities. A nonvalue-added activity is one that often has to be performed to move or deliver material or information closer to the customer but with no physical *value-add* taking place. Nonvalue-adding activities have received a bad reputation in the lean literature. All supply chains require some level of nonvalue-adding activities to operate. A third set of activities are those that are pure waste, or what the Japanese call *muda*. These activities add neither value nor move material or information closer to the customer.

Confusion sometimes exists regarding the differences between nonvalue-adding activities and waste. In fact, the two terms are often used interchangeably. One way to think about this is to realize that all wasteful activities are nonvalue adding. Waste creates only additional costs, therefore wasteful activities are immediate candidates for elimination. However, the reverse is not entirely true. Nonvalue-adding activities are not necessarily wasteful. In fact, customers are often willing to pay for these activities. Consider the movement of a product or material from one point to another. No change occurs to a product's physical value when moving across a supply chain, yet transportation is required to move a product closer to the *place* where a customer wants that product.

Another example involves machine setups or changeovers. During changeovers no physical value or enhancement takes place. Who would argue, however, against the importance of setups? Without setups nothing gets produced. The challenge here is to identify that portion of the setup that can be improved upon or even eliminated. Supply chain designers should minimize or improve nonvalue-added activities whenever possible. It's hard to imagine a supply chain that does not have some nonvalue-adding activities.

The traditional wastes...

Defects	Increasing the cost of non-conformance through quality errors
Excess inventory	Maintaining excess inventory due to overbuying, overproduction, or poor inventory management
Excessive processing	Performing more tasks or steps than what a process requires
Unnecessary motion	Any wasted motion during movement or processing
Waiting	Sitting idle in anticipation of further value-adding processing
Overproduction	Producing more than current demand requires
Unnecessary transport	Unnecessary material handling and transportation within and between work centers and sites

Plus some more...

Too many bits and bytes	Creating and disseminating unnecessary digital information
Untapped creativity	Failing to utilize human resources to their fullest potential
Poor measurement	Measuring too much, the wrong areas, incorrectly, or promoting unintended behavior
Excessive overhead	Time and cost waste from unnecessary staff
Overdesign	Designing in too many components and product features
Duplication of effort	Developing duplicate processes across similar sites or locations
Poor planning	Failing to align the supply and demand segments of the supply chain

Figure 1.1 Sources of supply chain waste

Types of Waste

If waste is the enemy of lean, it becomes helpful to know what the enemy looks like. Most lean proponents have at least heard of the seven kinds of wastes as articulated by Toyota. While understanding these wastes is important, they reveal a perspective that is internal, production-focused, and clearly from an earlier era. The top half of Figure 1.1 presents these traditional wastes, partly because they are frequently mentioned. They also provide a good set to build upon when broadening our thinking about waste.

To reflect modern thinking this figure includes additional wastes that appear across the supply chain. Digital waste reflects the redundant or unnecessary data that are collected, managed, transmitted, or stored for no tactical or strategic reason.[5] On a personal level, one only has to think about the dozens or even hundreds of emails received daily to appreciate digital waste. While storage space is practically free, the time to wade through hundreds of messages is not.

Duplication of effort refers to the tendency of larger companies to allow each operating location to develop its own internal processes or work methods, even though these locations usually share commonality in the things they do. Does every site have to develop its own process for developing products, selecting suppliers, or conducting quality training? Would it make sense to develop some common processes that build in best practices that are shared across an organization?

Another category of waste involves poor measurement, a category that creates more waste than anyone realizes. Chapter 6 will present some examples of the waste that results when managers and employees try to *make their numbers* without a solid plan to back them up. We can also have too many measures, too few measures, incorrectly calculated measures, and measures that do nothing to promote strategic objectives. Type I and Type II quality errors, for example, are often the result of poor measurement during statistical process control charting.

Unused employee creativity reflects the waste, often in the form of lost opportunities, of not tapping into the creative contributions of employees. Overdesigning reflects the tendency of engineers and marketers to pack products with as many features and as much functionality as possible, even if customers have no particular use for these features.

We could extend the waste list even further. How much overhead waste is spent by managers in insignificant meetings each day? At one university even the simplest of changes must go through six levels of review and approval before they can be implemented. And how much waste does the inefficient use of energy resources create? There is usually no shortage of waste within a business and across supply chains. In reality, the categories of waste presented in Figure 1.1 are likely incomplete.

DEFINING SUPPLY CHAINS AND SUPPLY CHAIN MANAGEMENT

Since the underlying concept of this book involves the need to manage lean across an extended supply chain, it makes sense to describe some important terms. First, a supply chain is a set of three or more organizations linked directly by one or more of the upstream or downstream flows of products, services, finances, and information from a source to a customer. Figure 1.2 presents the extended supply chain model that provides the framework for the first half of this book. In reality, complex firms have many different supply chains that support their operations. Things are rarely as neat as presented here.

If supply chains are our focus, then supply chain management (SCM) becomes an important part of the equation. Anyone who has written about SCM has defined the term one way or another, making confusion about the definition a real possibility. According to the *Supply Chain Research Group*, confusion arises

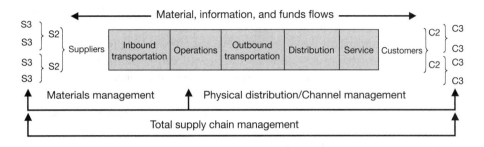

Figure 1.2 Lean extended supply chain

further when trying to define two concepts, SCM as a philosophy and SCM as a set of operational activities, with a single term. Actually, the same point can be said about lean. The confusion only gets worse when we introduce a *supply chain orientation* to the discussion.

A supply chain orientation is a higher-level recognition of the strategic value of managing operational activities and flows across a supply chain. Effective SCM, which requires managers to assume a higher-level recognition of the strategic value of SCM, involves proactively managing the two-way movement and coordination of goods, services, information, and funds (i.e., the flows) from raw material through end user. SCM involves the coordination of a wide range of activities and flows that extend across organizational boundaries. We often describe effective supply chains with words like simplified, coordinated, synchronized, integrated, and lean. While early definitions of SCM focused on the downstream part of the chain, nothing less than an end-to-end perspective will work today.

A large set of activities fall under the SCM umbrella. This is one of the reasons we need to expand our perspective of lean from an internal, operational view to one that encompasses entities and activities up and down the chain. A listing of activities under the supply chain umbrella includes purchasing and material releasing, inbound and outbound transportation, receiving, materials handling, warehousing and distribution, inventory control and management, demand and supply planning, order processing, production planning and scheduling, shipping, processing, and customer service. While the need to perform supply chain-related activities has been present for as long as businesses have existed, it is an organization's willingness and ability to coordinate these activities that is relatively new.

While many activities are part of SCM, an improved perspective visualizes supply chains as comprised of processes rather than discrete activities and tasks. A process consists of a set of interrelated tasks or activities designed to achieve a specific objective or outcome such as new product development, customer-order fulfillment, and supplier evaluation and selection. Supply chain processes are essential to SCM and lean.

To reflect current thinking, we must expand our thinking to include suppliers and customers that reside upstream and downstream from the focal organization. Multiple levels of suppliers and customers form the *extended supply chain* or *extended enterprise* where success is a function of effectively managing a linked group of firms beyond first-level suppliers or customers. The extended enterprise concept recognizes explicitly that competition is increasingly between coordinated supply chains or networks of firms.

Some lean observers will forgo any discussion of supply chains and instead focus on the term *value stream*. Womack and Jones define a value stream as the set of actions required to bring a good or service through three critical management tasks. These tasks include (1) the *problem-solving task* that runs from concept through production launch, (2) the *information management task* that runs from order-taking through delivery, and (3) the *physical transformation task* that proceeds from raw material to a finished product accepted by the end customer.[6] For our purposes the terms supply chain and value stream will essentially mean the same thing. Whatever approach or nomenclature is used (supply chains or value streams), we can't ignore the importance of an end-to-end perspective.

COMPARING THE PHILOSOPHIES

At various times companies are driven by different philosophies, or what some cynics might call the *flavor of the month*. While some of these philosophies last longer than a month, we probably get the idea. Each competing philosophy has its proponents, and purists will debate the technical differences between these philosophies. Lean, the Theory of Constraints (TOC), and Six Sigma frameworks all compete for our attention today. At times these debates almost become comical as the participants work to protect their ideological turfs.

Let's take a deep breath and recognize that while each framework has its own guidelines and proponents, the similarities and overlap between the three are much greater than their differences. The primary objective of Six Sigma is to reduce variability (i.e., inconsistency) within processes while the primary objective of lean is to reduce waste. But doesn't excessive variability in the output of a physical product create quality defects? And who could argue against the conclusion that quality defects cause waste?

A primary focus of TOC is to identify those constraints that cause bottlenecks while lean promotes the flow of goods, services, and information across the supply chain. But won't system constraints, which cause bottlenecks, constrict flow? Addressing system constraints supports better flow, increased throughput, and increased capacity through more efficient utilization of a fixed amount of assets. The lean application titled "Going with the Flow" (Chapter 8) will show how systematically attacking constraints resulted in triple-digit increases in productivity per hour within a candle-making operation.

Each philosophy has its own disciples who sometimes fail to recognize the overlap between these approaches. The position taken throughout this book is that all three philosophies are applicable, and even welcome, within a lean supply chain. They are complementary to each other rather than competitors to each other.

NINE MYTHS ABOUT LEAN

What should we really know about lean? And perhaps more importantly, what are some myths that often surround this concept? The following discussion, while certainly not an exhaustive list, presents some important myths and realities about lean. An important part of understanding lean is separating fact from fiction. Table 1.4 summarizes these myths and realities.

Lean Is about Cutting Costs

To some observers cost cutting is synonymous with lean. Cost reductions, when pursued properly, can remove waste from a supply chain. Lean purists are quick to point out, however, that lean is not about the short-term pursuit of cost savings that characterizes many organizations. Cost reductions achieved by eliminating important tests during product development or using lower-grade materials, for example, may not be supportive of a lean philosophy. A recent article in a respected business publication noted that the cost-cutting efforts at Home Depot, Northwest Airlines, and Dell have been quite costly in terms of lost market share and dissatisfied customers.[7]

Let's look at one cost-cutting measure that almost every U.S. firm has pursued with vigor. Sourcing from China, which can be a legitimate cost-cutting strategy, often delivers short-term unit cost savings. What is the total cost, however, of products that are recalled because they contain lead paint, or the total cost associated with the recall of tens of thousands of tires because the Chinese supplier omitted a key part of the manufacturing process? What waste is removed from a supply chain that is now 10 times longer than the previous one?

A recent study concluded that some, if not most or even all, of the cost advantages that have lured Western buyers to China are beginning to disappear. Long lead times that make planning difficult, delays due to congested ports, inventory carrying charges, increasing fuel and labor costs, changing currency values, and

Table 1.4 The myths and realities of lean

Myth	Reality
Lean is about cutting costs.	Lean is not about the short-term pursuit of savings that characterizes many organizations. Removing waste from a system is usually longer lasting than short-term, cost-cutting activities.
Lean is about internal production.	Lean principles can be applied internally to any area. Furthermore, ignoring the importance of lean across the entire supply chain shows an unhealthy adherence to an outdated idea of lean.
Lean is for manufacturing companies.	While some elements of lean are more conducive to manufacturing firms, the overall philosophy of removing waste is universal. Lean principles are robust and apply to any organization.
Lean is your most important strategic objective.	While lean is a key strategic objective, it is not the only objective that a firm should emphasize. Examples of other strategic objectives relate to sustainability, ethics, and supply chain integration.
Lean is a series of techniques.	Lean starts with a vision. After that vision becomes a strategic objective, various techniques and approaches can be put in place to help achieve the lean vision.
Lean means just-in-time.	Lean is a business philosophy while just-in-time (JIT) is a delivery system. Interchanging lean and JIT reveals a serious misunderstanding of lean.
You can't be too lean.	Firms that have drastically reduced inventory across their supply chain can face severe consequences when something goes wrong. Lean is not only about reducing inventories to their lowest possible level.
Lean is forever.	The pursuit of lean is a never-ending journey. Those firms that believe they have achieved lean often focus on new objectives and divert resources to other areas, making lean gains hard to sustain.
Lean stifles innovation.	Progressive organizations do not view creativity, innovation, and lean as mutually exclusive. When pursued correctly, lean thinking promotes rather than inhibits creativity and innovation.

pressure from the Chinese government to use suppliers that are further inland are combining to increase the total cost of doing business with Chinese suppliers.[8] Some companies, including Intel, have announced they are considering production sites in Vietnam instead of China.

One way to think about this is that many cost-cutting benefits are often short-term or even temporary, while rigorously pursuing lean improvements can be longer lasting. Throughout this book lean activities and cost-cutting activities, while often having some overlap, are not viewed synonymously.

Lean Is about Internal Production

If we are not careful we might conclude that lean is all about what transpires within internal production, a narrow view of lean that does not align well with today's competitive realities. A search of the Internet reveals information about a host of lean applications that include lean accounting, lean materials management, lean Six Sigma, lean training, lean product development, lean office, lean maintenance, lean systems development, and lean human resources, to name a few.

Placing lean in front of all these terms can be viewed two ways. A cynical view is that the term lean is now at the point where it has become so ubiquitous it is grossly overused and possibly meaningless. Take any organizational area or group and slap the word lean in front of it. It is inevitable that at any moment the masses will rise up and declare that enough is enough.

The second interpretation of lean recognizes the inherent soundness of the philosophy and the essential role it plays in helping organizations compete. This school of thought, and one that is endorsed here, is that the application of lean principles across these different areas is a good sign. It means that lean is capable of being applied to a wide range of settings and different kinds of organizations. The concept is robust.

Lean must also extend outside your internal organization. Ignoring the importance of pursuing lean across the entire supply chain again shows an unhealthy adherence to a narrow and outdated vision of lean. A broader view means we must also address lean supply, lean transportation, lean operations, and lean distribution.

Lean Is for Manufacturing Companies

Let's dispel a notion that comes across far too often in the popular as well as the academic press—the principles of lean apply primarily to manufacturing companies. In fact, many observers refer to lean as lean manufacturing. Nothing could be further from the truth, and continuing to stick to this narrow view demonstrates a remarkable lack of ingenuity. While some elements of lean are more conducive to manufacturing firms, such as closed-loop delivery systems, the overall philosophy of removing waste is universal. This book will purposely highlight many examples where lean is applied outside of manufacturing companies.

The second part of this book contains some in-depth lean applications. Only one of these applications features a company that is considered a traditional manufacturing company. The others feature organizations that are successfully applying lean principles in places that are far removed from our normal frame of reference.

Lean Is Your Most Important Strategic Objective

If we aren't careful we might just believe that lean is the most important thing your firm ever undertakes. While executive leaders should view lean as a key strategic objective, it is certainly not an organization's only strategic objective. It might be worthwhile to elaborate upon the words *strategic* and *objective*.

Something that is strategic has the ability to affect the integrated whole, which, for our purposes, means it has the ability to affect a firm's overall competitive or market success. An objective is an *aspiration* to work toward in the future. So, strategic objectives represent aspirations that can affect corporate or market success.

It would be a mistake to assume that all a firm has to do to be successful is to achieve a strategic objective of becoming leaner. A single-minded emphasis on lean will likely not guarantee longer-term success, just as a single-minded obsession with total quality does not guarantee success. Too many variables define the success or failure of complex organizations. Other strategic objectives can relate to sustainability, ethics, globalization, or supply chain integration, to name a few. In reality, most firms need to do a better job of showing how lean directly and indirectly supports the achievement of some other key objectives, and vice versa.

As an example of the danger of stressing one objective over all others, several years after winning the Malcolm Baldrige award,[9] the highest quality award in the United States, one of the winners entered bankruptcy. While this company could demonstrate its quality prowess, and has the award to prove it, market success required more than a commitment to total quality. Lean, like total quality, is a necessary but not sufficient condition for long-term success.

Lean Is a Series of Techniques

Organizations that view lean as a series of discrete techniques will likely fail to apply this philosophy across the entire supply chain. Recognizing that lean is an enduring philosophy, rather than a series of often narrow techniques, allows an organization to pursue its own vision of lean. Once the lean philosophy becomes firmly established as a strategic objective, an important step becomes one of customizing those approaches that work best for each unique situation. It all starts, however, with a philosophy, or what some might even call a vision, and a commitment to that philosophy.

Those who view lean as a series of techniques tend to follow a "cookie cutter" approach that comes largely from the manufacturing domain. So many managers talk about the need to emulate the Toyota Production System (TPS) that it begins to look as though these managers can't think for themselves unless Toyota thinks for them first. Simply copying a set of techniques that works in a certain industry, and believing these techniques are what defines lean, indicates a serious lack of understanding about this concept.

Lean Means Just-in-Time

Several decades ago U.S. business executives traveled to Japan to learn the secrets of Japanese quality. During their visits these executives witnessed statistical process control (SPC) charts being used extensively. After equating quality with SPC these executives returned and mandated the use of SPC charts. Now, we will have quality, too! Unfortunately, believing that SPC charting somehow leads to total quality reveals a misunderstanding about how leading companies achieve world-class quality. The same can be said about just-in-time (JIT). Saying that lean is about JIT deliveries reveals a misunderstanding about how leading companies achieve lean.

JIT is a delivery system that most organizations will never be a part of and, when a JIT network is in place, can actually lead to new waste if companies push their inventory back to suppliers, or if suppliers ship smaller quantities more frequently from a stockpile of inventory. While JIT can be an important part of lean, the two terms are not interchangeable. Chapter 2 will present a very convincing example of the waste that a poorly executed JIT system can create.

You Can't Be Too Lean

Can a company be too lean? At times the answer appears to be a resounding "yes." A study conducted by researchers at Michigan State University concluded that supply chains become increasingly vulnerable to disruptions as manufacturers pursue a lean inventory model.[10] It usually takes some catastrophe before a serious discussion takes place about risk and fragile supply chains. One knowledgeable observer commented that while lean is a demonstrably successful approach, a lean system is not a perfect solution. Under certain conditions its use can actually be bad for a company and bad for a supply chain. This can be the case when lean practices are overapplied or the system lacks flexibility.[11]

The following example reveals the dangers of taking lean to the extreme. Not too long ago an earthquake with a 6.8 magnitude struck central Japan. One of the companies affected was a supplier named Riken Corporation, surely a name that is not familiar to most readers.[12] Because this company could not supply a $1.50 piston ring after the earthquake, 70 percent of Japan's auto production shut down within days of the quake. Japan's supply chain simply had no buffer inventory. Companies affected by the supply disruption included Toyota, Honda, Nissan, Mazda, Fuji Heavy Industries, Mitsubishi, and Suzuki. In other words, just about anyone that makes a product with wheels attached to it was affected. Toyota temporarily shut down production at all 12 of its Japanese assembly plants.

What's the big deal here? After all, inexpensive piston rings are surely available from other sources. Well, maybe not. Most Japanese firms rely on one supplier for a purchase requirement, making the fallback to another supplier difficult, if not impossible, in the short term. To further complicate matters, each company specified custom-designed piston rings. A lack of standardization with something as basic as a piston ring contributed to bringing an entire industry to its knees. After the earthquake, Toyota's president said the company was going to examine its risk management policies.

Lean Is Forever

While some things are forever (like diamonds), the same is not necessarily true of the gains achieved from Total Quality Management and lean. Perhaps one of the greatest ironies right now involves Toyota, a company that many argue is synonymous with lean. While most of Toyota's Japanese production facilities and suppliers are located near Toyota City in Japan, the company assumed a different approach when it expanded in the United States. In its quest to ramp up U.S. production quickly and to create jobs in as many congressional districts as possible, the company established vehicle, engine, and parts factories in eight states—California, Kentucky, Texas, Alabama, West Virginia, Indiana, Missouri, and Tennessee.[13] This geographically dispersed network of facilities and suppliers has chipped away at the cost advantages the company has historically maintained from its lean network. Toyota seems to have let a new set of objectives override its lean objectives.

In another departure from its roots, Toyota's U.S. assembly facilities can only produce a single vehicle type compared with Japanese plants that produce up to six different vehicles. This inflexibility has affected Toyota's ability to respond to market changes (i.e., high gas prices) that have reduced the demand for trucks and increased the demand for smaller cars. In perhaps the most troublesome statistic of all, in a recent year Toyota recalled more vehicles in the United States than it sold in the United States that year, raising concerns about product quality. Let's not stop there. Toyota recently ranked 28th out of 36 vehicle brands in J. D. Power's overall customer experience ranking.[14]

Nobody expects Toyota to relinquish its status as the king of the automotive industry anytime soon. However, has the company's obsession with displacing GM as the world's largest auto company, perhaps sprinkled with the arrogance and complacency that sometimes affect those at the top, caused the company to stray from its roots? Even the best companies must work relentlessly to hold onto their advantages, advantages that other companies quickly learn how to duplicate. The model of lean that many companies continue to pursue is in need of some refreshing.

Lean Stifles Innovation

Innovation is one of today's hot business topics, and the need for innovation has worked its way into the strategic planning process at most firms. Hardly a week goes by without some leading business publication reporting on the topic of innovation, and it's not hard to find listings of companies that are considered innovators. For our purposes we define innovation as introducing something new or unique, such as a new idea, method, or device within any part of the supply chain.

A vocal school of thought is emerging that is critical of philosophies such as lean and Six Sigma, and the arguments these critics put forth have some merit. This school of thought maintains that the drive for efficiency and uniformity should not be applied to all organizational processes, particularly those that are somewhat unstructured. A massive attack on waste leads to conformity that counters creativity and innovation. One observer argues that under a lean system, companies emphasize narrowly bounded, well-defined process improvements at the expense of the radical innovations that can be the real game changers.[15] But does it have to be this way?

Progressive organizations do not necessarily view creativity and the drive for lean as mutually exclusive. Let's be clear here—we need to strike a balance between lean and innovation that lets us have our cake and eat it too. When performed correctly, lean thinking should promote rather than inhibit creativity. Lean transformations benefit greatly from out-of-the-box thinking. It is these creative moments that result in breakthroughs that improve performance, customer service, or remove massive amounts of waste from the supply chain. Creative thinking (sometimes referred to as brainstorming or divergent thinking) can be applied to lean applications as well as new product development. The second part of this book is full of examples that show how innovation supports lean objectives.

LINKING LEAN ACROSS THE SUPPLY CHAIN

This opening chapter would be incomplete without addressing how the various groups within the supply, transportation, operations, and distribution domains coordinate, align, and integrate their lean initiatives. Integration means bringing together different groups, functions, and even organizations, either formally or informally, physically or by information technology, to work jointly and often concurrently on a common business-related assignment or purpose. In our case the need to focus on lean objectives and projects is of primary interest.

The ways that groups work together to coordinate, align, and integrate their lean objectives are many. An obvious one is through a company's organizational design, which is defined as the process of assessing and selecting the structures and formal systems of communication, division of labor, coordination, control, authority, and responsibility necessary to achieve a firm's goals and objectives.[16]

Organizational design features that support lean alignment include cross-functional teams of various kinds, including product development and continuous improvement teams, co-location of support personnel with their internal customers, such as supply personnel physically co-located with operations personnel, and physical office and facility layouts that encourage the informal exchange of information. Another progressive design feature is a buyer-supplier council that includes executive representatives from a buying company and its key suppliers working together to coordinate their strategies and plans.

Crafting the right set of measures will encourage groups to align their lean efforts. Instead of relying on narrow functional measures that can be in conflict with one another, progressive firms adopt process or superordinate measures. Process measures are cross-functional by design, and superordinate measures are higher level indicators that cannot be achieved without some serious collaboration between supply chain groups. As Chapter 6 will explain, measurement systems can be your best friend or your worst enemy. Fortunately, you have some say in which one it will be.

The growth of cross-functional and cross-organizational information systems over the last 10 years is astounding. Shared and linked information technology systems, especially demand and supply chain planning systems, afford a great opportunity for groups to work across functional and business boundaries. Supplier and customer relationship management systems that allow on-line information sharing, collaboration, and negotiation also support this effort.

The development of strategies using a formal development process can also be an ideal way to align lean initiatives. Effective strategies result from an iterative process involving different groups, personnel, and even companies. Integrative strategies must support original corporate objectives as well as the objectives of other groups. Leading firms routinely hold formal strategy coordination sessions between their different sites, functional groups, and even with other key supply chain members. They also communicate widely the strategies of various functional groups, including through internal websites. The lean aspiration of any one group should not come as a surprise to other supply chain members.

The bottom line is that organizations have many avenues available to them to coordinate, align, and integrate their initiatives up and down the supply chain. Developing uncoordinated initiatives across a supply chain could create more harm than good. The view in this book is that pursuing lean across an extended supply chain is a coordinated rather than an uncoordinated endeavor. Do not view lean supply, lean transportation, lean operations, and lean distribution as independent pursuits.

CONCLUDING THOUGHTS

Lean is a robust philosophy that applies to any organization. The time has come to move from a narrow, internal view of lean to one that looks end-to-end across an entire supply chain. Truly lean organizations pursue improvement opportunities wherever they exist. And the pursuit of these opportunities is a never-ending journey.

Moving upstream to downstream, the chapters that follow examine how different, but interrelated, parts of the supply chain each contribute to a lean vision. Chapter 2 begins our journey across the supply chain by examining lean supply, an area that suffers far too often from benign neglect. Chapter 3 shows what it takes to create a transportation network that has the essential lean elements, while Chapter 4 presents the topics that are important for lean operations. Chapter 5 shows some creative ways to take waste out of distribution and marketing channels, while Chapters 6 and 7 lay out the measures and tools that support an end-to-end lean supply chain. Chapters 8–16 present detailed applications that show how diverse organizations are capturing some amazing benefits from their lean efforts, sometimes in the unlikeliest places.

ENDNOTES

1. D. Jones, P. Hines, and N. Rich, "Lean Logistics," *International Journal of Physical Distribution and Logistics Management* 27, no. 3/4 (1997): 153-173.

2. This example is adapted from D. Machalaba, "Crowds Heed Amtrak's 'All Aboard'," *Wall Street Journal,* August 23, 2007, B1.

3. Adapted from P. Prada and S. McCartney, "Clogged Arteries: Why Even Sunny Days Can Ground Airplanes—Flight 88 Got Stuck on a Congested Route; A Legacy of the 1920s," *Wall Street Journal,* September 28, 2007, A1.

4. This example is adapted from the Associated Press, "Newark Airport Screeners Good at Giving Back," *The Express-Times,* December 23, 2007, B5.

5. K. Vitasek, K. Manrodt, and J. Abbott, "What Makes a Lean Supply Chain?" *Supply Chain Management Review* 9, no. 7 (October 2005): 39.

6. J. P. Womack and D. T. Jones, *Lean Thinking* (New York: Simon and Schuster, 1996), 16-19.

7. B. Hindo, "Satisfaction Not Guaranteed," *Business Week* 3989 (June 19, 2006): 32-36.

8. W. Hoffman, "China's Advantage Slipping," *Traffic World* 271, no. 48 (December 3, 2007): 14.

9. A great quality irony is how often the name "Malcolm Baldrige," which is attached to the highest quality award in the United States, is misspelled. Many writers and editors want to place a second "d" in the name Baldrige to make it "Baldridge." Sometimes it is best not to trust your spell checker.

10. Staff, "MSU Study: Some Companies Get Too Lean," *Purchasing Magazine Online*, http://www.purchasing.com, July 15, 2004.

11. S. Melynk, "Lean to a Fault," *CSCMP's Supply Chain Quarterly* 1, no. 2 (Quarter 3, 2007): 29.

12. This example is adapted from A. Chozick, "A Key Strategy of Japan's Car Makers Backfires," *Wall Street Journal*, July 20, 2007, B1; and A. Chozick, "Toyota Sticks by Just in Time Strategy after Quack," *Wall Street Journal*, July 24, 2007, A2.

13. N. Shirouzu, "Toyota's New U.S. Plan: Stop Building Factories," *Wall Street Journal*, June 20, 2007, A1, A14.

14. D. Welch, "Staying Paranoid at Toyota," *Business Week* 4041 (July 2, 2007): 82.

15. See note 11, 30.

16. G. Hamel and C. Pralahad, *Competing for the Future* (Cambridge, MA: Harvard Business School Press, 1994), as referenced in D. Hellriegel, J. Slocum, and R. Woodman, Organizational Behavior (Cincinnati, OH: South-Western College Publishing, 2001), 474.

Web
Added
Value™

This book has free material available for download from the
Web Added Value™ resource center at *www.jrosspub.com*

LEAN SUPPLY

Our first stop across the lean supply chain takes us to the inputs that every organization relies on to succeed. Lean supply is one of the least recognized and pursued parts of a lean supply chain. There simply is not much written or available about this important topic. While suppliers can provide goods and services to any part of an organization, the primary focus here is on the direct materials that suppliers provide. Figure 2.1 positions where lean supply predominantly takes place within a supply chain.

Lean supply is not just about doing business with a set of suppliers that can ship on a just-in-time (JIT) basis, although that can be a major part of lean supply. The domain of lean supply includes selecting and then developing suppliers that practice lean principles; creating a physical supply network that features fewer suppliers providing more frequent deliveries of smaller quantities; and creating a supply organization that removes redundancy and waste from its supply management processes. This chapter addresses these three areas individually.

SELECTING AND DEVELOPING LEAN SUPPLIERS

The first of three major areas within the lean supply domain deals with evaluating, selecting, and then developing suppliers that demonstrate capabilities that support lean. A desire to work with suppliers that are actively pursuing their own lean initiatives should be a major objective for any supply organization. These suppliers should also demonstrate a strong commitment to continuous improvement, or what Chapter 1 referred to as striving for excellence. We are still waiting for the day when executive managers accept that supplier evaluation and selection is one of the most important processes they have in place today.

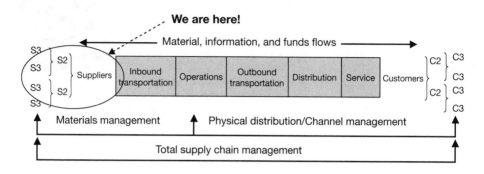

Figure 2.1 Lean supply

A reliance on lean suppliers is not only so the buyer can do business with suppliers that deliver smaller quantities more frequently, although that is important if the buyer expects to establish a JIT delivery system. A buying company may not want to place a supplier within a JIT delivery system or may not have the capability to develop such a system. Even when this is the case, a buyer will still want to maintain a group of lean suppliers. Ask yourself a simple question. If we expect our internal operations to drive out waste and become lean, why shouldn't we expect external providers to be lean?

Two concerns that keep supply managers up at night are how to remain cost competitive and how to secure enough capacity to satisfy demand requirements. The pressure to reduce costs is relentless and severe, and that pressure is not going away any time soon. Suppliers that focus on lean should have a definite cost advantage that can be passed along in the form of lower prices. After all, a lean supplier is one that has eliminated waste, and waste is nothing more than an addition to total costs. Lean suppliers will also have addressed the flow of material through their operations. The positive effect that flow has on capacity should not be underestimated, and subsequent chapters will go into this in more detail. Doing business with lean suppliers should be a primary objective during supplier evaluation and selection.

Frequently the selection decision suffers from benign neglect, which creates waste after the effects of poorly thought out selection decisions are realized. This is especially true when a buying firm has too many suppliers that receive shorter-term contracts. Supplier selection becomes almost a constant activity that is not performed well. The costs of poor selection decisions, while rarely measured formally, are nonetheless real. At times the selection process also takes too long, which presents its own kinds of waste.

Leading firms develop a process that includes best practices for guiding their selection decisions, and this process is shared with any internal site that selects suppliers. While this process can differ from company to company, it should include a step that involves the timely identification of supply requirements. This step is critical because it begins to define the criteria against which potential suppliers are eventually evaluated. The involvement of internal customers is essential for identifying the correct attributes, and eventually their weights, that will be used during a formal assessment. The ability of suppliers to adjust capacity quickly due to changing demand, for example, might be a critical requirement for the marketing group. Or a supplier's ability to demonstrate an active commitment to lean and continuous improvement might be an essential objective for the operations group.

Moving from Selecting Suppliers to Managing and Developing Suppliers

Once suppliers are part of the supply base, the emphasis shifts to managing relationships and developing supplier capabilities. Managing suppliers is one of the most important, and often challenging, responsibilities facing supply managers. Supplier performance management consists of the approaches and activities that supply organizations put forth to ensure a steady stream of conforming, and hopefully improving, products and services from suppliers.

As such, there is no one activity or approach that defines supplier performance management or supplier relationship management. Rather, these concepts comprise many different activities. A later section will provide a continuum of various supplier relationships. Knowing when, where, and how to apply an appropriate relationship is an area where supply professionals bring value to their organization.

The switching or churning of suppliers is simply not as great as it once was, making it important to work with the suppliers that will be around for a while. Firms that have the resources available often work directly with their suppliers to develop their performance capabilities, particularly in areas that support lean. Supplier development is a broad topic that represents any activity or effort by the buying company to improve the performance of suppliers, such as helping organize a *kaizen* event. Development efforts primarily fall into three categories: (1) working with suppliers to resolve a problem (reactive), (2) working with suppliers to continuously improve a performance capability (proactive), and (3) working with suppliers to create a performance capability where none previously existed (proactive).

The confrontational nature that has characterized too many buyer-seller relationships explains partly the reason for not pursuing supplier development activities. However, the need to focus on supplier development becomes quite clear if we think about the realities of today's marketplace. Leading firms have converged on a set of suppliers they view as critical to longer-term success. With a smaller supply base operating with longer-term contracts, improvement (which is a never-ending mandate) will occur primarily through enhancing existing supplier capabilities rather than from large-scale switching. Supplier development becomes an important strategy for working with lean suppliers.

Solectron, a world leader in contract manufacturing, is working diligently with its suppliers to remove waste from its supply chain. In an industry where costs steadily decrease rather than increase, an end-to-end commitment to lean is a strategic necessity. Solectron has conducted more than 1000 kaizen events with suppliers to eliminate waste. The company also plans to consolidate even more business with fewer suppliers so it can more fully tap into their expertise. Currently 150 suppliers account for 80 percent of Solectron's total annual purchases of over $9 billion.[1]

A Supplier Selection and Development Example

An example of working with suppliers with lean capabilities involves Hamilton Sundstrand, a United Technologies company that is a major tier-one supplier to the aerospace industry. Hamilton Sundstrand is benefiting from the trend that features buying companies identifying where they add the most value, and then outsourcing those areas that are not part of their core competencies or capabilities. Boeing has outsourced to Hamilton Sundstrand the design and manufacture of nine systems for Boeing's new 787 Dreamliner, including an auxiliary power unit, environmental control system, electric power generation and start system, and a remote power distribution system.[2] Boeing is relying on Hamilton Sundstrand for some serious technology and systems. A delay on any of these systems affects the delivery of the final product.

Hamilton Sundstrand is going through the same process as Boeing as it identifies those areas that are not the best use of company resources. Vertical integration is no longer part of the business model of most companies, including this one. The company decided to discontinue an internal machine shop in Colorado and transfer that work to an external supplier in Arizona. The Arizona supplier had a track record of perfect quality and delivery while remaining price competitive relative to its competitors. While the supplier's overall capability was not a concern, its capacity, particularly as it worked to absorb a large influx of work from Hamilton Sundstrand, was another story.

Hamilton Sundstrand dispatched a team of experts to work with its supplier, whose management was receptive about the development initiatives. In the words of Hamilton Sundstrand's Vice-President of Supply, "They saw the benefits that can be achieved from applying lean tools and ingraining lean into the company's culture. They saw lean as strategic to their vision to be in the business of supporting tier-one supplies to the aircraft OEMs." The Hamilton Sundstrand team worked at the supplier's location for several months and addressed the flow of material through the supplier's work cells and between buildings. As capacity increased due to faster flow, Hamilton Sundstrand realized even better performance from its supplier.

What is the point here? During supplier selection, companies such as Boeing must consider a supplier's capacity, its business plan regarding outsourcing, and how that supplier expects to work with its suppliers to advance lean. A break in any part of Hamilton Sundstrand's supply chain will have serious consequences on Boeing's ability to satisfy its end customers.

CREATING A LEAN SUPPLY NETWORK

The second major part of lean supply is the crafting of a lean supply network. A network is an *interconnected or interrelated chain, group, or system*. In this case, a lean supply network consists of a group of suppliers that are willing to work with a buyer to produce and deliver, more frequently and on a regular basis, smaller quantities of material. This ensures that material flows across the supply chain without any unnecessary buildup. While the principles of lean apply to any organization, it is also true that creating a lean supply network is a challenging part of an end-to-end lean organization. Because of their volumes and clout, larger firms will have obvious advantages when establishing a lean supply network compared with smaller firms. Manufacturing firms will also have a greater need for a lean supply network than nonmanufacturing firms.

Characteristics of a Lean Supply Network

A lean supply network is not merely about placing suppliers on a JIT delivery schedule. While this is certainly part of a lean network, by no means is it the defining characteristic. A lean network involves working closely with a select group of suppliers to remove waste and costs from the supply chain, even costs that are several tiers away from the buying company. The following presents the predominant characteristics of a lean supply network.

Fewer Total Suppliers. Working with suppliers to remove costs from the supply chain means working with a smaller set of suppliers. Most U.S. firms historically have maintained a supply base that is far too large to manage well. The logic behind relying on fewer rather than more suppliers is straightforward. The costs associated with maintaining multiple suppliers for each purchased good or service usually outweigh any perceived reduction in supply risk. We now know that risk has many dimensions and that maintaining too large a supply base in itself can increase, rather than decrease, supply chain risk and costs. Multiple suppliers for a single item create additional opportunities for variability and higher costs due to reduced leverage. Too many suppliers create waste.

A smaller supply base is a critical prerequisite for pursuing the kinds of cooperative activities that can truly make a supply chain leaner. One hundred suppliers will be easier to work with than 1500 suppliers we hardly know. This topic will be discussed further in a later section.

Purchases in Small (and Coordinated) Quantities with Frequent Deliveries. This characteristic is the one that most observers will associate with a lean supply network. Coordinating the purchase and delivery of smaller quantities on a more frequent basis requires close coordination with production planning, transportation, and logistics. The transportation aspects of a lean supply network are covered more thoroughly in Chapter 3.

Mutual, Consistent Improvement. Striving for excellence, a key lean objective, is equally important with suppliers as it is with internal operations. Buyers pursue this objective with suppliers by continuously measuring performance, helping suppliers directly when needed, and providing timely performance feedback. Progressive companies also offer incentives to encourage improvement. Examples of incentives include the opportunity for a supplier to become a preferred supplier, awarding a higher share of business as improvements are realized, and longer-term contracts.

Cooperative Buyer-Supplier Relationships. Different types of relationships are present within a supply network, and not all relationships are created equally. A continuum of relationships exists that features counterproductive on one end to collaborative on the other. Figure 2.2 describes the various relationships. After a buying company has reduced its supply base to a manageable size, the opportunity to pursue cooperative relationships with suppliers becomes more likely. A cooperative relationship, at a minimum, is required to support a lean network.

Supplier relationship management is rapidly becoming a key part of managing a global supply network. It's safe to conclude that suppliers will not be highly supportive of a buyer's lean objectives when the relationship is based on a win-lose approach and an absence of trust.

Efficient Communication Linkages. Establishing an efficient communication network involves both internal and external communications. There are many ways to promote accurate and more efficient communication linkages across the supply chain. Two important ways include (1) electronic data interchange (EDI) and (2) point-to-point communication.

A popular approach that supports efficient communication linkages across the supply chain involves electronic data interchange (EDI). EDI is a communications

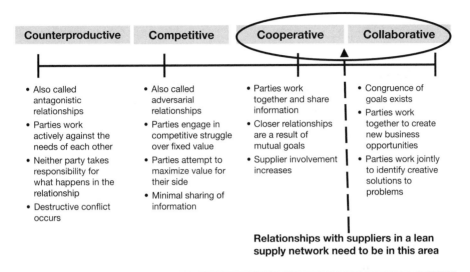

Counterproductive	Competitive	Cooperative	Collaborative
• Also called antagonistic relationships • Parties work actively against the needs of each other • Neither party takes responsibility for what happens in the relationship • Destructive conflict occurs	• Also called adversarial relationships • Parties engage in competitive struggle over fixed value • Parties attempt to maximize value for their side • Minimal sharing of information	• Parties work together and share information • Closer relationships are a result of mutual goals • Supplier involvement increases	• Congruence of goals exists • Parties work together to create new business opportunities • Parties work jointly to identify creative solutions to problems

Relationships with suppliers in a lean supply network need to be in this area

Figure 2.2 Continuum of supply relationships

standard that supports the electronic exchange of common business documents and information across businesses. While EDI is no longer considered leading-edge, it's hard to imagine a progressive supply organization not endorsing some sort of technology to promote efficient communication linkages.

The technology underlying EDI systems has changed dramatically over the last several years. The new version of EDI is called EDI XML, which is a standard-ized framework in which EDI-based business documents and messages are described using XML (extensible markup language) syntax. This form of EDI relies on virtual private networks (VPNs) supported by the Internet. This format is quickly replacing the use of third-party value-added networks (VANs) because it is less expensive and presents fewer standards issues.

Another important part of communication involves point-to-point commu-nication. In a traditional supply chain, procurement personnel are the primary conduit to the supplier through the supplier's sales people, as illustrated by Figure 2.3. Besides being inefficient, this model often limits, and at times even distorts, the flow of information between organizations. It does not support the intense communication that must occur between functional groups when managing a lean supply network.

Figure 2.4 illustrates a lean supply network that features a point-to-point communication model. Here, functional experts at the buying firm speak directly to their counterparts at suppliers on topics of mutual concern. Besides being more efficient, this heightened communication should promote higher levels of trust and cooperation across the supply chain. Interestingly, the procurement group has

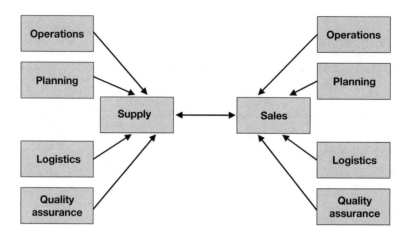

Figure 2.3 Communication linkages in a traditional supply chain

sometimes been the most vocal opponent of a point-to-point model. Perhaps it is a concern that engineers might make commercial commitments they are not allowed to make when talking with suppliers. Or perhaps the procurement group is worried about losing organizational power. The simple fact remains that a point-to-point communication network is essential to a lean supply network.

Recognizing that a point-to-point communication system might lead to issues that challenge the procurement group's authority levels, one company has come up with a simple solution. It developed bullet-point listings of what nonprocurement personnel may and may not talk about with a supplier. These do's and dont's are widely communicated internally and with suppliers.

Challenges to Creating a Lean Supply Network

Various challenges affect a company's ability to establish a lean supply network, particularly in the United States. After all, if there were no challenges everyone would be pursuing lean supply with zeal and intensity, and we know this is not the case. Some of these challenges are historical and have been addressed aggressively by firms. Other challenges are still present, such as longer material pipelines resulting from the growth in worldwide sourcing. Let's identify the historical and current challenges to a lean supply network and ways to overcome each challenge.

Too Many Suppliers. As mentioned, most U.S. firms have historically maintained a large supply base. Overcoming this challenge requires a methodical analysis by purchase commodity regarding how many and which suppliers to maintain. During the 1990s, over three-quarters of firms surveyed decreased the

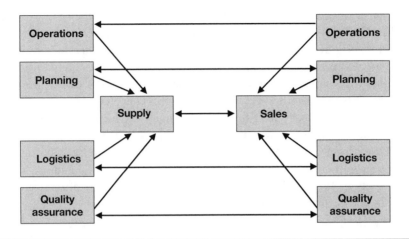

Figure 2.4 Point-to-point communication in a lean supply chain

total number of suppliers they maintained, some by up to 90 percent.[3] Another survey reported that over the last several years almost 50 percent of firms have reduced their supply base by 20 percent, another 15 percent reduced their supply base between 20 and 60 percent, and fully three-quarters of buying firms now commit 80 percent or more of their total purchase dollars with fewer than 100 suppliers.[4] Overcoming the challenge of a large supply base has resulted in an aggressive attempt by most firms to optimize their supply base. This topic will be discussed in more detail in the last section of this chapter.

Geographically Dispersed Suppliers. The geographic spread of suppliers around the United States, and now around the world, cannot be ignored as a major impediment to lean. Material pipelines seem to be lengthening rather than shortening. At one time the average supplier distance from Spring Hill, Tennessee, which was the primary location for producing Saturn vehicles, was 400 miles. Managing a JIT delivery network for Saturn is obviously a major undertaking. Unlike most companies, GM has the clout to entice suppliers to participate in a JIT delivery system.

Since the roots of lean are in Japan, it might be worthwhile to understand why geographic dispersion is something most Japanese OEMs have not faced. Japan is 145,843 square miles in size compared with 3.7 million square miles for the United States, and has a population of about 130 million compared with the U.S. population of roughly 300 million. Furthermore, approximately 70 percent of Japan is mountainous. Forgetting for a moment the willingness of Japanese suppliers to locate near their primary customers, something that is not as common with U.S. suppliers, it is easy to see why Japanese suppliers are located in major industrial areas near their prime customers. Where else were they going to locate? Supplier deliveries to customers are usually intracity rather than intercity.

Companies overcome the geographic dispersion challenge in a number of ways. One way is to establish a full-blown lean transportation system featuring a closed-loop transportation network. (Chapter 3 will discuss closed-loop transportation systems.) Another way to overcome this challenge is to encourage suppliers to locate physically near the buying company. Obviously, one has to be a large customer before this becomes a realistic option. At the extreme, some buying companies have carved out space within their production facilities for suppliers to locate their operations. With this option, material handling replaces transportation. While this option may initially appear to be attractive, it does make supplier switching costs very high.

Inconsistent Supplier Quality. Supplier quality levels that are nowhere near zero defects can still present a major challenge to lean. Inconsistent quality is not acceptable in a system that has zero tolerance for defects and maintains few, if any, safety stocks. Unfortunately, U.S. suppliers, as well as U.S. OEMs, were somewhat late to the quality management game compared to their major foreign counterparts. In the latter 1990s, the U.S. suppliers to a tier-one automotive supplier, for example, provided material at a 50,000 parts per million (ppm) defect level, while suppliers at this company's German unit received material from its European suppliers with a 5000 ppm defect level. There are some powerful ways to overcome inconsistent supplier quality:

- Supply base reduction helps eliminate those suppliers that are not capable of meeting or exceeding a set of rigorous quality standards.
- Supplier development efforts that focus on quality improvement are becoming popular as a means to ensure consistent quality.
- Most firms now weigh heavily on an assessment of a supplier's quality capabilities during supplier evaluation.
- Supplier performance scorecards almost always include a measurement rating for quality.
- Longer-term contracts often include clauses and language related to continuous supplier improvement.
- Many buying companies encourage their suppliers to pursue ISO 9000 certification.

Adversarial Buyer-Seller Relationships. It would be an understatement to say that historically buyer-seller relationships in the United States have suffered from a lack of mutual trust, a deficiency that has made the parties within a supply chain reluctant to work together. The activities required to make a lean supply network a reality demand cooperative and trusting relationships. Adversarial relationships have also contributed to a lack of communication and information sharing between supply chain parties.

A way to overcome a lack of communication and information sharing is to include critical suppliers during the buyer's supply chain planning process, perhaps even involving suppliers early during product development. A point-to-point communications system, which was discussed earlier, should also help overcome this challenge.

If strong relationships with suppliers are critical to a lean network, and the argument here is they are critical, then overcoming the challenge of adversarial relationships means understanding how to pursue stronger relationships. A sample of ways that a buying company can improve relationships with suppliers includes the following:

- Formally assessing the supplier's perception of the buyer as a customer
- Assigning individuals to manage critical relationships
- Practicing cooperative cost management techniques
- Conducting supplier development activities as needed
- Creating opportunities for communication
- Providing timely supplier performance feedback
- Inviting suppliers to be part of an executive buyer-supplier council

One outcome from a buyer's relationship management efforts should be the pursuit of activities that promote trust. Trust refers to the belief in the character, ability, strength, or truth of a party. Buyers demonstrate their trustworthiness through open and frequent communication, following through on promises and commitments, acting legally and ethically, and protecting sensitive information. Trust-based relationships also act on behalf of the relationship rather than narrow self interests.

Identifying Items and Suppliers for a Lean Network

Perhaps the best way to think about the kinds of items to include in a lean supply network is to think about what not to include. This first example involves large corrugated shipping containers, while the second example features a product where hundreds, if not thousands, fit into a shoebox.

I Want a JIT System, Too. This is a story about a guy named Big Roy. Roy is responsible for managing a sheet metal priming and packaging operation for an OEM. One of his group's responsibilities is to purchase corrugated containers to package large replacement parts for his company's aftermarket. His group also purchases corrugated shipping containers that hold parts during transit. Roy's facility ships sheet metal parts to distribution centers around the United States.

One day Roy was prominently featured on the front page of a company publication for implementing a JIT delivery system with a major corrugated supplier. Instead of large quantities of space-intensive boxes delivered every several weeks, the supplier now provided daily deliveries of smaller quantities. Instead of a storage area full of boxes, Roy's storage area now featured, well, nothing. The paper even had a picture of Roy smiling broadly as he stood in the middle of nothing. Roy definitely was the man of the hour.

Roy's newfound celebrity status did not go unnoticed by the package engineering group at the OEM's primary packaging facility 50 miles away. After all, this facility used some of the same cartons and suppliers as Roy. The head of the packaging engineering group decided that he, too, wanted a JIT system. He knew that if he did not at least match Roy he would never hear the end of it. This was now a matter of saving face! At least this manager's reason for pursuing a JIT delivery system was based on sound business principles.

Let's review a paraphrased conversation between the operations manager at the corrugated supplier and the packaging engineering manager who also wants his own JIT delivery system.

Packaging engineering manager: *I just read in a company publication that you are shipping large cartons on a JIT basis to Roy's facility.*

Operations manager at supplier: *Well, we didn't have much choice.*

Packaging engineering manager: *I want JIT deliveries, too.*

Operations manager at supplier: *I don't think so.*

Packaging engineering manager: *Why not?*

Operations manager at supplier: *Come visit our facility sometime and you'll see why not. I have had to lease public warehouse space to store all these cartons that I make but can't deliver. With our setup charges I can't make just a load or two of cartons at a time, and we don't have the room to hold a bunch of cartons. We have to ship them to the public warehouse and then bring up a few loads at a time to your pal's plant, which by the way is 50 miles from nowhere. Roy may think his new system is great, but all we see are higher costs and more hassles.*

Packaging engineering manager: *Then why are you doing it?*

Operations manager at supplier: *Because he is our biggest customer. I was told to do it.*

Packaging engineering manager: *I still want JIT deliveries.*

Operations manager at supplier: *Sure, but you're going to pay for it.*

Think about what transpired here. The supplier is delivering more frequently because of pressure from its largest customer. A visit to this supplier would reveal something interesting. The equipment to make large corrugated boxes is complex and involves major setup charges. It is not a simple matter to change from one box size or from one customer's logo to another. Large corrugators operate economically with larger production runs. As much as we may not want to accept it, there are still production processes that benefit from economies of scale. Not everyone is capable of running tiny lot sizes.

Roy's desire for smaller quantities was inconsistent with the realities of the supplier's production process. As a result, the supplier still produced large quantities as always but was now forced to store the inventory in another location. This new system did not remove costs from the supply chain. In fact, it created *new* costs, which can only be described as ironic since the aim of a lean system is to remove waste. At some point we might have to conclude that large corrugated boxes are not the best candidates for a lean supply network, at least with this supplier's current production process.

There are some great lessons to take away here. First, Roy *pushed* his desire for a JIT system, not to mention the inventory and costs that went with that desire, back to the supplier. There is no semblance of a cooperative relationship. Second, Roy really did not understand his supplier. One of the reasons companies reduce their supply base to a manageable level is so they can better understand their suppliers' individual requirements and constraints. Third, a lack of communication occurred between corporate facilities that should be sharing ideas. Even though they work in the same division, one packaging engineering manager had to find out about what the other was doing through a company publication.

The last lesson is that a change that was intended to reduce costs, at least in Roy's mind, actually resulted in higher costs across the supply chain. Think of the waste that is created by moving boxes to a public warehouse, storing the boxes, and then shipping smaller quantities frequently to the customer, who is located a fair number of miles away from the warehouse. Interestingly, the available space in Roy's facility was not replaced with any value-adding activities. Eventually, the supplier will attempt to recoup these additional costs, perhaps through higher prices, or will become more vocal in its displeasure with this new system.

Sophisticated suppliers are beginning to quantify the cost of providing additional value-added services that are requested by customers, including more frequent deliveries of smaller quantities. This calculation is called the *cost to serve*. Some suppliers will not be so willing to absorb additional costs in the future.

Should Standard Fasteners Be Lean? Let's look at another interesting attempt at lean and JIT. The owner of a small supplier received a letter from an OEM buyer informing him that his business must begin shipping his product on a JIT basis. The business owner was, to say the least, surprised. He supplied the OEM with low cost, standard fasteners shipped via less-than-truckload carriers. When this supplier sets up his equipment to make fasteners, the plan is to make gazillions of them. Like large corrugated cartons, this item also benefits from economies of scale. Why would a company want to receive frequent deliveries of an insignificant item in terms of size and cost?

Some probing by the supplier revealed that buyers were now being measured by the *percent of suppliers that are delivering on a JIT basis*. It doesn't take a rocket scientist to figure out that the easiest way to look good on this measure is to have suppliers ship on a JIT basis. And apparently all it takes is sending a letter telling the supplier to get with the program. Unfortunately, this measure is driving behavior that is counterproductive to a lean network.

By no means is this action removing any waste from the supply chain. More frequent deliveries of an insignificant item, additional paperwork, and increased material handling at the supplier and the buyer are creating higher costs. At least the fastener supplier did not have to lease public warehouse space. Chapter 6 will provide examples of the bizarre behaviors that sometimes result in a quest to look good on performance measures.

The economic case for managing fasteners on a JIT basis is weak since fasteners consume few dollars or floor space. Fasteners are part of the 80 percent of items that consume 20 percent of total purchase dollars. As a general rule it is probably best not to become too obsessed with these items. There are better opportunities to pursue.

Identifying the Right Items and Suppliers.   Now that we have explored some items that are not the best candidates to be part of a lean supply network, what are the characteristics of items that should be part of the network?

Two obvious characteristics working in favor of items becoming part of a network that features more frequent deliveries of smaller quantities are (1) the item's unit dollar value and (2) total space requirements. More frequent deliveries mean lower average inventory levels, which result in lower inventory carrying charges and reduced working capital requirements. Do not forget that inventory is treated as a current asset on a company's balance sheet.

The storage space that an item requires is also a consideration. Higher expenses naturally result from committing a large amount of square and cubic feet to bulky inventory items. Perhaps more importantly, this space cannot be used for

Table 2.1 Questions to ask when establishing a lean supply network

Question:		
Does the item have a fairly predictable demand and usage pattern?	Y	N
Is the supplier willing to participate in a lean supply network?	Y	N
Is the item high dollar or space intensive?	Y	N
Is the supplier in a location that supports being part of a lean transportation system?	Y	N
Does the buyer-seller relationship support working together?	Y	N
Is the supplier ready from a quality standpoint to ship smaller quantities more frequently?	Y	N
Is the supplier ready internally to support rapid changeovers and the production of smaller lot sizes?	Y	N
Does the item have any unusual transportation requirements, such as hazardous materials?	Y	N

more productive uses. Space-intensive items may not necessarily be cost-intensive items.

Table 2.1 provides a list of questions that can be asked when crafting a lean network. Some of these questions reveal why smaller firms are sometimes at a disadvantage compared with larger firms in this area. A supplier may not be willing to participate if the buyer's volumes are not important enough to that supplier. Predictability, in terms of demand requirements and supplier performance, is also important. Highly volatile items with frequent demand changes are not the best items for a system that is based on repeatability and stability. Unreliable suppliers are also a concern, although this discussion should help supply managers identify suppliers to eliminate from the supply base or identify targets for development opportunities.

It's important for commodity management teams to work with logistics and operations personnel when identifying items and suppliers to be part of a lean supply network. These decisions cannot be made in isolation, but rather must be part of a broader supply chain strategy. Consensus should be reached about the desirability of an item and a supplier to be part of the network.

A lean supply network must be approached from a total cost perspective. At an extreme, think about the logic of trying to receive daily deliveries of parts from Chinese suppliers. Electronic companies that receive frequent deliveries from overseas suppliers almost always have a stocking location near their facility to stage these materials. These materials are then shipped on a just-in-time basis from these storage locations.

Managing a Hybrid Supply System. Most firms, even those that are well along in the development of a lean network, maintain a hybrid materials management system. This means that some items will be part of a lean supply network and are provided by suppliers that coordinate their production quantities with their customer's demand requirements. It also means these suppliers willingly participate in a closed-loop transportation system featuring frequent deliveries and returnable containers. Coordinating production requirements and closed-loop transportation systems will be explained in Chapters 3 and 4.

Items that are not part of a lean network can still be managed by more traditional methods, such as an economic order quantity (EOQ) formula. The EOQ formula allows the calculation of an ordering quantity that represents the lowest total cost when considering an item's annual demand, ordering costs, and inventory carrying charges. Using the EOQ formula is a sure indication that an item is not directly part of a lean system. That doesn't mean, however, that this approach is wrong. It might just be the right approach for managing items that have no business being part of a network that features more frequent deliveries of smaller quantities.

SUPPLY MANAGEMENT PRACTICES THAT PROMOTE LEAN

The third part of lean supply involves various approaches that help remove cost and redundancy from the supply management process. Supply management is a cross-functional process for obtaining goods and services that features the active management and involvement of suppliers. It involves identifying a company's total requirements, developing supply strategies, evaluating and selecting suppliers, and then managing and developing those suppliers to realize performance advantages at levels higher than what competitors are realizing. Certain supply activities, whether it is their intended objective or not, can go a long way toward removing waste from the supply management process. The following describes some of the more powerful ways to drive waste from the supply management process. Each directly supports the objectives of lean supply.

Optimizing the Supply Base

Building a lean supply network involves determining the right mix and number of suppliers to maintain for each purchase item, category, or commodity. Talking about the right mix and number leads us to supply base optimization, an important concept that was presented in Chapter 1. Supply base optimization is a process that seeks to create a supply base that is as perfect, effective, or functional as possible. Most supply managers will associate supply base optimization with supply base reduction since most U.S. firms have maintained historically a large base. We will assume here that optimization usually involves supplier reduction.

A misconception surrounding optimization is that fewer suppliers mean fewer total supply chain members. At most companies, supplier reduction corresponds only to a reduction in first-tier suppliers. As buyers rely on suppliers to design and build entire systems, first-tier component suppliers often get pushed to the supply chain's second or third tier. The systems supplier is then slotted into the first-tier position. However, the need to source components did not go away. The responsibility for sourcing these components now often resides with the new first-tier super supplier. It is important that the first-tier supplier effectively manage second- and third-tier suppliers. Not doing so inevitably creates waste that ends up, literally, at the buyer's doorstep.

An optimized supply base usually results in supply managers working with fewer suppliers, something that supports the attainment of lean. Activities that require close cooperation between buyers and sellers simply are not feasible with an unruly supply base. Optimization efforts should also result in better supply chain performance and reduced risk. After all, who would knowingly eliminate their best suppliers? Fewer suppliers also support the leveraging of purchase volumes.

A major advantage of an optimized supply base is the opportunity to drive out redundancy and waste that adds minimal value. Think about what an optimized supply base means within the context of lean:

- Fewer contracts or purchase orders to negotiate and write
- Fewer material releases and receipts
- Easier material traceability
- Fewer supplier performance reviews
- Better communication with suppliers
- Fewer accounts payable transactions
- Improved supply base quality and delivery performance
- Lower purchase unit costs
- Opportunities for cooperative improvement projects

Except for unit price reductions that result from leveraging volumes, most organizations do not have a clue about how to measure the benefits of dealing with fewer suppliers. The transactions costs involved with dealing with suppliers, which are quite real, are usually buried in various overhead accounts. As long as the people in these overhead accounts are busy, an assumption is made they are being productive. Supply base reduction supports lean by reducing nonvalue-adding activities that are not immediately obvious.

Developing a World-Class Supplier Selection Process

The opening of this chapter discussed how supplier selection affects a firm's ability to create a lean supply chain. Supplier evaluation and selection is certainly not the only process that firms perform today. It is, however, one of the most important. The development of a selection process that also includes the tools and methods to support the selection decision can go a long way toward removing redundancy and waste from the supply management process.

Sometimes external forces demand that processes be performed faster and better. Many supplier selection decisions, for example, occur during product development. Given the steady decline in new product development times that is occurring across most industries, it seems logical that any supporting cycle times must also decline. Gone are the days when supply managers can spend months to evaluate, select, and negotiate supplier agreements. Now, major selection decisions often have to occur in weeks, perhaps even days. Supplier selection is a process that must be effective and quick.

There are many creative ways to shorten supplier selection cycle time without reducing the quality of the process. In fact, reducing the cycle time should actually improve the selection process as waste is removed and value-adding activities are streamlined. When performed correctly, a faster selection process requires supply managers to work smarter, be proactive rather than reactive, and be efficient. The following are some powerful ways to make the supplier selection process leaner without hurting effectiveness:

- Have supply managers participate on product development teams to gain early insight into selection needs
- Establish e-systems and templates so internal customers can forward supply requirements efficiently to procurement
- Develop pre-approved contract language to streamline negotiations
- Prequalify suppliers in anticipation of future needs
- Use International Purchasing Offices to evaluate foreign suppliers

- Send Requests for Information (RFI), Requests for Quotations (RFQs), and Requests for Proposals (RFPs) to suppliers electronically
- Use software to streamline the evaluation of supplier responses
- Use third-party data to financially prequalify potential suppliers
- Develop tools to support quantitative assessments during supplier site visits
- Create a preferred supplier list
- Segment supplier selection needs based on how critical they are and approach the selection decision accordingly

Reducing Redundancy across Buying Sites and Locations

Most firms do a poor or marginal job of coordinating their supply activities across their different business units, buying centers, and operating locations. As a result, redundancy and duplication of effort, and even conflict become a real issue as different units develop their own supplier selection protocols, measurement systems, strategy development processes, contracts, and information systems. Sometimes these internal units even approach the same suppliers differently, creating confusion within the supply chain. The importance of standardized approaches was touched upon in Chapter 1.

One way to reduce waste is to pursue a process called global sourcing. Global sourcing involves integrating and coordinating common materials and services, processes and practices, designs, technologies, and suppliers across worldwide purchasing, engineering, and operating locations. This differs from international or worldwide purchasing, which relates to a commercial purchase transaction between a buyer and supplier located in different countries with little or no coordination across locations within a company.

Table 2.2 presents some compelling evidence regarding the consistency or similarity that global sourcing firms achieve compared with firms that are not coordinating their worldwide activities. This table reports on the degree of similarity or consistency across some important supply management areas. These items are ranked by the largest average difference between firms that practice international purchasing and firms that practice global sourcing. A desired outcome from integrated global sourcing should be consistency across buying or operating units. Firms that engage in global sourcing are well ahead of their international purchasing counterparts in eliminating the dissimilarities that create waste within their supply management process. The time has come to take a globally coordinated view of supply.

Table 2.2 Supply management similarity across segments

	Global sourcing	International purchasing	Difference
Strategy development process	4.90	3.68	1.22
Supplier assessment practices	4.90	3.75	1.15
Purchasing or sourcing philosophy	5.04	3.96	1.08
Current purchasing strategies	4.96	3.96	1.00
Problem resolution techniques with suppliers	4.90	3.90	1.00
Contracting approaches	4.54	3.58	.96

1 = not similar or consistent, 7 = extremely similar or consistent

Source: R. J. Trent and R. M. Monczka, "International Purchasing and Global Sourcing—What are the Differences?" Journal of Supply Chain Management (Fall 2003): 26.

Developing Longer-Term Supply Agreements

The 1990s witnessed a major growth in the use of longer-term contracts. From 1990 to the latter 1990s, purchases represented by longer-term contracts increased from 34 percent to 50 percent of total purchase dollars.[5] This growth has continued through the 2000s. The amount of purchases covered by contracts is a common metric when evaluating a supply management organization, although be careful not to equate longer-term contracting with success. Buyers and suppliers have been known to lock themselves into some poor agreements.

Longer-term agreements are *legal contracts between two or more parties that are expected to be in effect for a time period greater than a year, and which usually address a greater range of price and nonprice issues than shorter-term or standard "boiler plate" agreements.* How do longer-term agreements help remove waste from the supply management process?

Longer-term agreements address many issues or topics that are not present in shorter-term contracts, including continuous improvement incentives, commitments to work jointly to improve performance, and mechanisms for better communication and relationships between the buyer and seller. These all offer the opportunity to remove waste and nonvalue-adding activities from the supply chain.

How else do longer-term contracts support lean supply? Effective longer-term agreements may remove uncertainty from a supply relationship, leading to better planning and less reliance on safety stock inventories. Furthermore, a longer-term agreement that leverages company-wide purchase should lead to further savings compared to a set of shorter-term agreements. Longer-term agreements with a reduced supply base also allow a buying company to move away from the cycle of perpetually reestablishing agreements, an activity that is generally considered to be nonvalue adding.

Contracting processes are also becoming more efficient as software becomes available to electronically sign and store contracts. A variety of companies have introduced easy-to-use software to affix electronic signatures to an agreement. Now, negotiation and the signing of agreements do not have to be face-to-face. Proponents of the signature technology tout its security, its ability to take time out of the contracting process, and its cost-effectiveness. Instead of sending one contract back and forth between parties so that all participants can sign the original agreement, or requiring the parties to be present in the same room, e-signatures allow the agreement process to be completed on-line.[6]

Establishing Low-Dollar Purchase Systems

Most people are familiar with the Pareto principle, which states that 20 percent of something is responsible for 80 percent of something. For example, 20 percent of suppliers may receive 80 percent of total purchase dollars, or 20 percent of customers may account for 80 percent of sales. A more troublesome ratio occurs when 20 percent of total purchases commands 80 percent of a supply group's effort. Unfortunately, this scenario is often too real.

Reducing the effort required to obtain low-dollar purchases remains an ongoing challenge. By improving how they manage low-dollar purchases, supply managers can begin to redirect their efforts toward value-creating activities while reducing the costs associated with obtaining relatively insignificant items. While the need to obtain low-dollar goods will never disappear, the effort required to manage their purchase should diminish greatly.

Many different systems help remove the transactions costs associated with relatively insignificant items. These systems often share one predominant trait— they allow internal users to efficiently obtain their low-dollar requirements, usually without help from the supply group. The following is a sample of systems that make the supply process leaner when obtaining low-dollar items:

- Procurement cards issued to internal users
- Blanket purchase orders that allow internal users to order directly from suppliers
- Online catalogues
- Electronic requisitions issued to procurement
- Electronic purchase orders issued to suppliers

- On-site suppliers to manage inventory
- Electronic funds transfer to suppliers
- Allowing internal users to issue purchase orders below a dollar limit

A study that focused on reducing the transactions costs of obtaining low-value goods and services found that the four highest rated benefits realized from these low-dollar systems, ranked in terms of importance, are (1) reduced costs per transaction, (2) increased attention given to more important items, (3) reduced time to satisfy internal user needs, and (4) a reduced number of transactions.[7] The benefits from these low-dollar systems align nicely with lean objectives.

CONCLUDING THOUGHTS

To view lean as simply what happens within one's four walls is incomplete. Furthermore, viewing lean supply as simply receiving smaller quantities on a more frequent basis from suppliers is also only part of the picture. If lean is a primary corporate objective, then executive managers must ask their supply managers what they are doing to support their organization's lean objectives. Asking anything less increases the probability that end-to-end lean management will be nothing more than an incomplete process.

ENDNOTES

1. This example is adapted from "Lean Drives Solectron's Sourcing," *Purchasing Magazine Online*, http://www.purchasing.com, January 12, 2006.

2. This example is adapted from "Hamilton Sundstrand Applies Lean, Quality Techniques to Supply Chain," *Purchasing Magazine Online*, http://www.purchasing.com, June 14, 2007.

3. R. Monczka and R. Trent, "Purchasing and Supply Management: Key Trends and Changes throughout the 1990s," *International Journal of Purchasing and Materials Management* 34, no. 4 (Fall 1998): 2-11.

4. A. Reese, "eProcurement Takes on an Untamed Supply Chain," *iSource* (November 2000): 108.

5. See Note 3, 2-11.

6. R. Buckman, "Signing Up for E-Signatures," *Wall Street Journal*, July 3, 2007, A9.

7. R. Trent and M. Kolchin, *Reducing the Transactions Costs of Purchasing Low Value Goods and Services* (Tempe, AZ: Center for Advanced Purchasing Studies, 1999), 10.

This book has free material available for download from the
Web Added Value™ resource center at *www.jrosspub.com*

LEAN TRANSPORTATION

This chapter takes us to the second major stop along the lean supply chain. It was not that long ago that most firms did not give much thought to their transportation needs, particularly for the inbound part of their supply chain. Transportation rates and service in the United States were governed by a comfortable blanket of economic regulations that were overseen by the Interstate Commerce Commission, the first commission established in the United States and one that no longer exists. Deviations from published rates rarely occurred, and any efforts to do otherwise yielded minimal benefit. It was easy to have suppliers arrange transportation, and when buyers did specify a carrier it was often "Ship via Best Way." When attention to transportation did occur, it was handled by a relatively insignificant group called *traffic*.

How the times have changed! The pursuit of lean cannot become a reality without a transportation system that supports lean objectives up and down the supply chain. This chapter begins by first explaining the concept of lean transportation, taking care to point out that a lean transportation system is not only about more frequent deliveries of smaller quantities. The effect that transportation deregulation has had on lean appears next, followed by lean transportation's essential elements. The chapter concludes with the important role that transportation strategies play within a lean organization. Figure 3.1 places this discussion along our supply chain model. While transportation occurs up and down the supply chain, it is the vital link between lean supply and lean operations.

WHAT IS LEAN TRANSPORTATION?

A primary objective of lean transportation, but certainly not the only one, is to provide predictable and more frequent deliveries to a specific point-of-use. Many

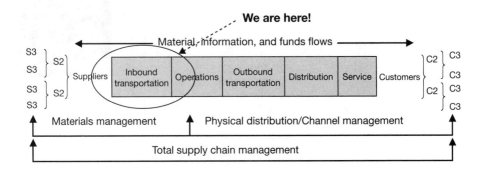

Figure 3.1 Lean transportation

transportation managers will argue that lean transportation means minimizing the number of miles traveled within a transportation system. This assumes, and this is an extremely important point, that a company has optimized its supply chain network. We can always reduce miles traveled, for example, by adding a bunch of stocking locations that are close to customers. But what would that do to inventory and overhead costs?

Transportation moves can occur upstream between suppliers and buyers, between locations of the same company, and downstream between a company and its channel members, including end customers. Of the major parts of a lean supply chain, the transportation portion may be one of the easier parts to put in place. The reason for this is firms are increasingly turning over responsibility for transportation to third-party experts that make their living managing transportation systems. Many companies have simply decided that transportation, while an essential part of a successful supply chain, is not a core capability.

A challenge with lean transportation is that the steps transportation managers often have to take to support lean are normally not what these managers are predisposed to do. Given that most transportation managers are measured on how well they reduce transportation costs or minimize miles traveled, moving smaller quantities of goods more frequently doesn't seem quite right. After all, economies of scale are as applicable in transportation as they are in manufacturing. It is not unusual, although not necessarily a given, that some transportation costs could actually increase in a lean supply chain. This is an area where supply chain managers must address trade-offs and conflict.

Lean transportation is an integral part of some important supply chain trade-offs. Trade-offs require a balancing of factors, or objectives, that cannot all be attained at the same time. The presence of a trade-off means giving up one thing in return for another. Functional groups that are unwilling to give anything up as they concentrate on their own, and often narrow objectives frequently find themselves in direct conflict with other groups. A process engineering group that is responsible for production efficiency and product quality at a battery manufacturer has become increasingly vocal, for example, about its discontent with suppliers from far-flung geographic locations. The engineers are mystified that purchasing continues to select suppliers, site unseen, based on product samples and low prices. When the engineers suggest that purchasing should visit suppliers before selecting them, the purchasing group suggests that perhaps the engineers should make these visits. The Las Vegas odds are 50-1 in support of the proposition that the purchasing group is measured on price reductions rather than total cost reductions.

Some important supply chain trade-offs involve transportation, making it the case that lean transportation does not necessarily mean low-cost transportation. A lean system is one that effectively manages trade-offs from a total cost perspective. While supply chains are never short of trade-off choices, five of the most important ones include the following:[1]

- **Lot Size-Inventory Trade-Off.** While larger lot sizes provide production efficiencies, demand rarely comes in large or standard lot sizes. Large lots lead to high inventory that is held in anticipation of demand.
- **Inventory-Transportation Cost Trade-Off.** Aggregating material movements allows fewer and larger shipments and reduced transportation costs. Less frequent material movement, however, requires holding inventory and possible decreases in customer service.
- **Lead Time-Transportation Cost Trade-Off.** Transportation costs are lowest when large quantities of items are transported between stages of the supply chain, creating longer-lead times and higher inventory carrying costs.
- **Product Variety-Inventory Trade-Off.** Increased variety and features create new part numbers, which affects forecasting complexity, product placement across the supply chain, product costs, transportation costs, and inventory levels.
- **Cost-Customer Service Trade-Off.** Increased customer service levels usually require higher inventory levels and faster delivery, which increases inventory and transportation costs.

It is simply a matter of fact that lean transportation must operate within the context of these trade-offs. At times transportation costs, due to frequent deliveries of smaller quantities, may actually rise. This is acceptable if inventory-related costs decline by a greater amount. Lean transportation is more about supporting supply chain and corporate objectives than about achieving the lowest possible transportation costs.

Some observers will use the term lean *logistics*, rather than lean transportation, when talking about the movement of goods. This implies a broader treatment of the subject. As an interesting aside, some observers present the term logistics with a lower case *l* while others use an upper case *L*. Believe it or not, the differences are meaningful to purists. A narrower view of logistics usually relates primarily to the physical movement of goods across a supply chain. A broader view of logistics includes all the parts of the supply chain that plan, implement, and control the efficient, effective flow and storage of goods, services, and related information from the point-of-origin to the point-of-consumption in order to meet customers' requirements.[2] This broader view is essentially describing supply chain management. Our focus in this chapter is primarily in terms of the narrower view.

Transportation managers, or third-party providers if transportation has been outsourced, must work closely with and support lean supply and lean operations. The timing of material pickup and delivery will largely be dictated by an operations' schedule that determines when and where something is required. The schedule and its volumes will also dictate the kinds of equipment, such as trucks and returnable containers, that will be required. Working with transportation representatives, the supply management group will have responsibility for identifying those suppliers capable of participating in a lean supply network. It is essential for supply and transportation managers to coordinate their efforts.

While a good part of lean transportation deals with more frequent deliveries of smaller quantities, we could make the argument that any transportation effort that results in the elimination of waste qualifies as part of lean. Wal-Mart, for example, has instituted a *Remix* distribution program that consolidates less-than-truckload (LTL) shipments and increases truckload deliveries to stores.[3] Full truckloads that move goods directly between two points can be highly efficient and effective as long as the use of full truckloads does not adversely affect other supply chain units or cost categories. A solid 80 percent of what U.S. companies spend for transportation services goes to trucking, and about half of that is for full truckload movements. Smaller shipments may also be aggregated by freight forwarders with goods from other shippers to achieve transportation discounts. While neither truckload shipments nor consolidated shipments with freight forwarders feature more frequent deliveries of smaller quantities of goods, they both have the potential to remove supply chain waste.

TRANSPORTATION DEREGULATION—A CATALYST FOR LEAN

In the late 1970s and early 1980s, Congress passed a series of legislation, which President Jimmy Carter signed, that economically deregulated transportation modes and carriers operating in the United States. (Safety regulation still exists and is managed largely by the Department of Transportation as well as other miscellaneous government boards and commissions.) The primary objective of these new laws was to make the entire transportation system more efficient. This legislation included the *Air Cargo Deregulation Act* in 1977, the *Air Passenger Deregulation Act* in 1978, the *Motor Carrier Act of 1980*, the *Staggers Act* in 1980, the *Transportation Industry Regulation Reform Act* (TIRRA) in 1994, the *ICC Termination Act* in 1995, and the *Ocean Shipping Reform Act* (OSRA) in 1998. In retrospect, these laws were a primary catalyst for the evolution of lean transportation. Table 3.1 provides some key points about each law.

Recall from the opening of this chapter that prior to deregulation, transportation rates and service in the United States were governed by a comfortable blanket of regulations that were overseen by the Interstate Commerce Commission. The changes brought about by these laws created new opportunities that directly supported the reduction of waste. In this context, waste reduction extended across the entire U.S. economy.

The primary objective of each law was to make the U.S. transportation system more efficient by allowing increased competition, rate-making flexibility, and other nontraditional shipping arrangements that are formalized through contracts. Prior to deregulation, for example, the Interstate Commerce Commission enforced something called *The Rule of Eight*, which mandated that no trucking company with contract carrier authority could have more than eight contract customers. One estimate is that 70 to 80 percent of freight in the United States that is not moving on private fleets now moves under some form of a contract rather than a standard bill of lading.[4]

One only has to look to the *Staggers Act* for a seemingly minor legal change that resulted in far-reaching transportation changes. A change provided in this law allowed a form of intermodal transportation called *piggyback*, or *trailer-on-flat-car* (TOFC). Intermodal transportation between rail and motor carrier further promoted a leaner transportation system by combining the efficiencies of line-haul rail movements with the pickup and delivery flexibility of trucking. The growth in intermodal transportation over the last 25 years has been nothing short of astounding.

For transportation providers the changes were major, and sometimes even gut wrenching. Carriers now had to compete against new entrants, against existing carriers, and even against aggressive carriers from other transportation modes. They also lost their blanket of economic protection, making it look like the Wild West all over again. Organized labor, such as the Teamsters, clearly did not favor deregulation. Reduced barriers to entry allowed thousands of nonunionized carriers to begin service, and since 1980 no new unionized carriers have offered transportation services.

Table 3.1 Major transportation deregulation acts

Law	Comments
Air Cargo Deregulation Act (1977)	• Eliminated economic regulation and permitted air carriers to publish cargo rates without approval of the Civil Aeronautics Board • Allowed rate negotiation between shippers and carriers • Reduced the barriers to entry for new carriers
Air Passenger Deregulation Act (1978)	• Freed carriers from government regulation over passenger fares • Reduced barriers to entry for new carriers
Motor Carrier Act of 1980	• While still requiring published tariff rates, the law allowed carriers to offer discounts from published rates • Made it easier to obtain a Certificate of Public Convenience and Necessity, opening the door for new entrants to offer service • Allowed public and private carriers to haul a wider range of goods • Ended restrictions on contract carriage
Staggers Act (1980)	• Provided rate-making flexibility • Allowed railroads to enter into long-term contracts with shippers • Deregulated a form of intermodal transportation called "piggyback"
Transportation Industry Regulation Reform Act (TIRRA) (1994)	• Deregulated intrastate trucking • Eliminated the need for carriers to file rates and notices of rate changes • Provided rate-making confidentiality between carriers and shippers • Allowed off-bill discounting • Removed some antitrust exemptions for rate-making bureaus
ICC Termination Act (1995)	• Eliminated most remaining truck regulation • Established the Surface Transportation Board • Formally eliminated the Interstate Commerce Commission
Ocean Shipping Reform Act (OSRA) 1998	• Allowed carriers and shippers to enter into confidential service contracts • Although contracts are still filed with the Federal Maritime Commission, they are no longer public

For shippers (i.e., the buyers of transportation services) the changes brought about by deregulation offered an opportunity to leverage their transportation volumes with longer-term agreements, an activity that usually resulted in deep rate discounts. Shippers that relied on motor carriers saw the choices available to them increase dramatically, increases that are still occurring today. In 1995, for example, there were 346,000 interstate motor carriers operating in the United States. By 2003, this number had increased to almost 675,000. The number of marine vessel operators and Class I railroads has actually declined during this same period.[5]

Deregulation resulted in some painful changes, but they also created opportunities for taking waste out of the transportation network. One example that shows the kind of innovative thinking that emerged after deregulation involved an unlikely arrangement between an automotive company's national distribution center and an orange juice company. Using a private fleet the juice company shipped oranges from Florida groves to a juice processing plant located near Detroit, Michigan. Unfortunately, prior to deregulation private carriers were prohibited from hauling freight for other companies, often forcing empty return trips. Empty back-hauls are a terrible waste of resources.

Transportation managers came up with an innovative idea. After unloading the oranges from Florida, why not send the empty trailer over to the national distribution center located three miles from the juice plant? The national distribution center in Michigan could then load the trailer with replenishment inventory for the Orlando regional distribution center. After the trailer was unloaded in Orlando it would proceed to the orange groves for more oranges and a trip back to Michigan. This idea was truly win-win—the orange juice company covered the expenses for return truck trips to Florida while the national distribution center gained a lower-cost transportation option. Post-deregulation ideas like this sprouted everywhere.

Beyond anecdotal evidence, did deregulation accomplish the objective of making transportation more efficient and less wasteful? The answer appears to be a resounding "yes." From 1980 to 2004, the cost of logistics, which here includes inventory carrying charges, but not the value of the inventory, and transportation declined from over 16 percent of gross domestic product (GDP) to less than 9 percent of GDP![6] Transportation costs declined from over 7 percent of GDP to less than 6 percent, and inventory carrying charges declined from over 8 percent of GDP to less than 3 percent of GDP. A good part of the decline in inventory carrying charges can be attributed directly to the benefits derived from transportation networks that feature fast, reliable, and more frequent deliveries of smaller quantities.

Total logistics costs as a percent of GDP are now over 10 percent largely due to higher fuel costs, driver shortages, and congested ports of entry. Looking back over the last 25 years, however, the economic effects of transportation deregulation have been positive. Supporting a growing economy with a smaller portion of a nation's resources is called efficiency, and efficiency and lean are the best of friends.

ELEMENTS OF A LEAN TRANSPORTATION SYSTEM

At the company level there are some specific elements that tend to characterize lean transportation systems. While not all lean transportation systems will feature each element presented here, the following characteristics will come up in most conversations when lean and transportation are combined into the same discussion.

Contract and Third-Party Logistics Providers

Many firms operate lean and efficient transportation networks because they have decided not to operate their own networks. Instead, they rely on others who may, or may not, have their own physical assets to manage a client's transportation and logistics needs. The last 25 years has seen a steady increase in the use of contract and third-party transportation providers, making a better understanding of this part of lean transportation a must.

Some powerful trends are at work that should ensure the growing reliance on contract and third-party logistics (3PL) providers continue. Perhaps the greatest driver behind transportation outsourcing comes from a relentless pressure to reduce costs, making the efficient use of resources a mandate. Supply chain managers will increasingly look to transportation outsourcing as a way to lower costs and remove waste from the supply chain. Next, many firms are becoming increasingly specialized in what they do. In other words, we can't be everything to everybody. Increased specialization leads to focused investment in a process, technology, or capability, which leads to greater cost differentials between firms. Third, firms will increasingly focus on what they excel at while outsourcing non-core areas. More and more companies are formally defining their core capabilities and competencies to help guide their outsourcing decisions. And more and more companies are deciding that transportation, while an integral part of an effective supply chain, is not part of their core business. A focus on core capabilities and competencies combined with cost reduction pressures may be the two strongest drivers behind the outsourcing of transportation and logistics services.

Other good reasons exist for believing that transportation and logistics outsourcing will continue. The way that companies win in the marketplace is increasingly through speed and responsiveness. Shorter cycle times encourage greater outsourcing with less vertical integration. The time to develop a capability or capacity internally may exceed the window of opportunity available to exploit an opportunity. Last but not least, Wall Street recognizes and rewards firms with a higher return on assets. Since managing a private transportation fleet usually requires an assumption of fixed assets and increased human capital, pressure from financial analysts are causing supply chain managers to look to outsourcing as a means to enhance the all important return-on-assets metric.

Transportation Classifications. An understanding of lean transportation requires some familiarity with the kinds of transportation classifications that exist. The three most familiar classifications of transportation carriers are (1) common, (2) contract, and (3) private carriers. Much of the freight that moves as part of lean transportation moves on dedicated contract carriers that are often managed by 3PL providers. A significant amount of material still moves on private carriers. And, as delivery reliability by common carriers becomes more precise, the reluctance of some managers to use standard transportation options (i.e., common carriers) should begin to lessen. The following summarizes three predominant classifications of transportation carriers:

- **Common Carriers.** These carriers are for hire and serve the general public without discrimination. To satisfy its public service requirements, a common carrier cannot refuse to transport a particular material that is within its scope of operation. All shippers generally receive similar service from a common carrier.
- **Private Carriers.** These carriers are owned by a company whose primary business is something other than transportation. The private carrier essentially serves that company's needs as well as any subsidiaries and are not for hire by the general public.
- **Contract Carriers.** These carriers serve only those shippers with whom the carrier has entered into a contractual agreement. Contract carriers usually perform specialized services for a shipper, such as regular pickup and deliveries in a closed-loop, just-in-time (JIT) system. Some industry experts also refer to contract carriers as *dedicated fleets.*

While it may be hard to believe, private trucking fleets make up the largest segment of the U.S. trucking industry, comprising an estimated 45 percent share of the $700 billion motor-carrier market.[7] Most companies that rely on private fleets do so to move full truckloads of goods to distribution centers or directly to their customers. What this means is that private fleets are used primarily for outbound rather than inbound transportation. In fact, less than one-third of companies use their private fleets for inbound shipments.[8] Many firms with private fleets also rely on contract carriers, LTL carriers, and other third-party alternatives.

Companies that maintain private fleets indicate the reason they do so is because they believe these fleets provide superior service levels. These companies may also have unique operating requirements that require specialized equipment. Private fleets also experience far less annual driver turnover (14 percent annually) compared with for-hire truckload companies (100 percent annually).[9] Most private fleet managers express confidence they will handle more rather than less freight over the next few years, indicating that outsourcing does not seem to be a concern to them.

On the flip side, some transportation experts argue quite vocally that a continued reliance on private fleets, particularly for long-distance movement of goods, is a wasteful use of corporate assets. One expert maintains that "private fleets are complex operations with their own unique set of requirements and regulations. They take time, energy, and above all else, money to run efficiently and at peak performance."[10] Other studies suggest that most private fleets lack the economies of scale required to establish a competitive cost structure. These studies also suggest that private fleet assets are constrained by the limits of their own network structure and demand profile, leading to a greater percentage of empty miles compared with contract or common carrier assets. We will have to see how the debate between private and contract carriers plays out, particularly as it relates to a lean supply chain.

Contracted Transportation Services. One area where managers can exercise some real creativity involves negotiating agreements with contract carriers. U.S. commercial law is generous regarding what two or more parties may agree to in a contract. And let's not forget that deregulation opened the door for negotiating rates and discounts. Virtually anything in a transportation contract is negotiable as long as the contract satisfies some basic conditions:

- **Offer and acceptance.** An offer is a proposal to do something and acceptance is agreeing to the offer.
- **Consideration.** Each party must agree to give up something of value during the performance of the contract.
- **Legality of subject matter.** Contracts can only cover topics that are legal.
- **Legal capacity.** Only those individuals who are legally or mentally qualified to enter into a contract may do so. In commercial applications this deals with legal agency.

Why not use standard LTL common carriers instead of dedicated contract carriers to support our lean transportation objectives? A supply chain mapping exercise performed at one company revealed that a traditional supply chain using LTL shipments builds in an unusually large number of steps or activities, something that can extend delivery times and increase the opportunity for theft and damage. A traditional inbound shipment relying on LTL common carriers can require 33 steps or activities to move an item from a supplier's production process to a buyer's production process, which Table 3.2 details. This table assumes the movement of material over several hundred miles rather than down the street.

A delivery system that features dedicated contract carriers with suppliers that coordinate their build schedule with their customer's demand schedule should require only eight steps. We can probably conclude that a good portion of the 33 steps in a traditional transportation system involves waste or other nonvalue-added activities. This includes inventory waste due to slower velocity of inventory through the upstream portion of the chain, multiple handling with no new value being added, increased packaging, and a greater chance of in-transit damage. Furthermore, this exhibit shows only a single link between a single first-tier supplier and a buyer. Imagine how much waste and nonvalue-added activities take place for a complex product requiring hundreds of first-tier suppliers and potentially thousands of subtier suppliers, all operating within a traditional production and transportation network. Lean transportation clearly offers the potential for dramatic supply chain improvements.

The early days of JIT networks relied almost exclusively on private or contract carriers. Shipping by LTL was simply too unreliable for planning a time-sensitive flow of material across the supply chain. LTL carriers provided *delivery windows* that could be in days rather than *specific delivery dates and times*, and the technology to track shipments did not exist. Now, carriers such as Roadway Express, FedEx Freight, USF Holland, Averitt Express, Old Dominion Freight Line, and Con-way Freight (to name but a few) all offer faster delivery with tight delivery windows. These LTL carriers are becoming so precise in their delivery and tracking abilities that new cost-effective options are available for planning shipments across the supply chain. This is only good news for those who manage transportation networks.

There certainly is no rule that says material movements within a lean system have to be with contract or private carriers, particularly if all a shipper wants to accomplish is a delivery at a certain date and time. Common carriers may not be the best or most economical option for bringing returnable containers or other returns back to their point of origin, however, something that closed-loop systems are designed to do quite well.

Determining the best option (common, contract, or private carrier) to support a lean supply chain will require detailed transportation analyses, something that 3PL providers are usually quite capable of doing. Furthermore, detailed assessments of specific carriers must also occur, looking at the total cost of doing business with a carrier as well as each carrier's speed, reliability, capability, and availability.

3PL Service Providers. The previous discussion has made several references to 3PL providers. What exactly is this thing we call a 3PL? A third-party logistics

Table 3.2 Comparing traditional and lean transportation steps

Traditional LTL shipment	Closed-loop JIT delivery
At the supplier:	**At the supplier:**
1) Move material from production to packaging.	Move material in returnable containers from production to the shipping area.
2) Package material for internal storage.	
3) Move and store material internally.	
4) Cycle count material as required.	
5) Pick material for shipment when ordered by customer.	
6) Move material to shipping area.	
7) Get material physically ready for shipment.	
8) Prepare shipping documents.	Prepare shipping documents.
9) Load LTL common carrier.	Load dedicated contract carrier.
By the carrier:	**By the carrier:**
10) Local delivery truck picks up material and transports it with other loads to a local terminal.	
11) Unload truck and consolidate material for transport to break-bulk terminal.	
12) Reload truck with material for break-bulk terminal.	
13) Transport material to break-bulk terminal.	
14) Unload truck and consolidate with loads for next break-bulk terminal near customer location.	
15) Reload truck with material for next break-bulk terminal.	
16) Transport material to next break-bulk terminal.	
17) Unload truck and consolidate with loads for local terminal that serves the customer.	
18) Transport material to local terminal.	
19) Unload truck and consolidate orders by customer.	
20) Reload local delivery truck with customer orders.	
21) Transport material to customer.	Transport material to customer.

Table 3.2 Comparing traditional and lean transportation steps (continued)

Traditional LTL shipment By the customer:	Closed-loop JIT delivery By the customer:
22) Unload material at receiving area.	Unload material at receiving area and load returnable containers.
23) Receive material into the receiving system.	
24) Forward receipt information to accounts payable.	
25) Inspect incoming material.	
26) Attach move tickets.	
27) Move material to inventory until needed.	
28) Stockkeep material and record location.	
29) Cycle count material as required.	
30) Retrieve material when needed from storage.	
31) Move material to required usage location.	Move material to required usage location.
32) Dispose of packaging.	Move returnable containers back to receiving area.
33) Update records.	Update records.

provider is essentially an organization that manages and executes various logistics functions on behalf of another company.[11] The 3PL can be asset-based, which means it has its own assets in place to provide logistical services, or it can be nonasset-based. Nonasset-based 3PLs coordinate logistical networks and use the services of for-hire or contracted transportation and logistics providers. Recent estimates indicate that U.S. firms spend upwards of $90 billion a year in the 3PL space, a figure that is expected to increase. This compares with just over $30 billion in 1996.[12]

Many transportation carriers have evolved to the point where they now offer a broad range of logistics services. NRS, for example, started service in 1953 with a single truck. The firm now offers warehousing, distribution center, and consolidation services for the nation's largest retailers.[13] J. B. Hunt is known as much for its value-added logistical services as it is for trucking. There are literally thousands of 3PL providers offering services to clients today, making the choice of an ideal provider increasingly complicated.[14]

The migration of transportation companies toward becoming full-service logistical providers is a prime example of how suppliers are moving up the value creation stream to satisfy the needs of demanding customers. The 3PL selection process requires the careful crafting of Requests for Proposals (RFPs) that contain detailed shipping history, desired services, and performance expectations. A trucking company does not wake up one day and suddenly announce it is now a 3PL provider, although that has been known to happen. The logistics provider must have the capabilities to support its claims.

Closed-Loop Delivery Systems

Many observers equate lean transportation with JIT deliveries in a closed-loop system. For many companies, particularly larger ones such as GM and Deere, closed-loop systems are a critical part of their supply chain. A closed-loop system, also called a *milk run*, features regular pickup and deliveries across a supply chain with return trips. The term milk run has its roots in an earlier period when a milkman made regular deliveries to homes. After dropping off full bottles of milk the milkman brought empty glass bottles back to the bottling plant. If you understand the idea of a milk run, then you understand the idea of a closed-loop transportation system.

Closed-loop systems are used in various places. A closed-loop system can feature a material handling loop within a single facility. Many distribution centers, for example, have installed automatic guided vehicles (AGVs) that take a predefined route around the facility. These vehicles have the ability to exit onto a spur to drop off material as required. They also have the ability to pick up and transfer material to other areas. The route is regular and repeatable.

The inbound part of the supply chain is also a major opportunity area for closed-loop systems. The next section will provide a detailed example of an inbound closed-loop system. Transportation between company facilities, such as manufacturing plants and distribution centers, as well as material movement between a company and its customers, are also popular closed-loop destinations. Chapter 5 will present an example of a closed-loop system between a distribution center and automotive dealers.

Closed-loop transportation systems are probably the best-known part of lean transportation. The only problem is that most companies lack the size, sophistication, or even the need for such a system. Furthermore, any freight moving on rail carriers, and a great deal of freight in terms of tonnage does move via rail, is definitely not part of a JIT system featuring a closed-loop transportation network. The same is true for goods arriving from around the world via oceangoing vessels.

It is a mistake to believe that all JIT deliveries are part of a closed-loop system. Material can be delivered at a specified time when needed by a contract or even a common carrier without being part of a system that features a regular pickup and delivery schedule. And not all deliveries involve returnable containers that must be returned to an upstream location. The continued growth in air cargo shipments reflects a desire for material to arrive JIT without scheduled return trips in a closed-loop system. Unfortunately, statistics regarding the amount of freight moving via closed-loop systems are hard to come by.

Closed-Loop Examples. This example features the development of a closed-loop delivery system between an OEM producer of transportation equipment and several suppliers.[15] Perhaps the best way to appreciate what a closed-loop system has done for this company is to look at the before and after picture of a logistics system that involves two suppliers, cleverly named Suppliers A and B, located in Indiana. The OEM's production facility that these suppliers support is located several hundred miles away.

Supplier A provides the OEM with fans, producing a total of four different part numbers. As shown in Figure 3.2, before the development of a closed-loop delivery system this supplier shipped its parts via LTL carriers to the production facility two times a week. Recall that LTL shipments go through their own series of steps between the shipper and the customer, which is illustrated in Table 3.2 Any unneeded inventory at the OEM's production facility was transferred to a third-party warehouse to join the other excess inventory awaiting a call to action. On average the warehouse maintained 32 days worth of inventory from Supplier A.

Supplier B provides hoods and side panels, comprising a total of nine part numbers, for two product lines. Before the development of the closed-loop system this supplier shipped full truckloads of material directly to a third-party warehouse three times a week. On average the warehouse maintained 20 days worth of inventory from Supplier B. A third-party would transfer material from the warehouse to the OEM's production facility on an as-needed basis. Empty returnable containers would then be sent from the production facility to a separate cross-dock facility. These containers sat in this facility until enough were accumulated to justify a truckload trip back to the supplier. It should be obvious that neither the production materials nor the returnable containers passed the flow test.

One thing that should be immediately obvious is that the demand schedules between the OEM and the two suppliers clearly were not in sync, a topic that Chapter 4 will address. The redesigned system, which Figure 3.3 illustrates, is like a breath of fresh air (as long as you are not standing downwind from the trucks). The OEM's supply management group worked with the two suppliers to ensure that a closed-loop system was feasible. The supply group also selected a contract carrier to handle pickup and deliveries. The new network, which is approximately 800 miles in round-trip distance, now features pickup and delivery according to a regular schedule. The two suppliers ship only the quantities that are required directly to the OEM's facility five times a week. The third-party warehouse and cross-dock facility are no longer part of the transportation network for these suppliers.

Before

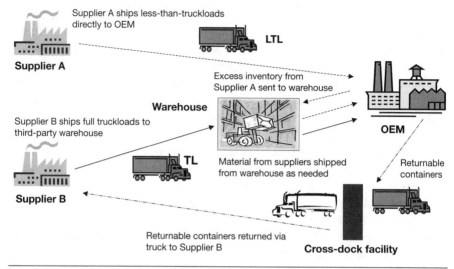

Figure 3.2 A traditional transportation system

After

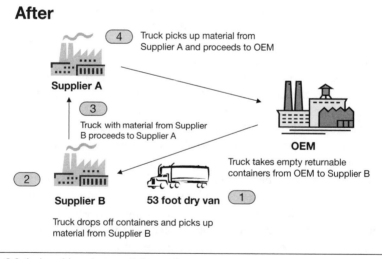

Figure 3.3 A closed-loop transportation system

The OEM has put in place a process to help analyze and implement closed-loop delivery opportunities with suppliers. The major features of this methodology include the following:

- Gather and map supplier data
- Use packaging information to design trailer layouts

- Meet with tactical and strategic buyers to verify feasibility of the closed-loop system and develop implementation strategies
- Create route specification sheets, route timelines, and trailer diagrams

This company has done a thorough job of calculating this system's value. The original system, which featured multiple transfers of inventory between facilities, holding inventory for extended periods, and extensive transportation, resulted in total logistics costs of almost $700,000 annually. The closed-loop system, which eliminated multiple handling and storage of inventory, resulted in annual total logistics costs of just under $300,000 annually. This company can certainly come up with better ways to use $400,000 than to tie that capital up in logistics costs.

Streamlined pickup and delivery systems are not only important in manufacturing environments. Any nonindustrial setting that uses maintenance, repair, and operating items (in other words, everyone) can use distributors to provide delivery directly to departments or individuals. The delivery personnel also take any items that are going back to the distributor. While the distributor's delivery schedules change day to day based on how customers order, the system still features a closed-loop capability. One eastern university found that using distributors that offer direct delivery has enabled it to eliminate its central stores and internal delivery trucks. As part of their contract, the distributors provide on-line ordering, reliable point-of-use delivery, and automated billing data for the efficient management of accounts payable. Lots of good stuff here!

These examples highlight a major question that the architects of a lean supply chain should continually be asking. This involves a thorough probing of every link and entity in a supply chain to determine its value contribution. Remember our battle cry here—minimize nonvalue-adding activities, entities, and tasks while eliminating waste. Here, third-party warehouses, central stores, holding inventory, handling items numerous times, and excess transportation are wasteful.

Returnable Containers

Returnable containers play a vital role all across the supply chain. Without meaning to insult anyone's intelligence, let's be clear on what is meant by a returnable container. Returnable containers, totes, or pallets, usually made of steel or plastic in a variety of sizes, are designed for repeated use. Some sources use the terms *returnable* and *reusable* containers interchangeably. Unlike corrugated containers that are primarily used for a one-way trip before being disposed of or recycled, returnable containers are intended to return to their point of origin over and over again. It is not unusual for a returnable container to have a five-year useful life.

What is the attractiveness of returnable containers within a lean system? For starters, these containers are used repeatedly over a period of years, making for a long-lasting financial payback. Prior to switching to returnable containers, Yuasa Battery in Reading, Pennsylvania, used corrugated honeycomb pallets, trays, covers, and spacers to ship its product at a cost of $110 per container. This company realized the payback from a returnable container after only three cycles.[16] Next, these containers are durable. They rarely break during handling or transportation. And if they do get damaged many of the plastic containers come with easy to remove and replace panels.

Another nice feature is the ability of these containers to interlock when stacked, similar to Lego pieces, which reduces shifting during transportation. This prevents loads from collapsing upon each other, making damaged freight a distant memory. And finally, the containers fold down and nest into a fraction of their upright dimension. This makes it more economical to handle and ship the containers back to an originating location. While returnable containers might not be as good as sliced bread, they are darn close.

Returnable containers are used at various places along the supply chain. One area is the link between external suppliers and a buying company's manufacturing, distribution, or retailing facilities, usually within a closed-loop delivery system. The closed-loop system is designed to pick up and return empty containers to suppliers after delivering full containers to the buyer.

Another area that often features returnable containers is the link between a manufacturer and distribution centers. Some activities, such as unit packaging, storing, labeling, or shipping of products to customers, are not economical in a higher-cost manufacturing environment. Products are often shipped in returnable containers to another location for further processing, perhaps in support of a company's postponement strategy, a concept discussed in Chapter 5. A third area includes the link from distribution center to distribution center. This model is common for companies that maintain a central or national distribution facility that replenishes regional distribution centers.

Shipping goods between a distribution center and a customer, such as a retail outlet, is also a popular use for returnable containers. This often involves using smaller containers called *totes*. Finally, the internal movement of material between work centers often features returnable containers. To not use returnable containers internally would violate some fundamental principles of lean.

If returnable containers are such a good idea, why aren't they used just about everywhere? The thing about returnable containers is they have this little quirk—they must be returned back to some location. And that's the stumbling block. Companies that do not have a closed-loop transportation system in place or some economical way to bring the containers back will have difficulty justifying the expense of the container system. Except for smaller totes and pallets, most returnable containers are relatively low-value items that are expensive to ship back using common carriers (although some companies will return these containers using common carriers). Chapter 10 describes the use of returnable containers in detail, including how to estimate the number of containers to populate within a system, how to make the financial case for returnable containers, and how these containers find their way back home.

Given that returnable containers have been around for a while, it would seem their use is mature and that the technology underlying the containers is well established. While this is largely true, it does not mean the innovation process has stopped cold.

One segment of the returnable container market that is now benefiting from innovation is pallets. The wooden pallet, a *technology* that is now over 60 years old, is starting to get a makeover. iGPS, an Orlando, Florida, company that manages pallet pools (i.e., pallets for rent), embeds a radio frequency identification (RFID) tag in every plastic pallet it manages. The company is the first to order millions of RFID tags with corresponding GRAI numbers. GRAI, which stands for *global reusable asset identifier*, is a unique identifier for reusable packages and other transportation equipment assigned by the standards organization European Article Numbering.Uniform Code Council (EAN.UCC).[17] The U.S. military has used GRAI numbers for some time.

Besides being 30 percent lighter than wood pallets, plastic pallets are marketed as more hygienic and reusable with the ability to be tracked across a supply chain. This assumes, of course, that companies have the infrastructure in place to read the RFID tags. Most companies are still in the pilot phase of their RFID programs.[18]

Another innovation surrounds something called *smart containers*. Smart containers contain embedded sensors and systems linked to satellites to track a container's physical location.[19] While ocean containers are the early target for this technology, its use will likely expand to include smaller containers and sealed motor vehicles. A Stanford University study estimates that the widespread use of smart container technology will lead to a 50 percent increase in access to supply chain data, a 38 percent reduction in theft, a 14 percent decline in excess inventory, and a 29 percent reduction in transit times.[20]

Smart container systems will eventually have the ability to detect container tampering or theft, or, if the container is carrying illegal contents such as drugs, weapons, or even humans. Basic detection technology using satellites is already available from companies such as General Electric and GlobalTrak.[21] Like the claims that have accompanied RFID technology, we will see how this technology evolves.

Modified Shipping and Handling Equipment

It is not unusual to require specialized shipping and handling equipment to support lean transportation. A challenge with conventional transportation equipment, particularly trailers, is that material is loaded from the back and placed progressively into the front. In accounting terms, this is a LIFO system (last in, first out). Unfortunately, the order that material is picked up may not be the order that material will be unloaded at a receiving facility. Increasingly, material is being transported and unloaded near its point of use, particularly when shipping to distribution centers. State-of-the art centers have dozens of receiving and shipping docks interspersed around the facility. This allows for the unloading of goods at a location that reduces congestion and unnecessary travel during material handling.

One example of modified transportation equipment involves side-loading trucks. These trucks, which are usually shorter than standard 53-foot trailers, allow material to be loaded and unloaded from the side rather than from the back. This is conceptually similar to soda and beer trucks that make frequent stops to deliver relatively small orders. The objective here is to provide easy access to material regardless of the sequence in which the material was loaded. The next time you find yourself staring at a parked UPS truck take a look inside. While they are not side-loading vehicles, they allow easy access to any package in the truck. They are also designed to allow natural light to enter through the roof, thereby making the job of locating packages even easier. Crawling around the back of a dark truck is not most peoples' idea of a good time.

Information Technology

A worthy goal across supply chains today is access to real-time data. The days of queuing data into batches for nightly processing just won't cut it in a lean environment. While real-time information technology can be collected in many supply chain areas, our interest here is with transportation.

Perhaps the most exciting innovation in real-time technology involves satellite-based global systems that provide real-time vehicle, rail car, and container tracking. This is often combined with onboard computer systems that allow efficient communication between a driver and operations managers who are overseeing the transportation network. Some firms have created nerve centers to watch for developments, such as adverse weather, that can affect JIT delivery networks. These centers are tangible evidence of a desire to manage supply chain risk that can affect timely deliveries and flow. Companies that are serious about controlling their supply chain will want to do business with carriers that have these real-time capabilities. Be sure to include queries about this capability in all RFPs.

What's the big deal with IT-based systems? Think about how the following real-time data and efficient communication systems examples directly support the objectives of lean transportation, particularly the flow of material across a supply chain:

- The arrival time for trailers arriving with material should not be a surprise to anyone. Knowing the precise time a transportation vehicle will arrive allows a receiving crew to make sure an open door is available, prepare any receiving documents, and preassign workers to process the vehicle. Combining GPS capabilities with advance shipment notices that detail the contents of transportation vehicles is powerful stuff.

- Nasty acts of nature (floods, snow, tornadoes, hurricanes, etc.), road construction, accidents, and traffic congestion can all alter the timely flow of goods across a supply chain. A sudden snow squall that reduced visibility to next to nothing in central Pennsylvania, for example, caused 64 cars and trucks to pile up within minutes on I-81. This closed the freeway for many hours as rescue crews attended to injuries and damaged vehicles. Knowing about problem areas, combined with the ability to communicate efficiently in real-time with drivers, can help avoid troubling delays.

- A supplier that is part of a closed-loop system is scheduled to have material ready for pickup on Wednesdays at 10:00 a.m. Unfortunately, the supplier had a power outage that will delay the pickup by three hours. In real-time an adjustment can be made and forwarded to the driver's pickup schedule, thereby avoiding some serious dwell time. These systems help build flexibility into the transportation system.

An exciting development that taps into real-time data involves smart engine sensors that are linked through satellites to a carrier's command and control center. While not yet commonplace, the idea is to identify potential problems before they become serious problems by constantly assessing vehicle performance. Proponents of this idea visualize a day when these sensors routinely detect potential issues early and direct a driver to the nearest service center. The service center will receive information about the potential problem, allowing the center to make any necessary preparations.

The objective with smart sensors is to prevent a situation from worsening while reducing the time a vehicle is out of commission. Technologically, this scenario is not unrealistic. GM's OnStar system performs monthly diagnostic checks of a vehicle's systems. The OnStar system forwards the data from the vehicle to a satellite and then back to earth. The vehicle owner receives an easy-to-read diagnostic report via email. The report includes diagnostic checks of the integrity of all major systems, including maintenance recommendations if the system detects an issue. The report also contains information about scheduled maintenance that is due and remaining engine oil life. Vehicle owners can also receive a diagnostic check upon request.

Tracking systems, such as the kind that FedEx uses, are integral for following the progress of individual shipments across a supply chain. While these tracking systems only provide real-time data when a package is scanned, the scanning occurs at enough points to provide a solid audit trail. Today's lean transportation networks are as much about bits and bytes as they are about physical assets.

THE IMPORTANCE OF TRANSPORTATION STRATEGIES

The concept of developing lean transportation strategies is so important that it warrants its own discussion. Centrally led or coordinated transportation strategies that align with and support the aspirations of other groups are essential to the success of a lean supply chain. Effective transportation strategies enable various lean objectives up and down the supply chain to become a reality.

A clear indication that a transportation group is pushing itself in the right direction is the presence of strategies that are formalized through formal contracts. Most individuals think of a strategy as a longer-term plan, which is only one piece of the equation. A timeless definition of strategy within an organization, or a subunit of a larger organization, views strategy as a conceptualization, expressed or implied by the organization's leaders, of the long-term objectives or purposes of the organization, the broad constraints and policies that currently restrict the scope of the organization's activities, and the current set of plans and near-term goals that have been adopted in the expectation of contributing to the achievement of the organization's objectives.[22] An effective strategy, including transportation strategies, basically consists of objectives, constraints, plans, and goals.

Strategy development occurs at corporate, business unit, functional, and departmental levels. Our concern here is how transportation supports lean business strategies as well as the lean strategies of other functional groups. Figure 3.4 identifies the sequence of events that are part of the process for creating lean transportation strategies. The steps for developing these strategies are not necessarily linear, although they appear so in this exhibit. Some activities should occur concurrently.

Transportation is clearly a service that supports other groups up and down the supply chain. It is strongly recommended that managers give some thought concerning how they will integrate not only their transportation strategies but also their transportation personnel, whether they are internal or third-party providers, with other functional groups. Some possible ways to promote human

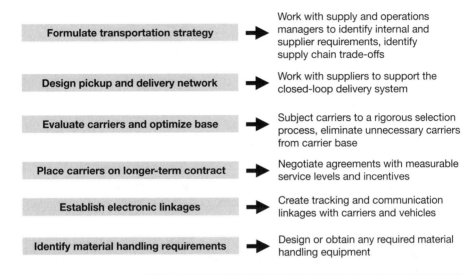

Figure 3.4 Creating a lean transportation system

integration include placing transportation or logistics representatives on new product development teams, and collocating transportation personnel with supply and distribution personnel. When you make your living as an internal service provider, practicing total quality demands a thorough understanding of customer (internal and external) requirements.

CONCLUDING THOUGHTS

Transportation is more than picking up the phone and calling a carrier to pick up or deliver goods. The reality is that transportation occurs all across a supply chain, and few should doubt that it is increasingly an important enabler of a firm's strategic objectives. There are many ways that transportation supports the attainment of a lean supply chain. Believing that lean transportation is about more frequent deliveries of smaller quantities reflects an outdated view about how transportation supports lean.

As firms become more focused, perhaps even more specialized in what they do, we should expect a greater reliance on third parties to design and manage lean transportation networks. The challenge will become one of identifying which third parties best understand and can support a company's unique supply chain objectives. Incorrect 3PL selection decisions will have long and far-reaching consequences. It will also be a challenge reconciling the goals of lean transportation with supply chains that are stretching around the world.

ENDNOTES

1. Adapted from D. Simchi-Levi, P. Kaminsky, and E. Simchi-Levi, *Designing and Managing the Supply Chain: Concepts, Strategies, and Case Studies* (Boston: McGraw-Hill Irwin, 2003).

2. This is the adopted definition of Logistics from the Council of Supply Chain Management Professionals (CSCMP).

3. W. Hoffman, "Cleaning Up on Distribution," *Traffic World* 271, no. 2 (January 15, 2007): 10-12.

4. D. Sparkman, "The Dedicated Logistics Revolution," *Traffic World's Guide to Dedicated Contract Carriage,* Supplemental Publication to *Traffic World* (2008): 8.

5. J. Sutherland, "Collaborative Transportation Management: Enhancing Supply Chain Adaptability and Resiliency," presented to the Center for Value Chain Research, Lehigh University, February 16, 2006, citing http://www.bls.gov/publications/national_transportation_statistics/2005/html/table_01_02.html.

6. From data collected annually for the CSCMP *Annual State of Logistics Report.*

7. H. Lehmann and P. Svindland, "How to Make Dedicated Fleets Work for You," *Traffic World's Guide to Dedicated Contract Carriage,* Supplemental Publication to *Traffic World*(2008): 22.

8. D. Sparkman, "Blurring the Lines," *Traffic World's Guide to Dedicated Contract Carriage,* Supplemental Publication to *Traffic World* (2008): 31.

9. See note 8, 28.

10. See note 4, quoting Clifford Lynch, 10.

11. From http://www.eyefortransport.com/glossary.

12. See note 5, citing data from Armstrong & Associates.

13. See note 4, 18.

14. *Inbound Logistics* magazine is an excellent source of information about 3PLs. The magazine recently provided a listing of what it considers the top 100 3PL providers as well as an on-line 3PL decision support tool.

15. The author would like to thank Brian Fugate, Ph.D. for sharing this example.

16. The author would like to thank Rick Newberry for sharing this example.

17. This example is adapted from S. Lacefield, "Is RFID Ready to Jump into the Pool?" *DC Velocity* 5, no. 11 (November 2007): 61.

18. See note 17, 62.

19. J. Giermanski, "Tapping the Potential of Smart Containers," *Supply Chain Management Review* 12, no. 1 (January/February 2008): 38-44.

20. See note 19, 39.

21. See note 19, 40.

22. This discussion in this section on strategy draws from R. Vancil, "Strategy Formulation in Complex Organizations," *Sloan Management Review* 17, no. 2 (Winter 1976): 1-18.

4

LEAN OPERATIONS

Our third stop across the supply chain takes us to lean operations. By design this chapter is titled "Lean Operations" rather than "Lean Manufacturing." It would be a serious error to limit our lean discussion to manufacturing companies, although that often happens. While many concepts presented in this chapter have evolved from manufacturing, many of these same topics can be applied across any industry.

This chapter presents five essential elements of lean operations, another of those topics that justifies its own book. With that in mind we will take a scaled-down view by looking at setup time reductions, facility layout changes, pull systems, uniform loading, and level scheduling. These elements are those that companies should perfect internally while also expecting suppliers to demonstrate their prowess in these same areas. Figure 4.1 positions this chapter within our supply chain framework.

SETUP TIME REDUCTION

For some very good reasons, the first area that companies usually address as they "lean out" their internal operations is to reduce setup or changeover times. An organization that can't get its setups or changeovers to the point where they are essentially a nonevent can kiss a good part of their lean aspirations goodbye. Setup time reduction is the *systematic process of minimizing downtime between part number changeovers or when moving from one condition to another.* An analogy is to move from a traditional tire change to a NASCAR or Indy pit stop. The goal is to take something that previously required hours and reduce it to seconds or minutes. Organizations that have no intention of pursuing the more complex parts of

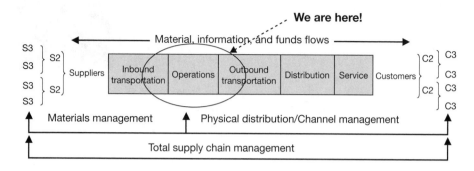

Figure 4.1 Lean operations

lean operations, such as pull systems and level scheduling, will still benefit from faster changeovers. Reduced setup times provide internal flexibility, a competitive attribute that most companies desire.

Changeovers affect not only the machines and equipment within a producer's internal operations, making a focus on suppliers an important element within this topic. All supply chain members have processes that allow them to move from one state or condition to another, or changeovers. An airline, for example, has thousands of changeovers daily as planes arrive from one destination and must go through a changeover before they can fly to their next destination. A plane that sits on the tarmac is not a large revenue generator, and any reduction in changeover time can have a financial impact. Or consider the U.S. Navy. After Trident submarines arrive back to their home port after a 70-90 day deployment, they require about 37 days of retrofit work before they are again ready to sail. Retrofits that involve the installation of new technology can take as long as 120 days. Any decrease in the changeover time represents additional time that a submarine can fulfill the mission it was designed to do.

It is safe to view setups or changeovers as essentially nonvalue adding, but important, activities. Recall from Chapter 1 that our primary focus with nonvalue-adding activities is to minimize their impact on our ability to pursue value-adding activities. Even if an organization is not pursuing lean, changeovers impede flow, and impeded flow affects throughput, productivity, and capacity. Nothing much happens in the way of value-added activity when equipment or a work center is shut down for a changeover.

Setup reduction is an issue that the entire supply chain must address. Suppliers that have not addressed setup improvements can really affect the aspirations of downstream customers. A U.S. company that made custom-fitted shoes from computer images of customers' feet recently closed its doors.[1] A major part of the company's problems were due to suppliers that could not (or would not) supply the shoelaces, leather, and other basic materials in smaller batches. The supplier that provides the small metal rings, called eyelets, that line the lace holes, for example, wanted minimum orders of 100,000. The shoe producer only needed 5000 eyelets in two different finishes.

A shortage of very specialized bolts and fasteners, while not the only challenge that Boeing faces with its 787 program, is affecting the plane's build schedule. So what is the problem? The suppliers that make these bolts, and there aren't that many, want to make thousands each time they run their production equipment. Each specialty bolt must be made individually on a lathe, a time-consuming process by anyone's measure. Because each lathe has a high setup time, the fastener supplier prefers to make thousands of the bolts during a production run. Unfortunately, and in the words of one Boeing executive, "Problem is, we don't need thousands of bolts right now. We might need ten of one kind."[2] Let's be clear here—these are not everyday nuts and bolts. A titanium fastener that is 1 inch in diameter can support the weight of 50 midsize automobiles.

Setup Time Reduction Objectives

The overarching objective of rapid changeovers is to support an organization's ability to produce smaller lot sizes within a pull environment. Setup times that are essentially a nonevent also allow greater responsiveness to changes in demand patterns. This capability allows a work center to reject scheduling work based on economic formulas, which are usually driven by local factors (i.e., ordering costs, carrying costs, etc.) rather than supply chain demand. Recall that Chapter 2 presented some examples where small lot sizes were impractical and that the economic order quantity (EOQ) model is used out of necessity. The lean application titled "Why Push When You Can Pull?—The Lessons Learned" (Chapter 12) features a company that failed to address setup times when introducing a new scheduling system. This failure affected the company's ability to package smaller volumes of more part numbers rather than higher volumes of fewer part numbers.

The ability to make setups a nonevent can be a competitive weapon, and an absence of rapid changeovers can create a serious disadvantage. Few would argue that product offerings and varieties are multiplying rapidly. Think about how many varieties and types of shampoo are available today. Proctor & Gamble, for example, has at least 10 kinds of its *Head and Shoulders* brand shampoo on store shelves. And how many variations of *Tide* detergent are available? The ability to shift easily between part numbers and produce smaller quantities economically can lead to new product offerings and market growth.

Even if a company continues to operate in a push environment, reducing setup times still offers an opportunity to remove waste and increase flexibility by not being constrained by setups. Many good things occur when setup times are reduced, regardless of whether we operate in a push or pull environment. For example, an operation may remain competitive in its current location rather than outsourced to China.

How Do We Reduce Setup Times?

No single way exists to reduce setup or changeover times. Rather, the quest to shorten these times involves various approaches, ranging from rigorous time-motion studies that detail movements down to the second, to purchasing additional equipment. The quest to reduce setup times has renewed the importance of industrial engineers. In fact, a focus on lean and supply chain management has resurrected what was a declining discipline. The following presents some smart ways to reduce setup times.

Improve Changeover Methods. Improving setup or changeover methods involves detailed analyses of setup movements. Often, firms employ sophisticated video analysis to perfect their methods. The lean application that features NASCAR pit crews (Chapter 9) will show how these high-performing teams are relentless in their pursuit of ever-shorter pit stops, or what we refer to as changeovers.

There are many ways to reduce setup times through improved methods. Practicing setups until they become routine is one way. Another way is to use wheels and rollers to easily move parts and tools without the use of material handling equipment. The reader might also be aware of the concept of SMED (single minute exchange of dies), another approach for streamlining equipment setup times. Other improvements include eliminating the use of nuts and bolts, and reducing the need to fit, adjust, and calibrate tools or equipment directly on a machine. Any transfer of internal setup or calibration work to external work will help eliminate time-consuming equipment adjustments. Setup times should also benefit from simplified and standardized equipment and tooling.

Another powerful way to reduce changeover times includes using operators rather than specialized setup personnel to perform changeovers. Specialized setup personnel often have responsibility for maintaining more than one piece of equipment. Based on personal experience, it is inevitable that two or more pieces of equipment will require a changeover at the same time. Besides resulting in longer downtime, machine operators are often idle while a specialist works on a changeover. This idle time, which makes planning the flow of work over the course of a day more difficult, can be a tremendous source of operational waste and bottlenecks. Unfortunately, employees often look forward to these down times.

Plan and Stage. Planning and staging may be one of the most important concepts that support not only setup reductions but better flow across the entire supply chain. This concept has not received the attention it deserves in the lean literature. Essentially, planning and staging means that some entity, whether it is a facility awaiting a supplier shipment or a work center that is processing a sequence of jobs, has access to information that enables it to know what is coming next and when a change will occur. This allows employees to have the required tools, personnel, equipment, documents, and materials ready to support the change.

Planning and staging allows work to be done concurrently in anticipation of a need. It is a powerful concept. Here are some examples that illustrate planning and staging:

- Planes that arrive at airports proceed to gates where ground crews are prepositioned with the personnel, equipment, and fuel they need to quickly turn that plane around for its next flight
- NASCAR pit crews know when pit stops will occur and are ready to jump over the wall with whatever tools, equipment, and materials the pit stop requires
- Suppliers forward advance shipment notices (ASNs) that allow downstream customers to plan and stage documents, workers, and equipment in anticipation of the material's arrival

A more detailed example brings home the advantages of planning and staging. Each day a regional distribution facility receives trailers with replenishment inventory from a national distribution center. The national center also transmits an electronic listing of the load and their contents within the trailers. When the regional center receives confirmation that the trailer is only several hours away, the facility transfers (i.e., formally receives) the trailer into its inventory system. This allows the facility to preprint the bar-coded move tickets that correspond to the contents of each load. The tickets are then placed in packets that are eventually affixed to the loads as they are taken off the trailer and moved to an appropriate facility location. The inbound supervisor also makes sure that an open door is available before the trailer arrives, which further promotes a continuous material flow across the supply chain. Visibility into each trailer's contents also allows a supervisor to determine how many employees to assign to unload the trailer, the type of material handling equipment needed to unload and transfer the material, and the number of employees required to put the material in its proper location. Plant managers estimate that planning and staging has reduced the time required to unload a trailer by over 30 percent, which makes the material available for sale that much quicker. The lean application titled "Why Push When You Can Pull?" (Chapter 11) will further illustrate the power of planning and staging.

Use New and Duplicate Equipment as Required. New equipment is increasingly being designed with shorter setups in mind. At one packaging facility, certain high-speed packaging equipment, clearly designed for long production runs in a push environment, was not supportive of the smaller production runs that a pull environment requires. Fortunately, new equipment has become available that replaces manual changeovers that require a half hour or more with automated changes that require just minutes.

A company might also want to buy additional equipment to help shorten setup times. As one piece of equipment is operating, a second piece of equipment is being set up for the next job. This can be a tough sell for some financial types, and a strong business case will have to be made that the flexibility and improvements which result offset the additional equipment costs.

Track Setup Reduction Progress. Tracking setup improvements demands a set of metrics that focus on setup reduction progress. This means that a measure must be created to track every area where setups or changeovers occur. We need to be clear about several points here. First, the measures normally do not track the amount of effort put into a changeover. Rather, the measures track the amount of elapsed time between completing one job and starting another. NASCAR pit stops measure the amount of time a car is in the pit, not the total time expended by the combined crew members. Second, once setups become a routine event within the desired time frame the setup time metric should go away. A setup time measure is simply a transitional rather than permanent measure that helps us to know when the journey from one state to another has occurred. Continuing to measure setup times when setups are routine is wasteful.

FACILITY LAYOUT CHANGES

Every organization that has facilities—whether this facility is a production plant, distribution center, service center, airport terminal, maintenance shop, retail store, or office—has physical layouts that constrain or promote the flow of work. After setup time reduction, welcome to the next most popular area where companies focus their lean transformation efforts—facility layout changes. In fact, many *kaizen* events, a topic discussed in Chapter 7, address physical layout improvements. Several of the lean applications featured in the second part of this book illustrate how layout changes support better flow and throughput.

A continuing problem is that too many facility layouts create waste through excessive material handling and movement, workers who are too specialized across separate and largely disconnected work centers, and material tracking systems that are often way too complex. Large manufacturing facilities often feature process layouts where parts and materials move from one work center to another as they progress through production.

Traditional facilities are organized around specialized work centers that group similar equipment and technology together, such as work centers for storage, assembly, testing, painting, inspection, finishing, or packaging. Parts earn some serious frequent flyer miles as they move back and forth across a facility, and of course a tracking system is needed to follow all this movement. These movements are usually excessive and create no new value. They also create a need for material handling and tracking systems.

Before creative managers figured a thousand and one uses for bar codes, early bar code technology focused primarily on tracking material as it moved throughout traditional facilities. Interestingly, the Japanese have never been big adopters of bar code technology. Part of this is due to the historical capability of Japanese production systems to produce smaller lot sizes in work cells, or what manufacturing companies call cellular manufacturing. With a cellular design, smaller lots of material do not travel extensively around a facility, thereby reducing the need for tracking systems. When Japanese companies went on a buying spree and purchased various U.S. companies in the 1980s, one of the first changes they made was to dismantle the conveyors and material handling systems that moved material between process work centers.

The Importance of the Right Layout

Research with many companies, as well as extensive personal experience, reveals that many advantages are possible when firms pay close attention to physical layouts. It is not exaggerating to say that improvements to a physical layout can lead to some positive outcomes, including reduced production cycle times, reduced work-in-process inventory, and reduced floor space requirements. Other outcomes include less material handling, less complex scheduling and control systems, improved product quality, enhanced operating flexibility, and lower total costs. Perhaps most importantly, certain physical layouts create a stronger ownership among employees for the success of a product from start to finish.

While at times all that is needed are tweaks to an existing layout, at other times a comprehensive review should take place to ensure the physical layout supports your lean objectives. Some firms that rely on a project layout, which features a stationary production system with workers and tools moving in and out of the process, find that a shift to an assembly line process may be valuable. The lean application titled "Lean Takes to the Skies" (Chapter 13) presents Boeing's shift from a project to an assembly line layout when building 737 and 777 model aircraft. At one time Specialty Records, the manufacturing arm of Warner, Electra, and Atlantic Records produced CDs in batches. A conversion to a continuous process using work cells changed the time to make a finished CD from days to minutes. Compaq, now part of Hewlett-Packard, also appreciated the value of layout changes after the company shifted from making its Presario personal computer on an assembly line to a work cell. An assembly process that previously required several dozen employees now only requires four employees working as a team.

For many companies, particularly those that operate in a batch and job shop environment, the answer to inefficient layouts is to change the layout so it overcomes the wasteful practices of specialized work centers. For many firms this means adopting a cellular layout or work cell. Cellular layouts feature grouping *dissimilar* operations and equipment together, often in a U-shaped work cell, rather than grouping similar operations and equipment together. The cell layout lends itself to clear visibility of work, minimal material movement, simplified scheduling, and worker flexibility.

Work cells provide a setting for employees to work cooperatively in true teams. In fact, a key feature of cellular layouts is their use of self-directed work teams. Far too often we address the physical aspects of facility changes without thinking about the human aspects. Self-directed teams have significant authority to manage their work. This could include responsibility for hiring new members, determining work schedules, and identifying ways to improve performance.

Work cell employees usually have direct responsibility for products from start to finish, especially when compared with their counterparts who work in process or assembly layouts. Process work centers are notorious for a lack of accountability as work zips between work centers. Members of self-directed work teams, by definition, hold themselves mutually accountable for start-to-finish success.

Figure 4.2 illustrates the convoluted path that batches of men's dress shirts take as they progress from start to finish within a process layout. Pieces of shirts move all over the facility in large batch sizes because of the high setup times required for cutting the shirt patterns, which happens at the start of the shirt-making process. Now, new equipment is available that allows faster setups that support smaller batch sizes, rather than large work-in-process batches, for pattern cutting. Work cells organized around the primary shirt-making processes of cutting, sewing, inspecting, ironing, and packaging would likely increase throughput, minimize excessive handling, simplify the tracking of work in process, make the work area visible, and energize employees as they work in self-directed teams. If the flow of shirts looks confusing in Figure 4.2, imagine what it's like in real life.

Challenges with Layout Changes

All physical layouts should undergo regular reviews as part of the continuous improvement process. Leading companies are increasingly using computer simulation models to evaluate potential layout changes and their effect on operating

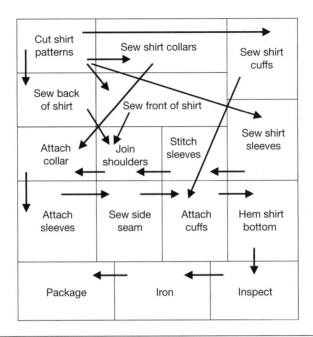

Figure 4.2 The travels of dress shirts in a process layout

performance. At times a change to a layout will be nothing more than a rearrangement of existing equipment that is designed to improve work flow. The change to the sorting area of a distribution center, which will be presented shortly, is an example of a low-cost change to improve flow. At other times, particularly as process technology and physical layouts are changed simultaneously, the changes can be dramatic and costly. The Alaska Airlines example presented later features process technology and physical layout changes that will require years to complete.

Besides the obvious fact that rearranging a physical layout can be a major task, other challenges often present themselves, particularly when creating work cells. Some equipment does not lend itself to be placed alongside different equipment, a defining characteristic of a work cell. A facility may also be too old to support a new layout. This is an issue when work is performed on different levels, or when older buildings prohibited the widespread wiring of computer cables. Fortunately, wireless systems have helped alleviate this latter issue.

Equipment may also be too large to move (think of a 10-ton press), or generates emissions or hazardous waste that prohibits it from being placed in a general work area. Specialty Records, the company mentioned in the previous section, relies on work cells to make CDs from raw material to finished products in a matter of minutes—except for one important step. The silk screening of artwork on the product must occur in a controlled area due to the hazardous materials involved. This restriction places some limitation on product flow through the facility.

At times new layouts require the purchase of new equipment, particularly if the layout changes also involve a process technology change. When this is the case the layout change may quickly turn into a capital project. Specialty Records, for example, purchased entire work cells that cost upwards of $1 million each when it shifted from a batch process to continuous-flow work cells. Making the financial case presents an entirely new challenge that managers must address. The lean application titled "What Goes Around Comes Around" (Chapter 10) defines the steps for developing a financial analysis for a capital project.

A final challenge mentioned here is that any physical changes that alter the normal routine or job responsibilities of employees can easily run into resistance, especially when operations are covered by union work rules and job classifications. Worker or departmental specialization must often give way to a flexible and responsive workforce. Management may have to renegotiate work rules, modify work classifications, provide training so employees can work within a new system, and guarantee that no positions will be eliminated as a result of any changes. While this particular challenge only consumes a paragraph of this chapter, the reality is that this single topic may overwhelm the success of any changes.

Improving Performance through Layout Changes

Let's be clear about an important point. Any organization that has physical layouts can benefit from layout improvements. It just so happens, as with many lean topics, that manufacturing firms have received the most attention. This does not have to be the case, however. Most corporate and office buildings are now designed today to provide spaces for people to meet, often in informal rather than structured settings such as conference rooms. Many kaizen events now focus on changing the layout of offices to reduce movement and enhance work flow.

Anyone who has worked in a distribution center, a major part of any supply chain, knows that facility layout is a primary determinant of that facility's productivity. A primary source of waste in a distribution center is excessive movement as employees move from one location or another to cycle count, stockkeep, or pick parts. While movement is a necessary activity, excessive movement is wasteful.

Distribution center designers understand the need for layouts that minimize material and employee movement. One way they accomplish this is to build centers with many receiving docks so inbound trucks can be placed close to where their contents are stocked. Another powerful idea is to locate multiple loads of an item in flow-through racks instead of relying on an active location backed up by reserve locations scattered around the facility. Smart managers also know they should stock their fastest moving items near their outbound shipping lines.

Many centers also use carousels to stock parts.[3] With carousels, the parts rotate around in bins that come to the employee rather than the other way around (think of dry cleaners where a system brings the clothes to the employee). The employee remains stationary as the parts bins move. As an employee picks a part and readies it for shipment, the carousel simultaneously forwards to the next picking location. This process dramatically increases an employee's picking rate per hour. Many firms also assign one employee to pick from more than one carousel. From personal experience, carousels can be a real game changer within a distribution center.

The following presents three diverse examples of physical layout changes and improved material and people flow.

A Horror Story with a Happy Ending. Let's look at a facility change that will help us appreciate the powerful relationship between layout and lean. The facility featured here is a distribution center in the Northeast United States that was plagued with inefficiencies within the customer order sort area. Let's look at the way previous orders were picked and packed before redesigning the layout.

Employees picked orders in four waves through the distribution center each night. An employee might pick, for example, 175 part numbers for different customers in a wave (two delivery routes usually comprise a wave). Picking by location sequence rather than by individual customer helps minimize the distance traveled between order picks.

After completing their work assignment, which contained parts for the customers in that wave, employees brought their parts to the sort area, the focal point of this story. The facility had stationary bins where employees placed the parts they picked. Each customer had an assigned bin. These bins ran horizontally down an aisle and vertically had four levels. Large parts, some weighing as much as several hundred pounds, were picked and placed directly by the shipping dock. These larger parts were sequenced in the order they were loaded on the truck and matched up later with parts from the customer bins.

After the order pickers were through placing their parts in each customer's stationary bin, an order packer removed the parts and packed them in a returnable tote or corrugated box. Larger orders or parts that did not fit in a tote or box were placed in a returnable cage that rolled on and off the delivery truck.

So, what's the problem here? First, the fixed bin area was a single, two-sided aisle with multiple levels that was cramped and poorly lit. The aisle became even more cramped when employees brought their picking carts into the aisle, something that was quite common. Second, the dealer identification signs on the bins were small and difficult to see. Employees were constantly walking up and down

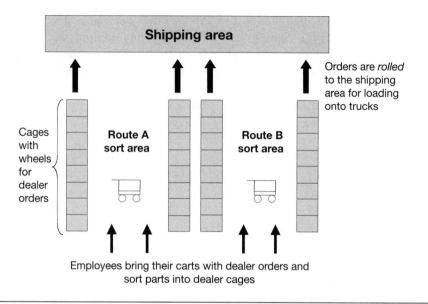

Figure 4.3 A distribution layout focusing on flow

the aisle to sort parts, bumping into each other, and often sorting parts incorrectly due to the congestion, poor lighting, and inadequate dealer signs. The flow was multidirectional and chaotic, and that was on a good day.

This process also featured excessive parts handling. Parts were placed in the customer bin by order pickers only to be taken out a few minutes later by order packers. Finally, larger orders or orders with loose pieces that would not fit in a tote or box were carried by an employee from the bin area and placed in a cage, a distance of 20 feet or more. Excessive handling and movement did not create anything worthwhile. There had to be a better way to sort and pack orders.

Figure 4.3 provides a schematic of the new sorting area. First, the stationary bins were completely dismantled, a process that required a weekend to complete. While this was occurring, electricians added additional lights and placed them physically closer to the sort area rather than in the ceiling, resulting in a brighter work environment. Smaller dealer route signs were replaced with signs that were five times their previous size.

The replacement of a fixed sort area with one that provided flexibility and visibility was the critical change. Under the new layout, which now is simply an open floor space, rolling cages are set up for each dealer in a route, dealer signs are attached to the cage, and the cages are sequenced to roll to the shipping area in the sequence they will be loaded on a truck. This path for loading is a straight line from the sort area to the shipping area. Recall that the shipping area is the point where the sorted parts for a dealer are combined with the larger parts in an order. At this point entire orders are loaded directly onto an outbound truck.

The order pickers place their parts in a returnable tote (or a corrugated packing box if totes are not available) that the order packer places in each cage when setting up the sort area. This eliminates the need for the order packer to rehandle the sorted parts. Parts that are not suitable for a tote are placed in a loose condition within the cage. After employees sort their parts, the order packer makes a determination as to whether the dealer has enough volume to receive a cage or the tote should simply be loaded on the truck. Cages that are not loaded on a truck become available for the next wave.

Dealers often receive cages because they protect loose parts during delivery. The cages are sealed with a plastic security seal, a step that deters theft or the removal of parts before a dealer can check his order in. Cages are also quick and easy to roll off a truck, and they are a convenient way for dealers to place any returns that are coming back to the distribution center. The delivery network is essentially a closed-loop system, a topic that Chapter 3 discussed.

Although not shown in Figure 4.3, this new layout provides another benefit. As the routes that constitute a wave are being readied for movement to the shipping dock, the sort area has enough room for the next wave to be set up concurrently without disrupting the previous wave. Because daily volumes fluctuate between the routes and waves, the ability to plan and stage helps ensure that unusually large routes do not delay the next wave, at least in the sort and pack area.

It's hard to overestimate how much a visible and flexible sort area supports this facility's lean objectives. After a brief adjustment to the changes, a 30 percent improvement in outbound productivity occurred as measured by lines shipped per hour per employee. Given the fact that no major changes occurred to the picking of parts or the loading of trucks, changes to the sort process resulted in some impressive productivity gains.

The new system also resulted in fewer sorting errors. This eliminated a host of wasteful activities, including fewer dealer calls about missing parts, less time researching problems, and lower costs due to fewer part losses. Never discount the value of a good layout!

A New Way to Fly. In a change that is being duplicated by other airlines, Alaska Airlines has pioneered a new self-service check-in process.[4] The result of this change is a doubling of passengers that check in per hour per agent hour compared with the previous process—all without any noticeable increase in physical space! This change is much more complex than the distribution center example just presented because it involves process technology and physical layout changes. It also involves changes at every airport where Alaska Airlines has check-in operations. The distribution center change did not involve any meaningful technology changes.

What did Alaska Airlines do that others want to copy? The airline formed an *Airport of the Future* team and charged it with creating a better way to move passengers through its check-in process. The team consisted of representatives of IT, marketing, facilities, and in-flight departments. While not telling the team what the check-in process should look like, the airline's chief executive officer was clear he wanted to take greater advantage of electronic ticketing technology and self-service kiosks. The airline provided the team with special warehouse space to create mock-ups and plan their new layout.

The team's final recommendation was an innovative *two-step flow-through* check-in process that earned the airline a U.S. patent. As passengers enter the Alaska Airlines check-in area, they proceed directly to kiosks that are spread around the check-in area. Those passengers that successfully complete their check-in at the kiosks are then instructed to proceed to a conveniently located baggage belt to drop off luggage for tagging.

During the kiosk check-in process those passengers requiring special assistance or requiring more time for check-in, such as a large group, a family traveling together, or someone with a pet, are instructed to proceed to a ticket counter for assistance. Passengers who check in on-line are instructed ahead of time whether to proceed directly to the baggage area or to the counter for assistance when they arrive at the airport. The on-line check-in and the kiosks act as a customer sorter, thereby supporting better flow of passengers through the check-in process. Passengers who check in on-line and have no luggage skip this process altogether.

Alaska Airlines has modified its check-in process at airports where the airline does not have physical check-in space, particularly at older airports, or where the volume does not justify the two-step flow-through process. The airline modified its two-step flow-through arrangement by mounting kiosks on ticket counters or by placing two kiosks on one podium with a baggage belt on either side.

What is the result of this new process and layout? A kiosk system mounted by ticket counters averages 21 passengers an hour per agent, two kiosks on one podium averages 31 passengers an hour per agent, and the patented two-step flow-through process yields an average of 42 passengers an hour per agent. The average transaction time with the two-step flow-through process is two minutes, a healthy reduction from earlier systems. In an industry that struggles every day to make a profit, endorsing lean practices is a necessity.

A Down-to-Earth Success Story. Allen-Edmonds is one of only two major companies that still make shoes in the United States. In an industry where cheap foreign labor has ensured that the shoe industry will never again be a major player in the United States, superb quality and an endorsement of lean practices have helped Allen-Edmonds to prosper.[5]

As part of its lean transformation the company completely gutted its main production plant in Wisconsin. This transformation started with a total cleanup of the plant, resulting in eight dumpsters of old shoe parts, desks, chairs, and floor fans being jettisoned. Anything that cluttered the plant and affected product flow was out the door. A cutting and sewing operation from a nearby plant filled over 4000 square feet of newly freed space, a move that replaced transportation between plants with material handling within a plant (always a nice trade).

Working with plant operators, company managers planned a new future for the plant. A major change involved the dismantling of a conveyor line. Next, the plant was repainted, a high-efficiency dust collection system and state-of-the-art lighting system were installed, new fans were secured in the ceiling, and an overhead electrical system replaced an on-floor system. New production equipment that was arranged into work cells and staffed by employee teams completed the physical transformation.[6] Employees were also cross-trained to perform multiple tasks, something that comes in useful when managing bottlenecks. Over a 16-day period the plant was transformed into what looked like a brand-new facility.

The results of these changes are impressive. The plant has significantly less overtime, more capacity, 60 percent less inventory as pull systems replace batch push systems, and double-digit productivity improvements. Perhaps most importantly, the company remains competitive in an industry that constantly scours the globe for lower labor costs. One executive commented that the changes were readily accepted by the workforce because it's "not that hard to give a crisis speech on shoe manufacturing in America."[7]

PULL SYSTEMS

As mentioned in Chapter 1, lean supply chains operate in a pull versus push environment. The concept of pull is integral to lean because no upstream activity occurs unless requested by a downstream entity. Pull systems feature action that is taken in response to a direct request rather than anticipating a need or request that may never occur.

The trigger to initiate an act in a push environment originates upstream with downstream entities managing the consequences. The trigger is often a forecast of anticipated demand that sets the supply chain in motion. As one manager described the push system at his company, "It's ready or not here it comes."

Push and pull does not only relate to production. We all have seen this concept at work with doctors and pharmaceutical companies. Pharmaceutical companies traditionally employed large sales staffs that would push new products onto doctors so they would eventually prescribe them to consumers. Now, pharmaceutical companies spend hundreds of millions of dollars targeting consumers with advertisements that urge us to talk to our doctor about one drug or another. The companies want the downstream consumer to initiate the pull signal through their doctor. This is clearly a shift from a push model to a pull model.

Working within a pull system requires a modified mindset, and this can present huge challenges. With a traditional push operation most work centers are concerned, perhaps even obsessed with equipment utilization or meeting sales targets. The performance measures within these centers will focus on efficiency, pieces produced per hour, and equipment utilization. We now know that operating equipment when there is no need to operate it is wasteful. Having equipment stand idle is better than producing unneeded components, assemblies, and finished products.

An analogy here relates to buying a new car. Since a new car is a capital asset it should be used, right? With this logic, no Sunday would go by without packing the kids into the car for a nice long drive, even if it were a drive to nowhere. After all, we need to utilize this expensive piece of equipment. It was not purchased to sit idle. Of course, this is a ridiculous scenario. At a personal level we know that operating a car when it is not needed is wasteful in terms of time, gas, and depreciation. So, why does it make sense to operate equipment at a business when it is not needed? Besides subjecting the equipment to unnecessary stress, downstream work centers may not require the output that is being produced. If a supply chain manager wants to make sure that behavior does not revert back to traditional ways, then he or she must pay close attention to the measures that are being used to drive behavior. Chapter 6 addresses this topic in detail.

A dramatic example of a push mentality involves the U.S. operations of Hyundai. Hyundai has a history of building factories that turn out vehicles with no related orders, and at one point recently Hyundai had about 32,000 unsold Sonata sedans parked outside its Alabama assembly plant.[8] The company establishes it sales targets on what it can produce rather than what it can sell. A Korean professor of auto economics commented that Hyundai's "production-oriented style of pushing all the time won't work anymore." One consequence of this push mentality is that Hyundai has had to tap rental fleet buyers, a move that diminishes the brand and resale value of the vehicles.

Visible Signals

Central to a pull system are visible signals, or what the Japanese call a *kanban*. A kanban is a signaling device that gives authorization and instructions from a downstream center for production or withdrawal of items from an upstream center. These signals, which ideally are nonverbal, can consist of cards, lights, spaces

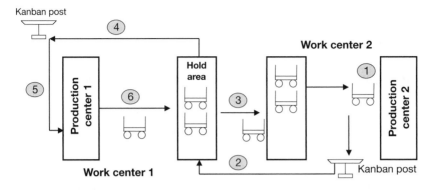

Figure 4.4 Two-card kanban system

in a rack, or squares on a floor. If a square on a floor is supposed to have a certain part number and quantity placed in the square, and that square is empty, then we can safely interpret the empty square as a pull signal to replenish that space with material. Kanbans are triggers to do something, such as produce or move material downstream.

Figure 4.4 illustrates how a two-card kanban system operates between work centers. A two-card system typically uses *P* and *C* cards. A *P* card, called a *production card*, is a trigger to produce whatever part and quantity is listed on the card. A *C* card, called a *conveyance card*, is a trigger to retrieve whatever part and quantity is listed on the card. Some refer to this as a transport card. An important point to realize here is that a card that is not attached to any material or load is a trigger to either produce or retrieve what is listed on the card. Material that has a card attached means that no further action is required until the material is used and the card is sent back upstream. The card system works best when build schedules are repeatable.

Referring to Figure 4.4, the following steps (represented by circles with numbers inside) show how a two-card system works:

Step 1: Work Center 2 (the downstream work center) uses material that was requested earlier from Work Center 1 (the upstream work center). The *C* card that was attached to the load is removed and placed in a kanban post. A *C* card that is not attached to material is a trigger to retrieve more material.

Step 2: An employee goes to the temporary hold area between the work centers with the *C* card. At the hold area the employee removes the *P* card from the load and inserts the *C* card.

Step 3: The load with the newly inserted C card is moved to Work Center 2, where the material is needed.

Step 4: The P card that was removed in Step 2 is sent to the kanban post in Work Center 1.

Step 5: The P card at the kanban post triggers production for the material and quantity listed on the card.

Step 6: The P card is attached to material in a returnable container and moved to a temporary hold area awaiting an employee to arrive with a C card to retrieve the material.

A balanced material flow between centers ensures that any inventory in the temporary holding areas, which in value stream mapping are called *supermarkets*, is consumed by a downstream work center. After all, the downstream entity was the one that requested the upstream entity to do something. The same logic of pull signals works between companies in a supply chain, although this is not as well perfected as managing the flow between work centers within internal operations.

UNIFORM LOADING

The underlying premise behind uniform loading is that each work center within a facility or across a supply chain is *not* independent, although far too often they act that way. The entire production process must be linked together and balanced so a steady flow of material throughout a facility or across a supply chain results in no shortages or inventory buildup. Batch sizes of subassemblies, for example, should not be calculated separately from the finished product's requirement. Uniform loading requires the sharing of demand information between work centers and among trading partners.

This part of lean operations was historically referred to as uniform *plant* loading. To phrase this critical element that way ignores the need to align the supply network with a unifying demand number. Some items are not that significant from a cost perspective, and these could be managed using traditional economic order models that are calculated independently. At least in theory, however, the 20 percent of items that make up 80 percent of a product's cost should strive for uniform build schedules that balance the flow of material across the supply chain against a key demand figure. Unfortunately, theory and reality are often quite different when it comes to this part of lean.

One of the best examples of uniform loading involves the Boeing 737. Previously, uncoordinated units across the company made thousands of parts on large machines (remember our discussion of long setups), which were then stacked, stored in buildings, warehouses, and even parking lots, and then moved between buildings as they awaited their next step in a prolonged journey. Now, dozens of internal feeder lines produce components and subassemblies according to the pace of the final 737 assembly line (the plane is actually assembled on a moving assembly line). Build schedules have become uniform. Suppliers are also beginning to build parts and subassemblies on a just-in-time (JIT) basis with receipts moving directly to the production floor.

The example about Boeing's bolts and fasteners for the 787 is clearly a case where different supply chain members have been unable to converge on a single demand signal. The result is too much inventory in one part of the supply chain or not enough in other parts. A sure indication that a supply chain is suffering from poor coordination is when the various supply chain members, including internal operations, are each producing according to their own demand figures.

Uniform loading demands open and accurate sharing of information up and down the supply chain. The adverse effects of not sharing demand information combined with a lack of data transparency across a supply chain can be considerable, leading to excess inventory, poor customer service, and higher production costs, to name a few. Minor demand fluctuations at the end customer or retail level often amplify as we move further up the supply chain. This amplification, known as the bullwhip effect, is the result of not knowing (and not sharing) the demand for an end product. Each link in the supply chain only knows what the preceding link ordered, and each link tends to react in ways that are not all that rational.

A common reaction in an uncoordinated supply chain is that each link increases its production to ensure it can cover an increase in orders, which amplify as the orders move further upstream. The cumulative effect of these increases is to cram the supply chain with inventory. Simulation after simulation shows that demand and supply are better balanced across a supply chain when open sharing of end-customer demand information (not just orders) occurs. At a macrolevel, uniform loading is about balancing the supply of material across a supply chain with the demand for material.

LEVEL SCHEDULING

Level scheduling involves scheduling and building the same product mix every day during a given period. This part of lean operations can be very difficult if not impossible for many companies, particularly those that compete in highly seasonal businesses or where demand is erratic. Level scheduling works best with fairly consistent patterns of customer demand, at least in the short run.

Companies that make a limited number of products on an assembly line are ideally suited to benefit from level scheduling. The assembly line tends to move at the same pace every day, making the daily routine predictable. It is not surprising why automotive companies are logical candidates for putting lean techniques in place. Each line makes a relatively small number of vehicle types, often only one type, at a steady pace. A bottling plant is also ideally positioned to think in terms of level scheduling.

As product offerings proliferate (think about how many variations of Colgate toothpaste are now available), and as industries move from traditional economies of scale with few product offerings toward a mass customization model featuring many offerings, predictable and level schedules may become a luxury that few supply chains will have. The added flexibility that improved setups and changeovers provide may help compensate for the added complexity that is occurring to build schedules. A concept called *postponement*, a topic covered in Chapter 6, may also help here.

An important part of level scheduling, and one of the few lean terms that is not a Japanese word, is takt time. *Takt* is a German word for the baton a conductor uses to create a steady and regular beat. Within lean operations the takt time is the rate at which customers demand a product. The demand rate establishes the takt time, so it is easy to see that an erratic demand pattern makes it hard to establish a consistent takt time. The challenge is to set up and staff a process that is synchronized to the takt time.

An example will illustrate the calculation and use of takt time. Assume a plant has six inbound lines to receive truckload receipts from suppliers and that each line is available to receive trailers seven hours a day. This makes a total of 2520 minutes of receiving processing time available (6 lines × 7 hours per line × 60 minutes per hour). Further assume that the facility receives an average of 10 trailers a day. The takt time for this process is 2,520 minutes/10 = 252 minutes. This means a trailer should flow into a receiving line every 252 minutes, or 4.2 hours. Takt time must be adjusted as available time (such as with overtime) and/or trailers (demand) fluctuates. If takt time is less than the expected processing time per trailer, we will likely have a backlog of work.

In another example, a work center with 50 hours of available machine time per week and a demand of 100 units has a takt time of 30 minutes. A completed unit must flow from the work center every 30 minutes given a demand of 100 per week. Obviously, the takt time will change if available machine time and/or demand changes.

Demand Is Not Always Level

Organizations with erratic demand patterns need to think about what they can do to smooth their work requirements. This could involve doing a better job of *managing* demand rather than reacting to demand. Sales personnel might work more closely with operations personnel, for example, when scheduling customer orders. Or a workforce might be cross-trained to allow the shifting of human resources from one work center to another as demand materializes. Creating a supply chain that is flexible across multiple dimensions will help compensate when level scheduling is a challenge.

Consider the physical distribution center featured during the facility layout discussion. The demand for replacement parts processed throughout the week is not consistent. Monday evening's orders, for example, are usually heavier because they include dealer orders from Saturday, sometimes Sunday, and Monday. The end of the week, particularly Friday, is often slower than earlier in the week.

This facility processes several kinds of dealer orders. Daily orders, the first order type, must be picked, packed, and shipped the day the order is received. Dealers use this type of order when they have an end customer order and cannot satisfy that demand from their internal inventory. The regional facility has no day-to-day control over these orders.

Stock orders, the second order type, are used once a week to replenish the dealer's internal inventory. Dealers receive a discount for items on these orders. Items placed on stock orders are not supposed to have any outstanding customer demand. These orders help the regional facility balance its daily workload from two perspectives. First, the regional facility has up to two days to ship stock orders from the day the order is received. On nights with fewer daily orders, the facility can pick some or all of any outstanding stock orders on their first day. On other nights, the orders might be held until their second day if that helps balance the workload. Second, dealers are assigned the day of the week when they can submit a stock order. Historical data help the facility determine when best to schedule each dealer's stock-order day.

While certainly not resulting in totally level work schedules, this flexibility goes a long way toward making the system less erratic from day to day. The ability to balance the workload not only has positive effects on workforce scheduling and hours, it also helps ensure the delivery vehicles assigned to a particular route match that route's needs. Erratic day-to-day volumes can wreak havoc on this outbound logistics system.

The idea of balancing work across supply chains should extend further upstream to the logistics arena. Continuing with our example of the regional distribution center, instead of dispatching trailers in batches from the national center to replenish the regional center, supply chain managers should attempt to time the truck deliveries to the regional center so they arrive consistently throughout the week, similar to takt time. Unfortunately, two or three trailers sometimes are waiting for unloading at the start of a day while on other days only a single trailer, if any, arrives. This uneven flow of work is very disruptive to the inbound receiving process at the regional center.

CONCLUDING THOUGHTS

This chapter addressed five essential elements that are part of lean operations. For firms that are not able to implement a pull system with level scheduling and uniform loading, there is no reason not to benefit from setup and layout improvements. Each organization needs to do what works best given its own situation. Lean operations are not an all or nothing proposition.

By no means are the elements presented here the only ones. Other elements that are often part of lean operations include the use of returnable containers for intrafacility movement, preventative maintenance programs, a flexible workforce and self-directed teams, a focus on continuous improvement, mistake-proofing, 5S visual management, and point-of-use storage.

It is probably safe to say that 90 percent of what has been published about lean deals with what happens within a producer's four walls. But if we really think about it, what is the value of having a lean operation when the rest of the supply chain is mired in waste? At best, a strict internal focus only gets us part way to our theoretical performance levels. It is important to never forget that lean operations must be part of a lean supply chain. The elements of lean operations that we hold ourselves accountable internally are the same set of elements we should look for in our upstream suppliers and downstream channel members.

ENDNOTES

1. This example is adapted from T. Aeppel, "U.S. Shoe Factory Finds Supplies are Achilles' Heel," *Wall Street Journal*, March 3, 2008, B1.

2. J. Lunsford and P. Glader, "Boeing's Nuts-and-Bolds Problem," *Wall Street Journal*, June 19, 2007, A8.

3. The author has extensive experience with carousel systems and believes every warehouse and distribution center should at least evaluate the applicability of this technology. For more information on carousel systems, go to: http://www.whitesystems.com.

4. This example is adapted from P. Avery, "A Better Way for Airport Check-in," *Kiosk Marketplace News*, http://www.selfservice.org, October 19, 2007; and from first-hand experience at airports that Alaska Airlines serves.

5. This example is adapted from P. Arnold, "Walk a Mile in Their Shoes," *MRO Today*, June/July 2004, http://www.mrotoday.com/archives.

6. For a history and photos of the company, go to: http://www.allenedmonds.com.

7. See note 5.

8. This example is adapted from D. Welch, D. Kiley, and M. Ihlwan, "My Way or the Highway at Hyundai," *Business Week* 4075 (March 17, 2008): 48-51.

5

LEAN DISTRIBUTION

Proctor & Gamble (P&G), a company that is recognized for its out-of-the-box thinking, recently made a strategic decision that will radically alter its global distribution network. P&G decided to reduce its network of worldwide distribution sites by 50 percent, from 450 to 225! The company expects to move more of its products via an extended transportation network that will deliver goods to customers faster.[1] Supply chain managers expect these distribution changes to result in better inventory management, reduced total distribution costs, and improved product availability. A progressive company like P&G would never discount the importance of lean distribution.

Let's compare P&G's actions to those of a medium-sized manufacturer of industrial components. At a meeting attended by managers from around the world, certain managers argued that this company's lean initiatives all involved internal manufacturing, a notion that others in the room did not discount. These managers said where they really needed help was in the distribution part of their supply chain, a costly area that is critical for supporting high levels of customer service. One manager wistfully noted that distribution seemed like "an afterthought" and that, except for some minor tweaks, distribution looked much like it did 15 years ago. No one was willing to claim that this company's distribution network was lean or world-class. When distribution is not your primary business, it's possible to get lost in the shuffle.

Welcome to the world of lean distribution, our final stop along the lean supply chain. This chapter provides an overview of distribution channels, including the important differences between warehouses and distribution centers. Next, the chapter focuses on ways to achieve lean distribution, including the need for perfect record integrity, improved demand estimation, form and time postponement, and delivery optimization technology. The chapter also presents cross docking,

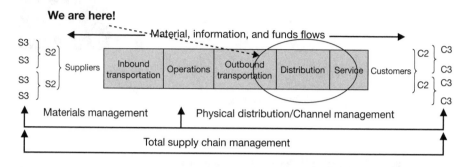

Figure 5.1 Lean distribution

make-to-order production strategies, optimized channel design, and the creative use of information technology as additional ways to make lean distribution a reality. Lean distribution is a broad topic that benefits from broad thinking.

A PRIMER ON DISTRIBUTION CHANNELS

Before talking about ways to make distribution channels leaner, it might make sense to briefly describe what is meant by a *channel*. Channels of distribution, sometimes referred to as *marketing channels*, consist of intermediaries that perform a variety of functions between producers and final customers or consumers. Figure 5.1 identifies lean distribution as the space (i.e., the channel) between a company's operations and its primary customers. These intermediaries can be owned by the same company that produces a good or service, or they can be owned or managed by third parties. Intermediaries can include warehouses and distribution centers, retailers, franchisees, wholesalers, brokers, dealers, and third-party logistics (3PL) providers. Whatever channel design a firm decides to use, each member must add value to that channel or risk elimination.

Lean distribution involves establishing ways to effectively and efficiently deliver a product or service from producers to customers. Increasingly, some distribution channels are shifting toward virtual channels in terms of product or service consumption. This is a real possibility when products can be digitized, such as music, movies, or news. Digital channels represent perhaps the leanest distribution channel possible.

Distribution channels usually consist of a variety of intermediaries, making the possibility of waste a real possibility. Channels can include, besides the producer, intermediaries that take physical possession, and sometimes even title, such as wholesalers, distributors, and retailers. They can also include intermediaries that do not take title or physical possession of goods such as brokers, sales agents, and manufacturers' representatives. Designing a distribution channel can be a complex undertaking.

The complexity of distribution channels varies widely by industry and company. The more complex the distribution channel the greater the opportunity exists to remove waste from that channel. One way, but certainly not the only way to think about distribution channels, is to segment firms by their customers. The *business-to-business* channel is usually very different from the *business-to-consumer* segment.

As a rule of thumb distribution channels are more complex in the business-to-consumer segment than the business-to-business segment. Colgate-Palmolive, for example, makes thousands of items in many shapes and sizes. To reach millions of customers Colgate has to manage a network of thousands of retailers and wholesalers located in over 100 countries, as well as channels that serve hotels, hospitals, governments, restaurants, export markets, and anyone else that uses the company's products. Making this even more complex is that all consumer product companies also engage in business-to-business transactions. At the other extreme is Boeing Commercial Aircraft. After Boeing completes the assembly and final preparation of an aircraft, the customer arrives to fly it to its desired destination. There is nothing too complex about that distribution channel.

Interestingly, the opposite is true on the inbound side of the supply chain. Boeing's supply network is perhaps the most complex in the world. The company relies on suppliers from around the world, for example, to provide the *millions* of parts that are required to assemble a 747. Colgate, on the other hand, relies on suppliers for packaging materials, raw or semifinished raw materials such as bulk chemicals, fragrances, and additives to produce many of its products. While not diminishing the efforts of those who manage Colgate's inbound supply chain, it is a bit less complex in relative terms compared with Boeing's inbound network.

A large part of lean distribution deals with the location of inventory before it reaches the final consumer. A big topic today concerns the right location and number of inventory stocking points to maintain. This invariably leads to a discussion of warehouses and distribution centers. As we proceed it is important to recognize that major differences exist between warehouses and distribution centers:[2]

- Warehouses are generally designed to store a wide range of items, particularly slower moving ones, while distribution centers usually stock fewer but faster moving parts.
- Warehouses follow a fairly standard process of receiving, storing, picking, and shipping. Distribution centers emphasize receiving and shipping with minimal storage.

- Warehouses provide few, if any, value-added services while distribution centers are often ideal places to add value. Loading software to personal computers, final packaging, or consolidating all the elements of an order into a single customer shipment, for example, may all be performed at distribution centers.
- Warehouses stress minimizing operating costs while distribution centers stress maximizing the profit impact from meeting stringent customer delivery requirements.
- Warehouses often feature batch information while distribution centers collect data in real time.

Warehouses and distribution centers are a common type of intermediary, and lean distribution initiatives must recognize the different roles that each plays. Any company that is serious about lean distribution will want to minimize warehousing wherever possible and emphasize flow-through distribution facilities.

WAYS TO ACHIEVE LEAN DISTRIBUTION

Not surprisingly, lean distribution is not thought about nearly as much as lean production, a situation that would benefit from a better balance. Literally hundreds of ways exist that can make distribution more lean and efficient. Each of the ideas presented here can help remove some serious waste from the downstream part of the supply chain.

Strive for Perfect Record Integrity

Perhaps the best place to begin when pursuing lean distribution is to undertake a serious analysis of your company's inventory control systems. The objective here is to have record accuracy or integrity that is as close to perfect as possible. Record integrity or accuracy exists when the physical inventory on hand for an item equals the electronic record on hand (POH = ROH), regardless of the quantity of inventory. (Inventory management is a separate topic from inventory control.) Any difference between POH and ROH represents error. This error can be the result of operationally mismanaging inventory, which affects the physical (POH) side of record integrity, or from systems-related sources, which affects the computerized side (ROH) of record integrity.

Perfect or near perfect record integrity is never an accident. It is the result of various activities and procedures designed to ensure the amount of physical material on hand (POH) in a distribution network (or at any point in a supply chain) is equal to the computerized record of material on hand (ROH). A record integrity level of 99.5 percent or higher represents world-class performance today.

Error in supply chains is often covered up with excess inventory, usually in the form of safety stock and safety lead times, and record integrity errors are no different. The wasteful effects of poor record integrity (i.e., error) on supply chain operations can be severe. When physical inventory exceeds the amount the computerized system believes is available (POH > ROH), the physical inventory cannot be sold or used to satisfy customer demand. An investment has been made in a nonproducing asset. When the record on hand is larger than what is physically available (ROH > POH), the risk exists that an item will be scheduled for production or even sold to a customer when in fact it is not available. This inevitably leads to unplanned backorder situations and dissatisfied customers. Unfortunately, few cost accounting systems, if any, quantify the damaging effects of poor record integrity.

It is surprising how many firms do not know their inventory record accuracy. Part of this is due to a lack of computerized inventory control systems, particularly at smaller companies. It is also surprising how many firms still count their inventory annually, or what inventory management specialists call a periodic inventory control system. Firms that are serious about controlling and then managing their inventory investment rely on a *perpetual* inventory control system that counts samples of parts each day or week. The level of inventory accuracy at any given time should not be a mystery.

When record integrity is lacking, steps must be taken to identify the sources of error with corrective action taken. This will require asking and answering some important questions that address both the physical and informational side of inventory control. Are record errors displaying a random or systematic pattern across stockkeeping units (SKUs)? How severe are the differences between physical stock quantities and electronic quantities? Are proper receiving, stockkeeping, and withdrawal procedures and systems in place? Are suppliers shipping quantities that match their documentation? Are effective cycle-counting procedures used? Is inventory scrap and obsolescence accounted for correctly? Is supply chain theft a problem? Are employees trained to properly move, handle, and disburse material? It is difficult to manage what we cannot control. Perfect record integrity must be one of your most sought after objectives.

Improve Demand Estimation Capabilities

Close your eyes for a moment and imagine you are walking along a beautiful beach. In front of you is a bottle, and when you pick up that bottle out pops a genie who is anxious to grant you a wish. If you happen to be thinking about lean distribution you will ask that genie for the ability to predict, with near perfect accuracy, the demand for your products or services. Let's be realistic here. You know the other things you initially thought about wishing for will only get you into trouble.

Perhaps the most important piece of information that moves across a supply chain is a demand estimate. Demand estimates include all the claims on your company's output for a particular period, including forecasts of customer demand, actual orders for which commitments have been made, spare parts requirements to support aftermarket needs, and adjustments resulting from changes in inventory stocking policies. One could argue persuasively that demand estimation is your company's most important supply chain process. Gain a strong understanding of demand and many good things follow. Eliminating waste is one of those good things.

Many companies fail to recognize the nasty effects of inaccurate demand estimation. The downside of poor demand estimation includes higher inventory volumes and carrying charges, poor customer service as inventory is unavailable or misallocated across locations and products, and excessive safety stock or higher minimum stocking levels. For companies that are serious about better inventory management, improving the quality of demand estimates, like improved record integrity, is a good place to start.

Consider the case of an east coast confectioner that develops demand estimates monthly in a make-to-stock environment. The supply chain group at this company analyzed its demand estimation error in its efforts to better manage its inventory investment. The company found an average error of 50 percent when comparing actual and estimated monthly demand using the mean absolute deviation (MAD) technique of error assessment. A closer investigation revealed some disturbing findings. First, material planners believed that a four-week safety stock for all items would alleviate the impact of poor estimates, thereby reducing the need to be concerned with demand accuracy. Furthermore, no single manager or group was accountable for the integrity of the demand estimate. Marketing, which technically had responsibility for generating monthly demand estimates, noted that estimating demand was not the best use of their time.

The investigation also revealed that material planners manually adjusted over half the programmatic demand estimates that are generated each month, a troubling statistic given that the programmatic estimates were correct more often than the overrides. An analysis across the company's 900 SKUs found that inventory was sometimes severely misallocated across geographic locations and product lines, creating problems in meeting delivery dates for customer orders. Finally, no individual or group actually understood the automated forecasting system the company had purchased. A world-class demand estimation process is so much more than having a computer with fancy algorithms that spits out some numbers each month. Most managers probably figured that other than these minor issues the system was operating quite well.

Table 5.1 Evaluating the demand estimation process

- Are demand estimates consistently over- or underforecasted?
- Are demand estimate errors randomly distributed?
- Is someone accountable for the accuracy of demand estimates?
- Are plans in place to continuously improve the demand estimation process?
- Do we understand why actual demand varies from estimated demand?
- When actual demand patterns change, is the system sensitive enough to realize the change or is there an unacceptable lag?
- Are better demand estimation tools or refinements available?
- Do we understand the demand estimation process that is used?
- Are demand estimates manually overridden by planners? If so, why?
- Is the time interval between demand estimates adequate?

The pursuit of more accurate demand estimates must be relentless, although this is one area where perfection is an unattainable state. Table 5.1 presents a set of questions that should be routinely asked when thinking about how to improve the demand estimation process. Chapter 6 will argue that an error measure that captures the difference between actual demand and estimated demand is one of the most important metrics in a lean supply chain. It is hard to overestimate the amount of waste that over- and underestimating demand causes. Life is much easier when we are working off the best information possible.

Pursue Form and Time Postponement

As a child we probably heard our parents or grandparents say, "Don't put off until tomorrow what you can do today!" Little did we know how incorrect that advice might be. Welcome to the world of postponement, a world that promotes deferring the time of shipment or the form of a final product until a customer order is received. Postponement is a strategy that counters what our parents and grandparents told us. With postponement, why do something today when we can put it off until tomorrow?

Postponement combines product design and channel management strategies. It applies primarily to firms that operate in a make-to-stock environment. As discussed later in the chapter, in a make-to-order environment a producer would not build a product until a firm order is received, making postponement less of an issue. Not all industries, however, are able to operate in a make-to-order environment.

The rationale behind postponement is that it is often more cost-effective to hold inventory in a semifinished state rather than trying to anticipate and build every final product configuration that customers will demand. It is simply easier to forecast at a base product level rather than trying to forecast for end items. Many observers also view postponement as a strategy for reducing supply chain risk.

Product development teams should consider postponement requirements during product design. This is the time when teams consider a number of objectives, or what some call *Design for X* where *X* represents whatever objective design teams want to achieve, such as design for total quality, sustainability, assembly, postponement, or total cost, to name a few. Postponement usually requires development teams to design product platforms that are finalized during production only after exact customer requirements become known.

Anyone who has been to a paint store has observed firsthand the principle of postponement. Once a customer selects a color an employee gets a base can of white paint, such as a gloss, semigloss, or flat, adds coloring, and gives the can some good shakes on a machine to arrive at the final color. Imagine the waste if every Sherman-Williams or Lowe's store tried to stock every one of thousands of possible colors. What would the machine changeover costs be to produce all those colors in a factory? Does anyone really know how many people in southern Alabama want a color called *Evening Sunset* in a semigloss? It is exponentially easier to plan at the total gallon level for flat, semigloss, and gloss paint rather than the individual color level. Paint represents postponement at its finest.

Some firms use postponement as a way to differentiate themselves. Follett Corporation, a medium-sized company located in eastern Pennsylvania, designs and manufactures beverage and ice dispensers for institutional and industrial use. One of its product lines is designed specifically for postponement. The base product, which is produced according to a forecast, is finished only after a customer provides a final order. Often, Follett's products are needed quickly as replacement units in restaurants, hotels, cafeterias, and hospitals. Postponement allows the company to ship customized products in days rather than weeks, thereby providing a lead-time advantage over competitors.

In their seminal paper, Zinn and Bowersox divided postponement into two primary types: form and time postponement. They further divided form postponement into four unique types: labeling, packaging, assembly, and manufacturing.[3] Let's look at the four types of form postponement with examples:

- **Labeling.** What if your product must be processed quickly to ensure freshness? A producer of canned tuna understood clearly that tuna must be packaged quickly to avoid spoilage. However, what if at the time of packaging the producer does not know its exact mix of orders between its own brand and store brands? The solution? Process and package the tuna quickly at a processing plant to ensure freshness but postpone final labeling until firm orders are received. This company knows that tuna are like house guests. Neither gets better the longer they hang around.

- **Packaging.** An automotive OEM ships replacement parts from its national center to its regional centers. Some of the parts, such as front fascias, take up a great deal of truck and warehouse space when packaged. The solution? Ship the large items to the regional centers in bulk containers just as they are received from suppliers. Do not package individual units for delivery until an order is received from a car dealer.

- **Assembly.** A major computer company places its PCs with a 3PL provider. The third-party processes orders for the computer company at its own location by assembling all the pieces (printer, cables, CPU, etc.) and then delivering the product to its final destination. The third-party may even install memory or other software to the computer as required by the final order.

- **Manufacturing.** The paint and ice dispenser examples presented earlier are examples of manufacturing postponement. With this type of postponement, changes occur to the final product beyond labeling, assembly, or packaging after receiving customer orders.

With time postponement a product is completed, but its placement at its final location in the distribution channel is deferred until an order is received. Once an order is received the product is quickly forwarded from a strategically placed location to its final destination. This helps avoid misallocating products and then relying on nonvalue-added cross shipments to get the inventory to the right location.

An example will help us better understand time postponement. A number of years ago General Motors (GM) established a short-term storage lot in Florida. GM stocked this lot with a large number of Cadillacs, which makes sense since Florida contains many of Cadillac's traditional buyers (although the newer Cadillac models appeal to new audiences). Normally these vehicles would be delivered and stored on each dealer's lot awaiting final purchase by a consumer. Traditionally, if a dealer did not have what the customer wanted, the dealer often had to have a vehicle delivered from another dealer or have the customer order the car, a process that takes months from order to delivery. The additional delivery involved with swapping cars in the distribution channel adds no value to the transaction. With the mega-lot, cars can be delivered anywhere in Florida in a day or two, and the customer has a huge selection of cars from which to choose. Placing cars in the big lot is time postponement, while adding any accessories to the car at the dealership is form postponement.

Convincing empirical evidence, along with an abundance of anecdotal accounts, supports the principle of postponement. One study by Johnson and Anderson revealed that an effective postponement strategy reduces both inventory holding costs and lost sales. Also, the ability to satisfy customer orders, as measured by fill rates, increases with postponement.[4]

The lean benefits of postponing versus not postponing become even greater as the number of final product derivatives increases. Johnson and Anderson found that a product with two derivatives had a customer fill rate of just over 85 percent with postponement versus just over 75 percent without postponement. A product with eight final derivatives had a customer fill rate of over 95 percent with postponement versus just over 75 percent without postponement. It becomes increasingly difficult to forecast as the number of final SKUs increases. Postponement offers a promising way to manage supply chain complexity.

Optimize Delivery Networks

Recall from Chapter 1 that optimization refers to making something as perfect (i.e., optimal), effective, or functional as possible. Sophisticated routing software and technology is enabling companies to operate optimized delivery networks with a minimum of waste. Any company that engages in daily or frequent downstream deliveries *must* think about route optimizers. The savings realized from these systems will compensate for what seems to be continuously rising fuel and labor costs. UPS and Air Products are two examples that show how leading companies use optimization technology to improve customer service and employee productivity while reducing costly waste.

Delivering the Goods at UPS. Few would question the notion that UPS manages one of the most impressive delivery networks in the world. In an earlier era (several years ago) UPS drivers employed maps, notes, and memory to determine the best route to deliver their packages each day. While this is obviously not the most efficient way to schedule deliveries, it gets even less efficient when substitute and part-time drivers take over a route.[5]

Over the last several years UPS has invested $600 million in a route optimization system that maps daily delivery schedules. Each day drivers check a handheld device that contains an optimized delivery schedule that minimizes the distance each driver travels that day. This system is so smart it even minimizes the number of left turns taken during the day, a feature that improves fuel mileage and reduces idle time. Without question the route optimizer has zapped waste and increased driver productivity. In a recent month UPS drivers logged 3 million fewer miles compared with the year before.

The optimization system also provides a platform from which other lean applications are evolving. UPS has added a feature that uses global positioning technology to warn drivers when they are in an incorrect driveway. Since the GPS system provides real-time information about truck locations, dispatchers can quickly send the closest driver to a customer after receiving a request for a package pickup. This system even allows customers to reroute packages that are in transit. A system that improves customer service while being brutal on waste is lean at its finest.

Optimizing at Air Products. Air Products, a global producer of industrial gases and chemicals, serves customers in the technology, energy, healthcare, and other industrial markets. As part of its efforts to differentiate itself in what is essentially a commodity business, the company has developed a telemetry system that allows it to efficiently manage gas inventories at its customer locations. Telemetry is the science of transmitting data using a telemeter, which is an electrical apparatus for measuring quantities, and transmitting that data back to a distant station.

Air Products has installed telemetry units at over 4800 tanks at 4000 U.S. customer locations. Customer inventory levels are managed by a group at corporate headquarters using what the company calls a dynamic target-refill system. As customer gas levels reach a predetermined point an electronic pull signal is sent to a centralized scheduling system. Each day drivers from around the United States log in to a computer network at their refilling terminals to download that day's optimized schedule into a handheld computer. As drivers make their deliveries various data updates are seamlessly sent to a centralized system, including the amount of gas delivered and each driver's hours of service data.

Optimized deliveries using remote telemetry is a winner for everyone involved. The system allows Air Products to optimize daily deliveries by employing advanced heuristics and algorithms. Customers benefit from having a third-party seamlessly manage their inventory remotely while guaranteeing no interruptions to their gas supply. The peace of mind offered by this system also helps the marketing group attract new customers. Chapter 14 presents this lean distribution story in detail, including the many benefits provided by this system.

Practice a Make-to-Order Production Strategy

Firms that are serious about lean distribution attempt, wherever possible, to implement a make-to-order production strategy. Some observers differentiate between assemble-to-order and make-to-order. For our purposes the differences are not material. Make-to-order means not producing an item until receiving actual customer orders. This practice supports a lean vision since customer orders are the ultimate pull signal and production does not occur until that signal is received. Distribution is streamlined within a make-to-order model because products are usually sent directly to customers after they are produced.

At times products may be forwarded to an intermediary, such as a logistics provider, for final assembly, packaging, or bundling with other items. Dell, the company that most associate with a make-to-order business model must still rely on third parties to match computers with keyboards, instruction manuals, peripherals, cables, and screens for a seamless customer delivery. Interestingly, Dell has begun to move some of its products through traditional retail channels as Hewlett-Packard and others make inroads into Dell's market share, particularly at the consumer level.

Not all companies or industries can wait until they receive actual orders before producing final products. Some industries do not have this luxury or are far removed from the ultimate customer (think of raw material extraction or agriculture) to engage in a make-to-order model. Other companies practice a hybrid model that features some make-to-stock (based on demand forecasts) and some make-to-order (based on actual orders). Home builders, for example, build model homes so customers can see their quality craftsmanship (make-to-stock), while also building houses based on a customer's specific preferences (make-to-order). Another hybrid model features postponement, a topic discussed earlier in the chapter. Postponement represents a willingness to take on a higher level of work-in-process inventory in anticipation of final orders.

Make-to-order companies have to be well versed in the topics presented in Chapter 4. In particular, this includes rapid setup times and layouts, such as cellular layouts, that are conducive to material flow. Flexibility and speed are essential attributes within a make-to-order environment. These companies also have to be at the top of their demand estimation game. A make-to-order environment actually increases rather than lessens the need for forecast accuracy. The impact from errors in estimating final demand, which affects the amount of raw and direct materials that are available to support a make-to-order policy, will be felt almost immediately. While there will be exceptions, most make-to-order companies do not receive customer orders and then decide to send material releases to suppliers. The required materials and components must be available when customer orders are received. Otherwise, the cycle time for fulfilling customer orders will become excessively long.

Make-to-order is an essential part of managing a firm's working capital requirements. Accountants and financial types will tell us that working capital represents the difference between current assets and current liabilities. From a lean perspective this is probably not the best definition, since supply chain man-

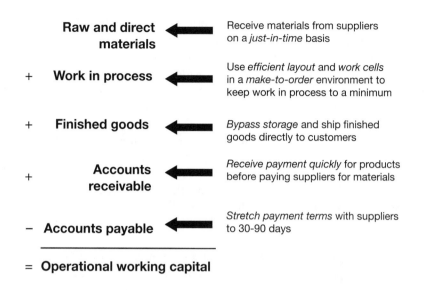

Figure 5.2 Managing operational working capital

agers do not directly affect or control some of the current asset and liability accounts. The amount of cash and short-term securities that a company maintains, both listed under current assets, does not usually fall under the supply chain domain. Supply chain managers need to manage working capital more from an operational perspective.

Figure 5.2 presents an operational definition of working capital. This formula shows that the resources allocated to working capital include the money tied up in raw materials, work in process, and finished goods inventory. Added to this is accounts receivable, which means that another entity is using your firm's resources without yet paying for that privilege. Accounts payable must be separated from the total because your firm is using the resources of another firm without yet paying for that privilege. Figure 5.2 shows how companies like Dell combine their make-to-order capability with other lean initiatives to manage working capital better than most other companies (not to mention achieving better return-on-net assets and return-on-invested capital). This figure supports the notion that lean practices have major financial implications.

Utilize Information Technology

Over the last 10 years the use of information technology to support lean objectives has grown almost exponentially. Whatever is said within this section is inadequate since the creative use of information technology to support lean warrants its own book. It's hard to imagine a company capturing the benefits of lean distribution without relying on some powerful information technology systems.

Many companies have installed enterprise resource planning (ERP) systems, such as SAP R3, to create a common IT platform. Unfortunately, these ERP systems, which are good at providing system breadth, are not as good at providing system depth. Consequently, many ERP systems are supplemented by supply chain planning and execution systems.

Supply chain planning software is intended to improve forecast accuracy, optimize production scheduling, reduce inventory and transportation costs, decrease order cycle times, and improve customer service. Supply chain execution software is designed to procure and manage the flow of products from suppliers, through operations, and through distribution. The primary objective of execution software is to ensure that the right product and quantity is delivered to the right place, at the right time, and to the right customer. This section focuses on two very important IT areas that support lean distribution: (1) distribution resource planning (DRP) and (2) warehouse management systems (WMS).

Distribution Resource Planning. As it relates to lean distribution, today's planning and execution systems include functionality that is traditionally associated with something called *distribution resource planning* (DRP). Like its upstream counterpart, material requirements planning (MRP), these venerable applications did not disappear with the development of new supply chain planning and execution systems. Instead, DRP applications are embedded into these new systems, which are widely available from third-party providers. The early days of MRP and DRP systems often featured larger companies writing their own computer programs, which is generally not the case today. DRP systems support a host of distribution capabilities that support lean distribution, including the following:

- Forecasting finished goods inventory
- Transportation planning
- Vehicle load scheduling
- Identifying optimal stocking locations
- Establishing correct min-max inventory levels at each stocking location
- Timing and replenishment of inventories
- Allocation of items in short supply
- Vehicle routing

Warehouse Management Systems. WMS are computerized systems that, when coupled with current technology such as bar code readers, pick-to-light systems, and voice recognition systems, support the effective and efficient operation of warehouses and distribution centers. WMS can prelocate inbound material, suggest how to relocate stock to minimize the distance traveled for picking, warn employees when physical cycle counts do not match system quantities, and provide changes to how orders are released each day for picking, to name but a few capabilities. One observer has commented that "Warehouse Management Systems have evolved into extremely powerful and sophisticated packages of software, real-time data collection, and automated equipment."[6] From personal experience, a WMS is a *must have* for any company with lean distribution aspirations.

Edward Frazelle, Ph.D., a recognized expert in warehousing and logistics, maintains that a full information technology solution for warehouse and distribution operations includes the following:[7]

- A computing platform such as a mainframe, client-server network, and/or network of personal computers
- A network of paperless devices such as radio frequency terminals, bar code scanners, light-directed systems, and voice headsets
- Warehouse management software
- Enterprise system interface software
- Material handling and paperless device interface software
- Databases that store relevant information

As a refresher, a database is a large collection of data organized especially for rapid search and retrieval.

ERP systems, supply chain planning and execution software, and WMS technology are all essential for supporting a lean distribution network. A recent survey that asked respondents how satisfied they were with their supply chain systems, on a 1 to 10 scale, revealed that most companies have a long way to go before we can feel "fully satisfied" about the state of supply chain IT.[8]

Transportation Management Systems. A nice complement to lean distribution systems is a transportation management system (TMS).[9] This system helps automate day-to-day freight management activities, including compiling rates electronically from carriers and managing payments to carriers. These systems also provide data that allow supply chain managers to identify ways to consolidate orders, often by consolidating less-than-truckload (LTL) shipments into truckload shipments. While TMS have been around for several decades, the choices available to system users, as well as system functionality, are better than ever. Many companies are electing to use the software provider's server to manage their transportation network rather than hosting the system internally. This reduces costs and accelerates implementation.

An example of how effective a TMS can be involves Jel Sert, a company that makes pudding, freezer bars, and freeze pops. In 2006, the company paid $15 million to move 20,000 shipments of products from its internal operations to its retail channel members. After installing a TMS in 2007, the company moved 21,000 shipments without an increase in its overall transportation costs. The efficiencies provided by the TMS offset what should have been higher costs due to increased fuel prices and higher volumes. Jel Sert also found the system helped it become a preferred customer with carriers. Using the payment module that is part of its TMS, Jel Sert eliminated the third-party freight payment service it relied on to reimburse carriers. Faster payments have made Jel Sert more popular with carriers.

Strategically Position Cross-Docking Facilities

Companies that are serious about lean distribution will explore the strategic placement of cross-docking facilities, which are also called *throughput* or *flow-through* facilities, within the supply chain. Cross docking is defined as the delivery of incoming shipments so that they can be easily sorted at an intermediate facility for shipment to downstream destinations.[10] These downstream destinations can include manufacturing plants, regional distribution facilities, retail outlets, or even customer locations. The primary objective of cross-docking facilities is to keep goods moving downstream toward customers. These facilities are not intended to be longer-term storage facilities. Rather, they are designed to break larger quantities (i.e., break bulk) from a single source, such as a supplier, into smaller quantities for downstream entities, such as regional distribution facilities.

Perhaps the best way to understand cross docking is through an example. Chrysler Corporation manages an aftermarket network that includes several hundred thousand part numbers, several national distribution facilities, and almost 20 regional distribution centers. Making sure replacement parts are available when automotive dealers require them is no trivial task. The company's Mopar unit was an early pioneer of cross docking supported by information technology.[11]

Chrysler's primary national distribution facility in Center Line, Michigan, receives dozens of truckloads daily with parts from suppliers located around the world. Upon receipt of these bulk loads at the national facility, which serves as the company's cross-docking facility, an IT system programmatically determines the quantity that each regional distribution center will receive. Bar-coded tickets that include the quantity that will be cross docked to each regional facility are printed and attached to the bulk loads. Bulk loads are then transferred from receiving to an outbound sorting area via automatic guided vehicles (AGVs). The material from the bulk loads is then sorted into shipping containers for the regional facilities according to the quantities determined by the IT system. These shipping containers are then loaded onto trailers that are operated by contract carriers. Material that is received in the morning at the national facility can be on its way to regional centers in Cleveland, Los Angeles, or Orlando within a few hours of receipt.

If suppliers do not provide enough material to satisfy Chrysler's national requirement, a fair share algorithm seamlessly takes over. The algorithm calculates the quantity to ship to each regional facility by considering backorders, current stocking positions, in-transit inventory from earlier shipments, and each facility's average weekly demand. Anyone who has worked in a flow-through facility appreciates the benefits brought about by cross docking supported by information technology. The strategic placement of cross-docking facilities can go a long way toward supporting material flow.

Optimize Distribution Channel Design

Most firms employ different kinds of intermediaries to provide spatial convenience or to perform value-added services such as breaking bulk. The key question becomes how many and where should these intermediaries be located? For most companies channel design is a strategic decision that has a tremendous impact on lean distribution. For example, more small companies, including service companies, are locating operations in Memphis, Tennessee, to be near FedEx's Super Hub. A later deadline for the pickup of packages and documents (up to 10:30 p.m.) allows more time to process documents and customer orders. These firms are using the logistical advantage provided by a key channel member to market themselves to customers and clients.[12]

It is not hard to find accounts in the popular press about companies that are addressing ways to remove waste from their distribution channels. Besides the P&G example presented at the beginning of this chapter, other examples include the following:

- Due to shrinking market share GM, Ford, and Chrysler have come to recognize they have too many dealers at the retail level. GM, for example, has 285 dealers for every point of U.S. market share.[13] Toyota, on the other hand, has only 104 dealers for every point of U.S. market share. A bloated retail channel creates obvious supply chain waste that automakers are being forced to address.
- In a radical redesign of its distribution channel, J.C. Penney has turned over the management of its dress shirts to a vendor in Hong Kong.[14] As shirts are sold at individual stores, the shirt supplier receives an electronic pull signal to produce and ship a replacement shirt directly to that store. Penney's distribution centers are bypassed completely, allowing faster inventory turnover as the supplier ships shirts directly from Asia to Penney's retail stores in North America as needed. This supports the lean principles of flow and simplification.

The supplier has migrated up the value creation stream and now helps Penney's with forecasting and product design.

In literal terms optimizing a distribution network means trying to find a channel design that achieves desired service levels at the lowest total logistics cost. Tools such as linear programming and other models that employ complex algorithms have the potential to converge on an optimal design.[15] The president of an inventory optimization software provider has commented that new technology has vastly multiplied the power of optimization tools.[16] In the past, businesses would optimize one distribution site at a time when determining inventory stocking requirements. Now, new software enables optimization across entire distribution networks.

In less complex terms (not everyone has the expertise to develop advanced network models) optimization gives way to something called rationalization, which means striving to find the right mix and number of intermediaries to place between a producer and end customers. Channel design involves proactively managing trade-offs, usually between inventory and transportation, at the highest supply-chain level. Chapter 3 discussed the idea of trade-offs.

CONCLUDING THOUGHTS

A challenge when discussing lean distribution is that this topic deserves its own book. This chapter presented a smorgasbord of powerful ways to remove waste from distribution channels. Unfortunately, too few pages and too many topics make it impossible to present everything that falls under the lean distribution umbrella. A major issue for many supply chain managers, for example, involves how to apply lean principles when managing reverse distribution channels. It's amazing how material that moves downstream in efficient master packs and neatly loaded trailers comes back looking weathered, damaged, opened, used, and a host of other words that end in "ed." For many firms effective reverse logistics is high on their agenda.

Another area that has huge potential for taking waste out of distribution channels is cooperative and collaborative planning approaches between supply chain members. Examples of these approaches include sales and operation planning (SOP) and collaborative planning, forecasting, and replenishment (CPFR). The purpose of CPFR is to provide guidelines and roadmaps for integrating demand and supply planning among raw material suppliers, suppliers of finished goods, and retailers. Various studies have shown that supply chain collaboration, particularly the sharing of demand data at the consumer level, offers tremendous potential for removing supply chain waste by better balancing the flow of material across the entire supply chain.

It is surprising how little attention lean distribution has received from practitioners and academics. Chapter 1 revealed that the search term *lean manufacturing* produced 270 or so *Google* hits for every single *lean distribution* hit. In ABI/INFORM, perhaps the most comprehensive database of business research publications on the planet earth, lean manufacturing publications outnumber lean distribution publications about 130 to 1. The opportunities for improvements within distribution likely exceed by a significant margin the opportunities that are still available within manufacturing.

ENDNOTES

1. W. Hoffman, "Cleaning Up on Distribution," *Traffic World* 271, no. 2 (January 15, 2007): 10-12.

2. Adapted from R. Dawe, "Reengineering Warehousing," *Transportation and Distribution* 36, no. 1 (January 1995): 102; and cited in D. Lambert, J. Stock, and L. Ellram, *Fundamentals of Logistics Management* (Boston: Irwin McGraw-Hill, 1998), 266.

3. W. Zinn and D. Bowersox, "Planning Physical Distribution with the Principle of Postponement," *Journal of Business Logistics* 9, no. 2 (1988): 117-136.

4. M. Johnson and E. Anderson, "Postponement Strategies for Channel Derivatives," *International Journal of Logistics Management* 11, no. 1 (2000): 19-35.

5. Adapted from Dean Foust, "How Technology Delivers for UPS," *Business Week* 4024 (March 5, 2007): 60.

6. R. Dawe, "What are the Odds of Winning with WMS?" *Transportation & Distribution* 38, no.12 (December 1997): 67.

7. E. Frazelle, *World-Class Warehousing and Material Handling* (New York: McGraw Hill, 2002), 204.

8. From a real-time survey conducted during a BetterManagement webinar, March 5, 2008.

9. This section is adapted from J. Cooke, "Can a TMS Really Save You Money? *DC Velocity* 6 (March 2008): 37-40.

10. R. Cook, B. Gibson, and D. MacCurdy, "A Lean Approach to Cross Docking," *Supply Chain Management Review* 9 no. 12 (March 2005): 54-59.

11. Mopar is an abbreviation for "Motor Parts."

12. Adapted from R. Flandez, "A Memphis Presence Gives Small Firms Logistical Advantage," *The Wall Street Journal*, July 10, 2007, B7.

13. N. Boudette, "Detroit Confronts Surplus of Showrooms," *The Wall Street Journal*, June 18, 2007, A10.

14. Adapted from G. Kahn, "Invisible Supplier Has Penney's Shirts All Buttoned Up," *The Wall Street Journal*, September 11, 2003, A1.

15. Industrial engineers at leading universities are increasingly focusing on mathematically modeling supply chain networks and systems. Companies that are looking to pursue this type of modeling are encouraged to tap into the expertise of these system modelers.

16. See note 1, 12.

6

MEASURING FOR LEAN

Management theorist Michael Hammer recently commented that measuring operational performance remains an unresolved challenge. He maintains this is remarkable for two reasons: performance measurement is so fundamental to basic management that it should presumably have been resolved a long time ago, and even though companies have developed sophisticated measurement systems over the last several years, too many managers still complain they measure too much or too little, measure the wrong things, or don't use their metrics effectively.[1] Consistent with these comments, a survey of the lean literature reveals a serious absence of any discussion about the importance of measurement or the kinds of measures that support lean across a supply chain. Measurement is an area we often take for granted, often with serious consequences.

This chapter explores measurement within the context of a lean supply chain. The first section addresses the importance of measurement, which is followed by a discussion of the dark side of measurement, including the wasteful actions that occur in the quest to make the numbers. The third section identifies a set of characteristics that are useful when evaluating the effectiveness of measures, followed by examples of measures that support lean objectives. The chapter concludes by showing the importance of linking lean accomplishments to corporate performance indicators.

THE IMPORTANCE OF MEASUREMENT

The reasons for measuring any kind of performance are relatively simple. Without question performance measurement motivates individuals to act in certain ways, so it's important we act in ways that support organizational goals rather than narrow and sometimes conflicting goals. Develop the right set of measures and the chances are good that the right kind of behaviors will result. Develop the wrong set of measures and be prepared to sit back and watch the results. Performance measurement also conveys what is important within an organization. If lean is important, then we need to create a set of metrics that convey that importance.

Measurement helps identify areas that are most in need of improvement, internal areas that might benefit from performance benchmarking, and rates of performance change. Measurement provides a picture of performance over time that managers can use to project into the future. This is essential since lean is a continuous journey that benefits from setting and then working toward milestones.

Measurement also supports some important principles of Total Quality Management. It allows managers to base decisions on objective rather than subjective analysis, an important quality principle. The measurement process is also an ideal way to drive continuous improvement. Once a performance target is reached it is a good bet that a new, more challenging target will emerge. Most managers do not even debate the relationship between measurement, motivation, effort, and performance. Measurement is also an ideal way to convey requirements between supply chain members.

THE DARK SIDE OF MEASUREMENT

A well-thought-out measurement system can do great things for an organization. Conversely, measurement can have a dark side that cannot be ignored. Having too many performance indicators, measuring the wrong things, or encouraging behavior that is not at all what management expected are all possible outcomes from poor measurement systems. Entire books could be written about the games people play in their quest to look good on performance measures.

Almost all performance measures have four parts, and it is critical these four parts are well thought out or we often see some strange outcomes. And here, we can safely assume that strange outcomes refers to wasteful activities and actions.

The first part of a measure relates to what the measure addresses, whether it is customer satisfaction, cycle time, quality, or delivery performance. Measuring areas that do not align with lean objectives can send the wrong message about what is important. The second part of a measure includes the performance target. Ideally these targets have an external focus, often developed through benchmarking, rather than representing internal performance levels that feature gradual improvement built in period to period.

The third component of a measure includes actual performance, which at times can be a challenge to arrive at if there is no information technology system supporting the measurement system. The fourth component is often absent in measurement systems, and it is this absence that can lead to some wild behavior. This includes the well-defined action plans that define how an individual or group will achieve a performance target. Along with these action plans is a clear identification of who has eventual accountability for success or failure of the measure.

The Games People Play

The unfortunate truth is that ill-conceived measurement systems, including an absence of well-defined plans about how to achieve performance targets, can cause people to engage in some strange, if not unethical behavior to make their numbers. The unintended consequences that measurement systems often create would almost be laughable if they weren't so wasteful. While measurement should be a vital part of lean, the sad truth is that measurement often works directly against lean objectives.

Consider the following outcomes that resulted from a desire to look good on various measures. When reviewing these snippets, ask yourself if these behaviors in any way support continuous improvement or the removal of waste from a supply chain. Each example, unfortunately, is real:

- A company that measures output rather than sales when evaluating the performance of its plants should not have been surprised when managers scheduled massive overtime in late December to make year-end production targets. The result was some serious overtime costs and production that had no corresponding demand. This excess inventory was stored in leased trailers outside the plant. Most employees were assigned to painting or other housekeeping duties in January due to a surplus of supply.

- The Board of Directors of a major corporation offered its CEO a bonus if the company's stock price stayed over $100 per share for an extended period. The CEO subsequently used company funds to initiate a massive stock buyback program that ensured the price would remain over $100. One board member later commented that a stock buyback was not quite what he had in mind when he supported the bonus incentive.

- A company implemented a new scheduling system that featured packaging smaller quantities of more part numbers rather than packaging larger quantities of fewer part numbers. This system would help ensure that only quantities that were needed by downstream entities would be packaged. Unfortunately, the company did not change its measurement system, which still based rewards on the number of pieces packaged per hour, a measure that additional changeovers adversely affect. Work centers ignored the scheduling system and continued to package unnecessary goods in order to gain efficiencies from higher volume runs and fewer changeovers.

- Managers at a St. Louis distribution center came up with a creative way to ensure they always exceeded their quality targets. They instructed their industrial customers not to submit formal quality claims for parts ordered but not received, parts that were received damaged, or parts that were received with incorrect quantities. Instead, customers were told to call the distribution center for replacement parts that would be sent with their next order. These off-the-books transactions were not recorded in the quality management system, resulting in elevated quality levels that less creative managers could only look upon with envy. Besides exhibiting questionable behavior, this approach did nothing to highlight quality problems.

- A company that manages its inventory through weekly cycle counts holds its plant managers accountable for the differences between physical inventories, which employees manually count, and the computerized system record on hand. These managers are also measured on how efficiently their facility conducts the cycle counts (i.e., cycle counts per labor hour). One clever manager figured out how to look good on these two measures. For parts with large quantities, he instructed his employees to go to a computer terminal, bring up the system records for those part numbers, and enter the system quantity in the handheld scanner the employees use to record the physical quantities. Not only did this facility have relatively fewer discrepancies between its physical and system inventory, particularly for larger quantity parts, recording quantities off a computer screen was also a highly efficient way to count parts. Unfortunately, this approach defeats the purpose of the cycle count system.

- To make their end-of-year sales target, salespeople at a major OEM asked their customers to buy heavily in the fourth quarter. The salespeople then made arrangements with these customers to return the material for a full refund after the distribution of sales bonuses. After some customers complained about the pressure the salespeople were placing on them, as well as the questionable business practices they were observing, these salespeople were discharged from the company.

- A plant manager failed to process customer returns at his facility because returns generated minimal credit to his operating budget. Budget numbers were earned for shipping orders out, not bringing them back. Not only did unprocessed returns stack up to the point they affected the flow of the facility, customers complained to corporate headquarters that they were not receiving their return credits. The plant manager, who on paper looked favorable on his operating numbers, was eventually reassigned to other duties.

- A major computer company measured its customer service people on how quickly they resolved customer problems. In this case the metric that was used focused on how quickly a service call lasted. The behavior that resulted because of this measure infuriated customers. Customer service representatives would simply transfer a customer's call to another representative or department, quickly disposing of the problem and looking good on the call duration measure. Some customers were transferred seven or more times during their service call. Unfortunately, customers who were victims of this game made their discontent known by shifting their business to other companies. This company has had to spend millions of dollars to improve its customer service network, not to mention the steps it has taken to repair its damaged reputation.

- An OEM that operates a network of aftermarket distribution centers measures the percent of customer orders that are shipped within their designated shipping time. Operations personnel quickly realized that a call to the manager that compiled this metric would result in an adjustment to show that any late orders were shipped on time. It should come as no surprise that the distribution centers across this company rarely achieved anything less than 100 percent on-time shipping compliance, at least on paper.

- A company that boasted its on-time delivery performance to customers was close to 100 percent was somewhat shocked when customers informed the company the true performance level was closer to 60 percent. A little checking revealed something interesting. Each time the company missed a shipping date it updated its system with the new ship date. Once an order was shipped the system did not use the original shipping date as a point of comparison but rather the most current date. An order could miss its target ship date five times, but as long as it hit its most current target date it was calculated as *on time*. Customers were not amused by this practice.

These wasteful examples can go on and on. One company measured its distribution center managers on the amount of inventory the center held at the end of the month. This resulted in frantic efforts to move as much stock at the end of the month as possible and then to work furiously to replace the inventory at the beginning of the month. A fast food chain measured its managers on the amount of food the restaurant scrapped each day, clearly a worthy sounding metric. Unfortunately, the employees deferred making food until customers ordered food. This had the effect of slowing down service since the physical process was not capable of operating in a make-to-order environment. Other managers allowed their food to sit a bit longer under the heat lamps than what the policy manual suggested. While scrap rates declined, so did customer satisfaction.

In each example no new value was created, and in fact waste was the inevitable result. In some cases problems were covered up rather than systematically addressed. And at other times people were discharged for their behavior. A performance measurement system can be your best friend or your worst enemy. These examples illustrate the worst enemy part.

HOW DO WE KNOW IF MEASURES ARE GOOD?

Before presenting a set of measures that should support lean objectives, it might be worthwhile to step back and present a set of characteristics that effective measures satisfy. If we want to avoid the dark side of measurement, we should know what good measures look like. Since measurement is so critical to lean success, let's do measurement right.

Perhaps first and foremost, effective performance measures *link to and support corporate strategies and objectives*. If a corporate objective is to pursue lean across the supply chain, then we should expect to see, for example, measures that relate to flow, pull, speed, cycle time, throughput, and delivery performance; measures that relate to total quality and customer satisfaction; measures that tell us how efficiently working capital and other financial resources are being utilized; and measures that relate to supply base performance.

Effective measures are also *presented in ways that executive managers appreciate*. Instead of simply reporting an improvement in inventory turns, for example, an effective measure will show how this increase in turns improved return on assets (ROA), cash flow, or working capital, all measures that are meaningful at higher organizational levels. This does not mean we should disregard operational measures. It does mean, however, that lean improvements need to be presented in ways that reflect their corporate importance.

As discussed earlier, effective measures *should not result in unintended consequences or behavior* that does not align with the spirit of the measure. How a measure is achieved is vitally important. Effective measures include well-defined action plans, or what some call tactics, that describe how to achieve each measure. The plans must also identify the individuals or groups who have ultimate responsibility for achieving a performance measure.

Effective measures also *use data from sources that are visible throughout an organization.* It should not be a mystery where numbers come from or how they are compiled. Furthermore, *the cost of obtaining measurement data should not outweigh the value of the data.* If that is the case the measurement process becomes wasteful.

Another characteristic is that *performance targets are reviewed and adjusted regularly.* These targets are based on world-class performance levels, ideally identified through external benchmarking. Setting objectives based on internal indicators tends to promote doing things the same way, often only incrementally better. Objectives that are not reviewed or adjusted on a regular basis become standards, and standards imply stagnation.

Solid measures also *promote teamwork and cross-functional cooperation* across the supply chain. A company that measures its customer service group on order-to-cash cycle time, for example, should not be surprised at the conflict that results if it measures transportation buyers on cost reductions. The customer service group will focus primarily on speed to get orders to the customer as quickly as possible. Unfortunately, in the transportation world speed usually means higher costs, and the pursuit of speed directly counters the buyer's performance measures. The conflict between these two groups is practically inevitable due to a misalignment of measures.

Effective measures *stress accomplishments rather than activities. Kaizen* events, quality improvement initiatives, and other lean activities are all activities. While it is natural to feel positive about activities that the prevailing wisdom says are good, activity means nothing unless it translates directly into desired outcomes. What did a kaizen event achieve in the way of improved performance? What benefits resulted from using self-directed teams in work cells? In short, what did these activities accomplish? We often interchange activity and accomplishment. Finally, effective measures *relate to what the customer really wants* rather than what managers think the customer wants.

Disregarding these characteristics affects the relevance of the measurement process and, oftentimes, leads directly to various kinds of waste, including wasted effort, conflicting goals, a disregard for the importance of measurement, and diminished business performance.

MEASURES THAT SUPPORT LEAN SUPPLY CHAINS

There are hundreds of possible measures that an organization can put in place. Unfortunately, the fact that there are hundreds of possible measures is one of the problems with most measurement systems. Having too many possible measures makes the task of finding the right set that much more challenging.

The right way to approach lean measurement is by identifying your organization's lean objectives and then creating the metrics that align directly with those objectives. Anyone who states that a standard set of measures exist that lean organizations should have in place is oversimplifying this issue. And there is no accepted measure of leanness. At best, we can provide examples of measures that could be part of your measurement portfolio if these measures align with your strategic objectives. It is your organization's responsibility to craft a final set of measures that align with an often very unique set of objectives.

Interestingly, most of the following measurement examples do not focus directly on costs and cost reductions unless the cost metric uses total costs. Recall from Chapter 1 that unit cost reductions and waste elimination are not necessarily the same thing. A strict focus on unit costs often results in behaviors that have longer-term consequences. A purchasing manager's relentless quest to obtain the lowest price from suppliers may lead to extended supply chains in terms of time and distance. Low-price material may also not match up well from a total cost of ownership perspective. A transportation manager who is driven to find the lowest cost carriers may see the effects of these price savings reflected in poor service, a lack of available equipment, unreliable delivery performance, and longer delivery times to customers.

To be consistent with the format of this book, the following sections present selected measures across the areas of lean supply, transportation, operations, and distribution. Measurement discussion relating to supply chain planning and control and customer value satisfaction are also presented. The following presents selected measures that might apply within a lean supply chain. Table 6.1 presents a more comprehensive set of supply chain (not corporate) measures sorted by application area.

Lean Supply Measures

Recall from Chapter 1 that lean supply consists of three major areas: selecting and then developing suppliers that practice lean principles, creating a physical supply network that features fewer suppliers providing more frequent deliveries of smaller quantities, and creating a supply organization that removes redundancy and waste from the supply management process. A supply organization can have measures that relate to each of these areas.

Supplier Scorecard Measures. Lean supply measures are often part of what are called *supplier scorecards* or *report cards*. While not as detailed as internal measures, supplier scorecards and their measures should nonetheless tap into some areas that reflect how well suppliers are performing, including delivery per-

Table 6.1 Possible measures within a lean supply chain

Supply chain area	Measures	Comments
Lean supply	Supplier scorecard measures	Includes regular reports of supplier performance, including performance areas that support lean objectives
	Supplier total cost measures	Combines unit price, nonconformance costs, and other relevant costs and savings
	Savings realized from supplier suggestion programs	Captures savings and reduced waste due to supplier suggestions
	Percent of suppliers producing from a buyer's pull signals	Reveals how well a major lean objective is accomplished upstream
	Percent of supplier volume produced from a buyer's pull signals	Another way to see how well a major lean objective is accomplished upstream
	Net savings from supplier development activities	Reflects the savings (less the costs) from supplier improvement efforts
	Return on investment from supplier development activities	A financial perspective showing the relevancy of development efforts
	Procurement overhead as a percent of total sales	Reflects the efficiency of the procurement organization
Lean transportation	Percent of receipts arriving with advance shipment notices (ASNs)	Information received in advance of a shipment supports planning and staging
	Percent of inbound shipments arriving under carrier contract	Negotiated contracts can provide benefits that standard transportation buying cannot provide
	Carrier performance	Evaluates various dimensions of carrier performance
	Transportation vehicle demurrage and detention charges	Higher charges indicate inefficient planning and management
	Percent of receipts delivered on a just-in-time (JIT) basis	Reflects the maturity of a JIT delivery network
	Total inbound and outbound transportation costs as a percent of sales	Cost measures will always be on the minds of managers
	Dwell (waiting) time ratios	Reflects the amount of time drivers and assets are idle
	Ratio of loaded miles to total miles	The degree to which deadhead miles are part of total miles

Table 6.1 Possible measures within a lean supply chain (continued)

Supply chain area	Measures	Comments
Lean operations	Percent of material or carriers unloaded upon receipt	Inbound receipts stored in a yard or on a vehicle impede flow
	Percent of volume that is cross docked	Reflects the amount of material that moves continuously to the next major link in the supply chain
	Percent of inbound receipts that do not move to storage	Reflects the amount of material that downstream entities within a facility require immediately
	Percent of output bypassing storage	Reflects physical output within work centers that bypasses storage
	Percent of production that is make-to-order versus make-to-stock	Measures how much production occurs because of customer pull signals
	Labor hours per $100 of sales	Used in production and distribution centers as an efficiency measure
	Overall equipment effectiveness	Measures the availability, efficiency, quality performance, and nonplanned downtime for equipment
	Changeover or setup times	Measures that capture how long setups and changeovers take
	Cycle time and throughput measures	Includes time-based measures that relate to flow
	Part-per-million (ppm) quality defect levels	A standardized metric that is used in many industries
	First-pass yield	Measures the percent of output that does not require repeated processing
	Scrap and reject rates	Captures the loss associated with nonconforming output
	Warranty return rates	Reflects charges related to products that have defects discovered by customers
	Total cost of quality	A composite measure that includes good and bad quality-related costs
	Average total cost per unit	This measure reflects total costs rather than unit costs

Table 6.1 Possible measures within a lean supply chain

Supply chain area	Measures	Comments
Lean distribution	Perfect customer order rates	The percent of orders that ship to customers with zero defects
	Order fill rates	Unfilled orders due to lack of stock create supply chain waste, costs, and lost sales
	Unplanned backorders	Orders that show a positive record on hand, but have no physical stock affect costs and customer service
	Order-to-cash cycle time	A popular measure that requires different groups to work together
	Conformance to customer-driven delivery dates	Measures on-time delivery at the customer's location rather than on-time shipping from producer's facility
	Average distance traveled between internal material movements	Provides visibility to a major source of supply chain waste
	Total miles traveled	A particularly relevant measure for customer delivery networks
	Distribution quality indicators	Includes indicators of wrong parts picked, wrong quantities, missed deliveries, and damage
	Total distribution costs (including transportation and reverse logistics costs) as a percent of total product costs or sales	Management is always interested in cost-related measures
Planning and control	Inventory record accuracy	Reflects the differences between physical and computer records for inventory across the supply chain
	Inventory write-offs as a percent of total sales	This reflects supply chain waste from poor planning or other supply chain problems
	Inventory carrying charges as a percent of sales	Reflects the true cost of holding inventory
	Demand estimation accuracy	This is a measure every company must have in place
	Raw material, work-in-process, and finished goods inventory turnover	Reflects how often inventory moves across the supply chain
	Percent of total transactions processed electronically	Reflects efforts to use systems such as electronic data interchange (EDI) and electronic funds transfer (EFT) to eliminate transactions costs

Table 6.1 Possible measures within a lean supply chain

Supply Chain Area	Measures	Comments
Customer value satisfaction	Customer satisfaction indicators	Firms often use third parties to capture customer satisfaction data
	Customer repurchase rate	When everything comes together, repurchase rates should be higher than industry averages

formance, quality performance, and total cost performance. Each of these areas is important to a lean supply chain.

Scorecards usually fall into one of three categories: categorical, weighted point, or cost-based measurement systems. For relatively unimportant items, categorical check-offs may be an acceptable way to evaluate suppliers. For more complex items, most firms use a weighted point system that includes a variety of performance categories, category weights, and measurement scales to determine a supplier's score within each category. The third type, cost-based systems, is the least used of the three types due to its complexity and difficulty collecting reliable data. Whatever type of system is used, supply organizations should apply a standardized measurement approach to avoid having each unit or location reinvent how it will measure performance, a type of supply chain waste identified in Chapter 1.

Supplier Total Cost Measures. A variety of measures attempt to evaluate suppliers based strictly on price, or what some call unit cost. One standardized total cost measure is the supplier performance index (SPI). The SPI is a total cost measure that assumes that any quality or performance infraction committed by a supplier, which contributes directly to waste, increases the total cost of doing business with that supplier. As an example, assume that a supplier delivers $150,000 worth of components to a company in the fourth quarter. The supplier also commits three nonconformances that result in $17,500 in total nonconformance costs. The supplier's SPI for the fourth quarter is 1.12 ([$150,000 + $17,500]/$150,000).

What does the SPI value mean? It means the total cost of doing business with this supplier is 12 percent higher than the total unit price. If the unit price of a supplier's good or service is $125, then the estimated total cost is $140 ($125 × 1.12). Because the SPI is a standardized statistic it also allows comparisons between suppliers. A supplier with an SPI of 1.12 has a 5 percent higher total cost than one with an SPI of 1.07. This measure supports the identification of nonconformances that are resulting in serious waste.

Conceptually similar to the SPI is a measure called *unit total cost* (UTC).[2] The two approaches (SPI and UTC) are very similar except UTC calculates a total unit cost presented in dollars per unit rather than a ratio. Both approaches recognize that supplier management must move beyond unit cost analysis, at least for critical goods and services.

Lean Transportation Measures

A variety of measures reveals how well inbound and outbound transportation systems support lean objectives. It is important to recall that many lean transportation networks are in fact managed by third-party logistics (3PL) providers. When this is the case, carrier performance measures will be critical.

Percent of Receipts Arriving with Advance Shipment Notices (ASNs). Lean supply chains rely extensively on information that provides insights into forthcoming requirements. A major enabler of planning and staging, an important concept presented in Chapter 4, is information that reveals what requirements are coming next. ASNs let a downstream work center know when receipts are arriving via the transportation network. Since ASNs are widely viewed as a good thing, it makes sense to have a measure that promotes their use. ASNs support workforce scheduling, flow, and short-term facility planning. They play a major role within an information-enabled supply chain.

Percent of Inbound Shipments Arriving under Carrier Contract. Almost all firms that are serious about a lean supply chain have in place negotiated contracts with transportation providers. These contracts are often longer-term agreements that address rate discounts, service guarantees, dedicated transportation equipment, and electronic linkages. Any company that operates a just-in-time (JIT) inbound delivery network will likely rely on contract carriers. While this is clearly an activity-based measure, it also promotes some desired outcomes.

Lean Operations Measures

Internal operations are where most organizations will see a preponderance of lean measures. These measures should relate to some important lean objectives, including total quality, pull, flow, cycle time, inventory management, and operating costs.

Cycle Time and Throughput Measures. Throughput and cycle time measures relate to speed and flow, aspirations that are fundamental to lean. Cycle time represents the average time between completing successive units or stages of a process.[3] Examples of operational cycle time measures include dock-to-dock cycle times (receiving materials from suppliers to shipping finished goods to cus-

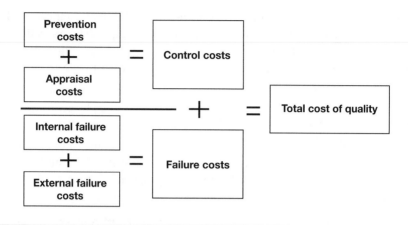

Figure 6.1 Calculating the total cost of quality metric

tomers), order-to-cash cycle time, and standard production cycle times. In reality, every task has a cycle time associated with it. Setup and changeover measures could also be part of this family of measures.

The concept of throughput is central to any organization that is pursuing flow as a key part of lean, making this an important measurement area. The throughput of a system is *a measure of the system's actual capacity to deliver output, usually expressed as a rate of units per time.* A focus on throughput helps explain why so many companies focus on reducing cycle times. Assume, for example, the throughput for a product with an average cycle time of 20 minutes per unit is three units per hour. If a process improvement or product redesign results in a new cycle time (i.e., faster flow time) of 15 minutes per unit, then the new throughput time becomes four units per hour. All else equal, reduced cycle times mean faster throughput and more units produced per hour, day, or month. It is hard to overstate the importance of throughput and cycle time measures when pursuing lean. Chapter 8 will show how faster throughput leads directly to higher production and greater capacity.

Total Cost of Quality. Some firms create measures that capture quality performance at a macrolevel. Figure 6.1 shows the conceptual format for calculating total cost of quality measures as defined by Joseph Juran, one of the preeminent quality thought leaders in the 20th century.

The challenge here involves capturing the data that are required to arrive at a total cost figure. The data are typically spread across different parts of the supply chain. Most cost accounting systems are not capable of separating overhead costs, for example, into their component elements for allocation. Other systems are incapable of capturing data that are spread across the supply chain and then assembling that data into a central database.

Lean Distribution Measures

Lean distribution can be quite broad since it includes any entity or part of the supply chain, including outbound transportation that resides between operations and the ultimate customer. This broad scope means that many measures could fall under this part of the supply chain umbrella.

Distribution Quality Measures. Like operations and production, distribution channels also have their own set of quality-related measures. Distribution centers will usually focus on how often customers receive wrong parts, damaged parts, missed deliveries, and quantities that differed from what they ordered. These are all errors that distribution centers control directly.

Labor Hours per $100 of Sales. Lean distribution channels are meant to be efficient. Therefore, it makes sense to have measures that tell managers how efficiently an entity is operating. A good efficiency measure, particularly within distribution centers, is labor hours per $100 of sales.

This measure tells managers at a glance how well an operation is performing. Any labor waste that occurs, including direct and indirect labor, will not escape capture by this measure. You can run but you can't hide, at least from this efficiency measure. As with any measure, the challenge is to establish a performance target that is meaningful rather than simply convenient.

Supply Chain Planning and Control Measures

Supply chain planning and control measures often look across the supply chain rather than at any single part of the chain. Perhaps the two most important supply chain planning and control measures are the accuracy of inventory records and the accuracy of the demand estimation process. These are also two relatively easy measures to manage.

Inventory Record Accuracy. Record integrity or accuracy, a popular measure for firms that rely on a perpetual cycle counting system, reflects the difference between physical material on hand (POH) and the computerized record of material on hand (ROH) for a part number. As mentioned in Chapter 5, record integrity exists when the physical inventory on hand equals the electronic record on hand (POH = ROH), regardless of the quantity of inventory. Any difference between POH and ROH represents error, and error creates waste.

This measure should be segmented into submeasures that capture record accuracy at different points along the supply chain. Record accuracy is essential for effectively managing components, work in process, and finished goods inventory. Inventory record accuracy is about control, and it's difficult to manage an investment in inventory when supply chain managers are not confident about the validity of their inventory numbers.

Demand Estimation Accuracy. As mentioned in Chapter 5, demand estimates include all the claims against a firm's output, including product forecasts. Too many companies fail to recognize the effect that inaccurate demand estimation has on supply chain performance. The downside of poor demand estimation includes higher inventory volumes and carrying charges, poor customer service as inventory is misallocated across locations and products, and excessive safety stock levels. Measuring the quality of product forecasts and demand estimates, like measuring record integrity, is a *must have* measure.

Customer Value Satisfaction Measures

Let's face it—all of the lean efforts in the world mean nothing if they fail to benefit the customer. Customer value satisfaction measures tap into the sentiments of business customers, such as dealers and retailers, and consumers. Almost all firms operate in a business-to-business (B2B) environment, and many also operate in the business-to-consumer (B2C) arena. Satisfaction data gathered by objective third parties along with repurchase rates will reveal whether we are delighting or frustrating customers.

LINKING LEAN TO CORPORATE INDICATORS

Demonstrating the true value of lean requires an ability to translate the impact that lean initiatives have on corporate performance indicators. Finance personnel will play an important role in this translation. Linking lean outcomes to corporate indicators helps demonstrate the strategic rather than the operational value of lean. Showing the impact that lean initiatives have on ROA, economic value-add (EVA), profitability, cash flow, working capital, return on invested capital (ROIC), and performance ratios such as assets to sales will capture the attention of executive leaders.

Let's provide an example that shows the relationship between lean improvements and corporate-level indicators. The CEO of an industrial company is not likely to get overly excited when he or she hears that various lean initiatives have increased inventory turns from 8 to 11 annually. (An abundance of research shows that lean organizations have higher inventory turns, on average, compared with counterparts that are less lean.) Executive managers simply do not think about or are not evaluated on the same set of performance criteria as the typical operational or supply chain manager.

Table 6.2 Identifying the corporate impact of lean initiatives

	Before	After
Sales ($millions)	$2300	$2300
Net profit	$184 (8% profit margin)	$184
Assets		
Cash	$220	$220
Securities	$85	$85
Receivables	$275	$275
Inventories	$287.5 (8 turns)	$209.1 (11 turns)
Plant and equipment	$450	$450
Total assets	$1317.5	$1239

Inventory turnover = sales/inventory ($2300/$287.5) = 8 turns annually, ($2300/$209.1) = 11 turns annually.
Asset turnover = sales/total assets ($2300/$1317.5) = 1.75, ($2300/$1239) = 1.86.
Return on investment = profit margin X asset turnover = (8% X 1.75) = 14%, (8% X 1.86) = 14.9%.
Asset-to-sales ratio = ($1317.5/$2300) = .57, ($1239/$2300) = .54.

Table 6.2 illustrates how to translate improvements from lean initiatives into their affect on return on investment, another important indicator that is watched closely. In this example, lean initiatives that increased inventory turns from 8 to 11 annually increased return on investment from 14 percent to 14.9 percent, or an increase of almost 6 percent. This increase is likely understated since improved inventory management should lead to lower inventory carrying charges, which should improve net profit. In this example net profit remained constant at $184 million. Executives will sing the praises of lean once they see firsthand the affect that lean initiatives have on corporate performance.

Identifying the impact of lean activities on return on investment is not the only way to demonstrate the value of these efforts. Lean activities can be translated to show their impact on earnings per share, economic value-add, return on assets, working capital, cash flow, profit margin, and the assets- to-sales ratio. The assets-to-sales ratio in Table 6.2 declined (a good thing) from .57 to .54. Demonstrating how activities that support lean affect key performance indicators and ratios is essential for moving lean from the operational to the strategic level. These indicators are also the kind that Wall Street analysts look at when evaluating firm performance.

CONCLUDING THOUGHTS

Whatever measures your organization uses, always step back and ask yourself if the measures align with your lean objectives, whether the measures conflict with other measures, and whether the measures are driving the right kinds of behaviors and outcomes. And increasingly, understand how operational measures link to and affect the corporate indicators that show the true value of a lean supply chain. Performance measurement should not suffer from benign neglect.

ENDNOTES

1. M. Hammer, "The 7 Deadly Sins of Performance Measurement and How to Avoid Them," *Sloan Management Review* 48, no. 3 (Spring 2007): 19-20.

2. M. Harding, "Gauging Total Cost, Supplier by Supplier," *CSCMP's Supply Chain Quarterly* 1, no. 3 (Quarter 4, 2007): 64.

3. A. Raturi and J. Evans, *Principles of Operations Management* (Mason, OH: Thompson Southwestern, 2005), 109.

7

TOOLS AND APPROACHES FOR CONTINUOUS LEAN IMPROVEMENT

The likelihood of becoming an organization that is lean from end-to-end will improve if employees at all levels have access to the kinds of tools and approaches that will support their efforts. There are literally dozens, if not hundreds of tools available that have some applicability to lean, and a thorough discussion of these tools would not only be impractical, it would also be redundant with the many books that already cover this topic.

This chapter is somewhat different from other chapters that appear in books about lean. While some sources do not address at all the tools and techniques that help an organization pursue its lean objectives, others present a fairly standard array of lean tools. This chapter presents a broad array of tools and approaches that should be part of any organization's lean arsenal. Some approaches presented here, such as *kaizen* events and value stream mapping (VSM), are associated by almost everyone with being critical to lean. Other tools and approaches, such as benchmarking and suggestion programs, are not associated nearly as often with lean. They are, however, very supportive of the lean journey.

KAIZEN EVENTS

Any discussion of lean would be incomplete without reference to *kaizen*, perhaps one of the most recognized Japanese words in the business world. The word *kai* means continuous and *zen* means improvement, or continuous improvement. Some will translate *kai* to mean change and *zen* to mean good, or change for the better.[1] Whatever the interpretation, the focus of kaizen is on smaller, incremental improvements or changes in a process. In Japan, kaizen is not so much about consciously thinking about continuous improvement activities as it is a philosophy ingrained in the minds of the Japanese. Raphael Vitalo, Frank Butz, and Joseph Vitalo, experts on kaizen, explain the concept this way:

> *Kaizen is a method that strives for perfection by eliminating waste. It eliminates waste by empowering people with tools and a methodology for uncovering improvement opportunities and making change. Kaizen understands waste to be any activity that is not value-adding from the perspective of the customer. By value-adding, we mean any work done right the first time that materially changes a product or service in ways for which a well-informed and reasonable customer is willing to pay.*[2]

A less recognized Japanese word is *kaikaku*, which is a rapid or revolutionary event rather than an incremental event. Proponents of reengineering will be more likely to endorse kaikaku.

The implementation of the kaizen process is usually through formal events. These events focus on one or more parameters that can be improved, such as improved throughput within a process, improved facility layout to improve flow, steps to improve process yield and quality, or any other performance attribute that affects the ability to serve the end customer.

The kaizen process consists of three phases.[3] The first phase involves getting ready for a kaizen event. This involves documenting a scope for the event, analyzing whether to conduct an event, and then preparing for the event. The second phase of the process involves conducting or performing the kaizen event. Finally, the third phase involves following up to ensure that any process improvements are permanent. Most kaizen events involve internal operations and have largely involved manufacturing firms. However, this process is ideal for companies to apply within any part of their supply chain.

The conditions for preparing for, conducting, and evaluating a kaizen event involve a series of milestones. An erroneous assumption is that kaizen, as a process, requires one week or less. While the actual performance of the kaizen event may involve a week or less, the milestones before and after the actual event require additional time. The following summarizes the milestones before, during, and after a kaizen event:[4]

- **Milestone A.** This initial part of the kaizen process defines the focus, boundaries, and expectations of an event in the form of a scope document. The scope document will also include an assessment of estimated costs and benefits, both soft and hard, associated with the kaizen event. This phase generally requires a minimum of one calendar week to perform.

- **Milestone B.** This part of the process includes an analysis and determination of whether holding the kaizen event is likely to produce the benefits sought by those requesting the event. This determination is then communicated to all stakeholders. This analysis generally occurs one calendar week from completion of a verified scope document.

- **Milestone C.** The objective of Milestone C is to increase the likelihood that the event will achieve its purpose by preparing people to participate and preventing problems from affecting the flow of the event. The kaizen leader acquires any needed information, prepares communications about the event, and readies the team and stakeholders to participate in the event. This generally occurs three weeks from the completion of a scope document that verifies the feasibility of a kaizen event.

- **Milestone D.** This milestone involves conducting the actual kaizen event, which generally lasts a week or less. During the event the kaizen leader and team evaluate the targeted work process, improve the process to solve the performance issue, measure results, and communicate these results to stakeholders. Each day of the event is carefully scripted regarding what occurs.

- **Milestone E.** The final milestone involves the kaizen leader verifying that the improvements from the kaizen event are being sustained. The leader and team also extract key learning and use this to improve the kaizen process, as well as improve the leader's personal performance. The kaizen leader also works to replicate at other sites the benefits from the event. The timing of this milestone can be up to six months after completing the event.

A company that uses kaizen events extensively is Crayola, a company that most of us remember fondly from our younger days.[5] The company has performed over 100 kaizen events over the last six years. One event in particular shows the power of kaizen to be applied in areas external to manufacturing. As the company expanded its product line by branching out into more complex toys and other creative applications, the package engineering group found that its workload changed dramatically in terms of scope and volume. A kaizen event, including extensive upfront preparation for the event, resulted in a clearer understanding of specific duties that packaging engineering must support as well as a refined flow of work through the department. Changes that resulted from this event are helping the company adjust to a changing business.

Perhaps the greatest value from kaizen is making this process a way of life to ensure a steady stream of continuous improvements. A company that is almost synonymous with kaizen is Toyota. Interestingly, Toyota discovered that its incremental approach to improvement with suppliers left it with higher component costs compared with Nissan, a company that had taken a more aggressive approach to cost reduction. Toyota also learned from internal studies that it was paying higher prices than GM or Volkswagen for similar parts.

This finding forced Toyota to rethink its procurement strategy with suppliers. A senior managing director for Toyota commented, "It may come as a shock, but if we're content with the little-by-little approach of kaizen, then we can't win."[6] While kaizen will still be applied to internal factory operations, the company is pursuing more aggressive actions with suppliers to achieve double-digit cost savings.

CREATIVE AND CRITICAL THINKING SESSIONS

By any chance were you or a classmate chastised in elementary school for coloring outside the lines? At some point we have all been pushed into a comfortable level of conformity that resides safely between the lines. For many organizations their battle cry might as well be "creativity not spoken here!" However, a need for continuous improvement and innovation has created an environment where we need to start working outside the lines. One of the most powerful ways to promote lean improvements across an enterprise is to create a culture that endorses the systematic use of creative and critical thinking skills.

Creative thinking involves coming up with as many ideas as possible using different points of view. Conversely, critical thinking, also called *convergent thinking*, involves the systematic analysis and critique of those ideas. These two types of thinking are interrelated. The general sequence of events involves generating ideas or solutions through creative thinking and then subjecting those ideas to rigorous analysis. Most of the approaches presented in this chapter, including group problem solving, value analysis (VA), and suggestion programs rely extensively on creative and critical thinking skills. Knowing when, where, and how to apply these thinking skills is essential when pursuing lean objectives.

Creative Thinking

While most people have some level of creativity within them, for many reasons we do not allow that creativity to surface. We are all bound by rules and procedures, day-to-day work, restrictive measurement systems, organizational cultures and norms, inertia to do things the way they have always been done, or fear of failure and ridicule.

Most organizations would benefit from a formal approach for generating creative ideas. Brainstorming is the most common type of a creative thinking session. The purpose of brainstorming is to put forth as many ideas as possible on a topic in a relaxed and stress-free environment. Facilitators should follow some general guidelines or ground rules when conducting creative thinking or brainstorming sessions:

- **Withhold Judgment.** Keep an open mind and defer the analysis of an idea until later.
- **Strive for Many Ideas.** The primary objective of these sessions is to generate as many ideas as possible.
- **Do Not Reject Ideas.** Ideas that seem to challenge our accepted norms or seem impractical may not be so impractical in the final analysis.
- **Make the Group Stretch.** Encourage the group to move outside its comfort zone. Go beyond obvious, practical, and safe ideas.
- **Remove Distractions and Allocate Enough Time.** Creative sessions should be free of day-to-day distractions with enough time to let the group think and digest its ideas.
- **Seek Combinations of Ideas.** Encourage participants to make new associations of linkages across ideas.
- **Do Not Attach Names to Ideas.** Ideas should be from the group rather than an individual.

An issue during creative thinking sessions is the desire to critique ideas, sometimes negatively, immediately after they are presented. Knee jerk comments such as "we tried that before," "this won't work here," "that's a stupid idea," or "so and so will never go for this" not only disrupt the flow of the session, they affect the willingness of participants to put forth any new ideas.

Critical Thinking

While the primary objective of critical thinking is to generate as many alternatives as possible, critical thinking involves comparing and contrasting those ideas. Critical thinking involves improving and refining promising alternatives, challenging the merits of an idea, reducing the list of ideas through discussion and analysis, and selecting a course of action. Similar to creative thinking, facilitators should follow some general guidelines or ground rules when engaging in critical thinking:

- **Avoid Early Closure.** Commit an adequate amount of time to give ideas thorough consideration.
- **Be Analytic.** Apply the tools that help the group rigorously analyze and display data.
- **Do Not Ignore Difficult Issues.** Be open about potential trouble spots, such as employee or union resistance to an idea.
- **Stress Objectivity Rather than Subjectivity.** Engage in fact-based decision-making but do not ignore the critical qualitative issues.
- **Remember the Implementation Plan.** The analysis of ideas is incomplete if a plan for making changes and improvements is not developed.

A number of good tools are available for analyzing ideas and displaying data. Tools for displaying data include cause and effect diagrams, histograms, and pie, Pareto, and run charts. Two particularly effective approaches for analyzing ideas include force-field analysis and cost-benefit analysis.

Force-field analysis requires the identification of those forces that will help and those forces that will hinder a particular idea from becoming a reality. When using force-field analysis, participants draw a line down the center of a page or flip chart. This center line represents the *as is* situation. The left side of the center line represents helping forces while the right side represents hindering forces. Along the right side of the page of the flip chart another line is drawn. This line represents the desired or *should be* state. The point of the exercise is to determine what must be done to move the center or *as is* line over toward the desired or *should be* line.

The helping and hindering forces are usually represented by arrows. The arrows for helping forces push the center line toward the *should be* state while hindering forces push the center line away from the *should be* state. Groups often rate the relative strengths of the forces. For example, a rating of 5 might equate with a very strong force while a rating of 1 means the force is relatively weak. After identifying the relative ratings we can begin to consider how to strengthen the helping forces while lessening the hindering forces.

Another powerful tool for assessing creative ideas is a cost-benefit analysis. This approach requires a group (or individual) to estimate the real cost and benefits associated with a solution or idea. It involves systematically calculating, or estimating as closely as possible, the known costs and expected benefits of an idea or proposed solution. The process often involves estimates and assumptions. For example, a cost-benefit analysis of a proposed returnable container system will have to make some estimates or assumptions about how long it will take for a returnable container to make a complete cycle through a closed-loop transportation network. The lean application titled "What Goes Around Comes Around" (Chapter 10) explores the use of a cost-benefit analysis in greater depth.

Linking Creative and Critical Thinking and Lean Improvements

What does a discussion about creative and critical thinking sessions have to do with a lean supply chain? More than we can imagine. The areas related to lean that would benefit from creative thinking sessions, such as greater innovation, are broad. Here are but a few examples of topics that might benefit from formal creative thinking sessions:

- How can we better manage working capital, including better management of inventory?
- How can we improve forecast accuracy and demand estimation?
- How can we reduce scrap from our production process?
- How can we use IT systems to remove supply chain transactions costs?
- How can we pursue better relationships with key suppliers?
- How can we reduce machine setup times and improve facility layouts?
- How can we improve the performance of teams?
- How can we improve performance measurement systems?
- How can we improve our global transportation network?

The ideas that are generated from these sessions are then systematically analyzed for feasibility during critical thinking. Those ideas that make the cut will then have an implementation plan developed.

GROUP PROBLEM SOLVING

Every organization has problems, and it is no stretch to say that problems cause waste, and sometimes even worse. So, what constitutes a problem? And how do we know when to apply a problem-solving methodology versus a continuous improvement methodology? While some might call any improvement scenario a problem, which is common with kaizen proponents, we will attempt to differentiate formally between problems and continuous improvement opportunities.

For our purposes, we will say we have a problem when we are falling short of a stated target or external benchmark. For example, let's say the performance tar-

Step	Question to be answered	Creative thinking	Critical thinking	Next step requirements
I. **Identify problem**	What needs to be changed?	Consider possible problems	Agree upon a problem statement	Describe desired state in observable terms
II. **Analyze problem**	What's preventing us from reaching the desired state?	Identify possible causes	Identify and validate key causes	Document and rank key causes
III. **Generate possible solutions**	How could we make the change?	Develop ideas on how to solve the problem	Identify most likely solution(s)	Create a defined solution(s) list
IV. **Select and plan the solution**	What is the best way to do it?	Evaluate potential solution(s) using various criteria Generate ideas on how to implement the solution	Agree upon solution(s) Agree upon implementation and evaluation plans	A plan for making and monitoring the change Measurement criteria to evaluate solution effectiveness
V. **Implement solution**	Are we following the plan?		Agree upon contingency plans (if necessary)	Solution(s) are in place
VI. **Evaluate solution**	How well did it work?	Identify and share lessons learned	Agree upon the effectiveness of the solution Identify any continuing problems	Verify the problem is solved

Creative thinking is also called *divergent thinking*. Critical thinking is also called *convergent thinking*.

Figure 7.1 Group problem-solving process

get for on-time supplier delivery is 98 percent but actual supplier performance is 90 percent. Or perhaps our target for fulfilling customer orders is three days, but the actual fulfillment time is five days. Actual performance is falling short of the targeted performance, indicating that we have a problem.

Conversely, let's say a firm has a stated goal of achieving a 5000 parts per million (ppm) defect level or better from suppliers. After consistently achieving the 5000 ppm level, the new target is adjusted to 3000 ppm. This is a continuous improvement opportunity, assuming that these internal targets are consistent or better than external benchmarks. If the industry standard for supplier quality performance is 1000 ppm, then this could be more of a problem than first realized.

Figure 7.1 presents a group problem-solving methodology. While a problem can theoretically be solved by an individual, serious problems should benefit from a group approach that brings together different knowledge, skills, and abilities. A virtue of this approach is that it is applicable across different settings and can be applied to any type of problem. The process is robust. It is also conceptually straightforward.

Another important feature is that this process includes, by design, creative and critical thinking requirements in each step. The process values different points of view while still recognizing the need to converge on some outcome before moving to the next step. When applying this process it will quickly become evident that Steps I-IV are internal to a problem-solving group while Step V requires taking a course of action outside the group. If resistance to a group's plan happens, it will likely happen in Step V. The requirement for the last step, verifying that the problem has been solved, is quite important. It is not uncommon to have more than one cause to a problem that forces a group to cycle back to Step II for further analysis.

Another team-based approach for problem solving is the 8D process in which 8D stands for eight disciplines.[7] The steps in this problem-solving methodology include (1) describing the problem, (2) establishing the problem-solving team, (3) developing an interim containment action, (4) defining and verifying the root cause, (5) choosing the permanent corrective action, (6) implementing corrective action, (7) preventing recurrence, and (8) recognizing and rewarding the contributors.

PROCESS MODELING AND REDESIGN

A tool that should be part of every organization's lean arsenal is the ability to model or map a process. Recall from an earlier chapter that a process is a set of interrelated steps and activities designed to achieve a specific objective. Examples of key supply chain processes include customer order fulfillment, supplier evaluation and selection, new product development, and demand estimation. Supply chains are composed of many different, but often interrelated processes that affect how well an enterprise operates. Often these processes are plagued by different kinds of waste. At a minimum processes should be evaluated to identify continuous improvement opportunities. Process modeling or mapping is an ideal tool for attacking waste and pursuing continuous improvement.

If processes are critical, and most knowledgeable observers would agree they are, then the ability to model (also called mapping) and redesign a process is a critical component of a lean organization. Models are representations of reality and can be physical, mathematical, which is common with supply chain simulations, schematic, or graphical.

Processes are often presented as flowcharts or maps. Technically, a flowchart is a graphical model of an existing or proposed process that uses simple symbols, lines, and words to display the activities and their sequence throughout a process. Three basic types of flowcharts include block diagrams, flow-process charts, and flowcharts using American National Standards Institute (ANSI) symbols.

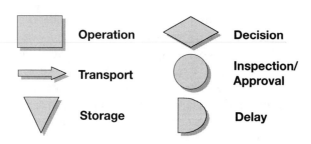

ANSI: American National Standards Institute

Figure 7.2 Standard ANSI process flowchart symbols

Flowcharts using ANSI symbols are perhaps the most commonly used technique for process modeling.

Process diagrams use a standard set of symbols to graphically portray a process. While some process maps simply use rectangular block diagrams, the symbols in Figure 7.2 begin to provide more detail about a process. The flowcharts can help us identify unnecessary and redundant steps, an inefficient sequencing of steps or use of resources, and bottlenecks.

When developing a process model it is important to portray the process as it currently exists. These illustrations can be at a higher level (the 25,000 foot level) or be quite detailed at the level of specific activities. At a later point we will redesign the process to appear as it should look. A more complex process, such as customer order fulfillment, may be broken down into a series of subprocesses or even individual tasks. Furthermore, individual events, such as ordering components from suppliers, can be further broken down into greater detail. The scope of a redesign effort is an important consideration when using this approach.

The ability to model processes is an important part of process improvement efforts, and continuous improvement is an important part of any organization that expects to become leaner. Organizations must clearly articulate the processes they rely on, identify those processes that offer the greatest opportunities for improvement, and create a culture that regularly applies process mapping. Process mapping must be a part of any organization's skill set.

VALUE STREAM MAPPING

Related to process design is value stream mapping (VSM), a tool developed by Taiichi Ohno at Toyota. VSM is a tool that helps us visualize the flow of material and information as a product or service progresses through a value stream. At Toyota, VSM is known as *material and information flow mapping* and is used as a tool to develop implementation plans to install lean systems.[8] The following defines some important concepts with VSM:[9]

- **Value Stream**—all the interrelated activities, value-added and other, needed to make a complete material or information product. James Womack and Daniel Jones argue that a value stream is the set of all the specific actions required to bring a product through the three critical elements of any business: (1) product design, (2) information management, and (3) physical transformation.[10]
- **Value Stream Map**—a set of drawings that make the flow of material and information visible.
- **Value Stream Mapping**—the physical effort that creates value stream maps.
- **Current State Map**—an illustration of a process or value stream as it currently appears.
- **Future State Map**—an illustration of a process or value stream that represents an ideal state after applying lean principles.

VSM differs from process mapping in a number of ways:[11]

- VSM gathers and displays a broader range of information than a typical process map.
- VSM tends to be used at a broader level, such as an entire value stream from receiving to delivery of finished goods.
- VSM is often used to identify where to focus future projects, such as kaizen events.
- VSM has its own set of icons that are different from the icons used with process mapping. These icons are specific to lean while process design icons are generic.

An advantage of VSM is the ability to provide a common framework and language across cultures. The process requires a thorough mapping and understanding of the current state of a value stream before a future state is determined. The future state represents a goal to work toward. VSM takes an integrated, holistic view of a value stream that is cross-functional, or horizontal, by design. Few, if any, value streams are purely functional.

Essential to VSM is the use of VSM symbols or icons. Unlike process mapping symbols, VSM icons are not standardized, although there are a fair number of generally accepted icons. It is not unusual for organizations to create their own symbols as the need arises. Figures 7.3 and 7.4 present a sample of current and future state VSM symbols. For a more thorough description of the icons used when creating current and future value streams, go to:
http://www.strategosinc.com/value-stream-mapping-3.htm.

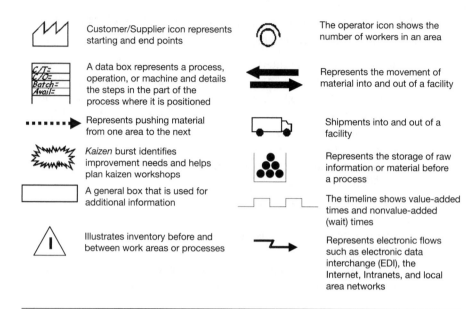

Figure 7.3 Selected current state icons

SIX SIGMA METHODLOGY AND PROJECTS

Six Sigma, today's version of Total Quality Management, has a philosophical and literal translation. As a philosophy, Six Sigma attempts to increase profits by eliminating the variability, defects, and waste that undermine customer loyalty.[12] It is hard to argue that defects, or what many quality people also call nonconformances, are not wasteful.

Literally translated, Six Sigma means that output within a process will conform to its specification target at a defect level of only 3.4 defects per million opportunities (DPMO), which is statistically misleading. A process that operates statistically at a Six Sigma level (sigma is a measure of dispersion around a mean) will produce output that has only two defects per *billion* opportunities. Those who originally developed the concept recognized that all processes have some natural drift or off-centering when they operate under actual conditions. This off-centering brings with it an increased probability of producing a nonconformance. In this case, the penalty is assumed to shift the process from 2 parts per billion defects to 3.4 parts per million defects. While this is not central to our discussion of Six Sigma, it is good information to know.

Central to Six Sigma is the define, measure, analyze, improve, and control (DMAIC) methodology. Table 7.1 presents the major features of each step. It should not be hard to see how this approach, when applied rigorously across an

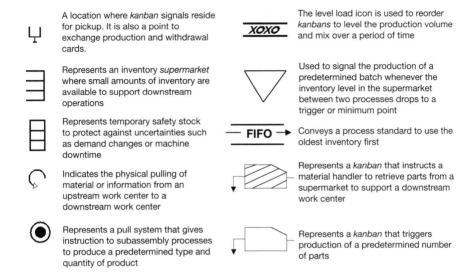

Figure 7.4 Selected future state icons

organization, is highly supportive of the lean objective *striving for excellence*. Six Sigma improvement projects are the obvious manifestation of the Six Sigma process. These projects are designed to address a specific quality improvement opportunity and their successful completion is often a requirement before an individual is granted his or her black belt. Black belts are Six Sigma leaders who are responsible for implementing improvement projects using advanced Six Sigma methodologies and statistical tools.

DMAIC is not the only Six Sigma methodology in existence, although it is almost universally accepted as the primary Six Sigma methodology. This methodology is best applied to existing products and processes that are not meeting customer requirements or performing as expected. There are a host of other methodologies that are used during product and process design. These fall under a broad acronym called DFSS (Design for Six Sigma). Different design methodologies include define, measure, analyze, design, and verify (DMADV); define, measure, analyze, design, optimize, and verify (DMADOV); define, customer concept, design, and implement (DCCDI); identify, design, optimize, and validate (IDOV); and define, measure, explore, develop, and implement (DMEDI).[13] The intent here is not to confuse the reader with a bunch of acronyms, although that is probably what just happened, but rather to point out that many different methodologies fall under the Six Sigma domain.

Table 7.1 DMAIC improvement process

Phase	Description
Define	**Define** the customer, their critical-to-quality (CTQ) issues, and the core business process involved • Define the boundaries of the improvement project • Define the process to be improved by mapping the process flow • Identify the customers of the process and their requirements and expectations
Measure	**Measure** the performance of the business process involved • Develop a data collection plan • Collect data from many sources to determine types of defects and metrics • Compare to customer feedback to determine shortfalls
Analyze	**Analyze** the data collected and the process map to identify root causes of defects and improvement opportunities • Identify gaps between current and desired performance • Prioritize improvement opportunities • Identify sources of variation
Improve	**Improve** the process by designing creative solutions to eliminate the root causes of defects • Create innovative solutions using technology and advanced tools • Develop and deploy an implementation plan
Control	**Control** the process to ensure improvements are maintained • Prevent reverting back to previous methods • Develop, document, and implement an ongoing monitoring plan • Institutionalize the improvements through the modification of systems and structures

Source: Adapted from the www.isigma.com dictionary.

Six Sigma faces some threats to its future use. As mentioned, a growing number of critics, including executives at some major corporations, are arguing for a reevaluation of the Six Sigma process. While the process may help remove waste and promote consistency, it may also have a detrimental effect on innovation. Some processes, so the argument goes, simply cannot be as defined or controlled as effectively as other processes. This school of thought argues that Six Sigma is being applied in areas where it may not be as applicable as other areas.

Another major threat to Six Sigma is the watering down of the requirements for becoming a black belt. In Six Sigma's earlier days becoming a black belt was a rigorous and special event. Today, just about anyone can take on-line classes that will help him or her earn a black belt. And many of these on-line providers advertise how quickly the black belt can be earned. An analogy is an MBA program that grants a majority of the credits required for graduation for life experiences. A personal belief is that no black belt should be awarded until the candidate has undergone rigorous training and completed a major black belt exam and project. David Drickhamer, an *Industry Week* columnist, noted, "Many certified Six Sigma black belts are as useless in factories as they are in dark alleys. They're being churned out of two-week seminars that are offered by every business school in the country. All black belts are not created equally."[14] Watering down the requirements makes a black belt less effective and the Six Sigma process open to skepticism.

VALUE ANALYSIS WORKSHOPS

Value Analysis (VA) is a lower cost but potentially higher impact technique that compares the functionality of a product or service against its cost. It is the organized and systematic study of every element of a material, component, system, process, or service to ensure it satisfies its intended function for the customer at the lowest total cost. It is a continuous improvement technique that aligns well with our lean objective of enhancing value as defined by the customer.

The core of VA is a systematic focus on value. In equation form, Value = Function/Cost. The objective of VA is to increase value by affecting the numerator and/or denominator of the value equation. It is a continuous improvement approach that is usually applied to existing products, services, and processes. Value engineering is the counterpart to VA that is applied during new product and service development. While VA was developed by Larry Miles at General Electric in the 1950s, this does not mean it is no longer an effective approach for managing costs. Some observers have a misconception that VA is product or service cheapening, which is simply not the case.

VA is often structured as group workshops. These workshops, as well as the VA process itself, are a combination of group problem solving, project management, process redesign, and continuous improvement efforts. VA benefits most from a cross-functional team approach that often involves suppliers, customers, packaging, logistics, supply management, design and process engineers, marketing, accounting, manufacturing, and even customers. Here's a sample of what each group brings to the value analysis table:

- **Management**—defines goals, ensures businesswide cooperation, develops return on investment (ROI) targets, and provides resource support

- **Procurement**—searches for new materials, technologies, and suppliers, provides cost data, works to gain supplier involvement, may train suppliers in VA techniques, and often is responsible for coordinating the process
- **Marketing**—identifies customer requirements, studies the effects of changes on customers and sales, and works to gain customer involvement
- **Engineering**—defines product functionality, reviews the technical feasibility of ideas, and checks the effect of changes on other parts, systems, or processes
- **Operations**—provides data on cost and productivity, provides process insights, and analyzes changes from an operational perspective
- **Suppliers**—provides an external perspective, submits ideas on materials, components, and processes, evaluates the impact of changes on their processes, and provides information on changing technical developments

Other groups that may become involved with VA include finance, information systems, transportation and logistics, quality, external customers, and plant maintenance.

The Value Analysis Process

VA workshops should follow a process with five distinct phases: (1) information gathering, (2) speculating, (3) analyzing, (4) recommending and executing, and (5) following up. Results should be tracked closely with improvements widely reported across the company. In fact, progressive companies establish annual improvement targets they expect to achieve through their VA efforts. When performed correctly, VA becomes a systematic approach for improving value, functionality, and costs. The following defines the five value-analysis phases:

- **Information Phase.** This phase involves putting together the right VA group and gathering data about possible VA opportunities.
- **Speculation Phase.** This phase benefits from creative *what if* thinking, a process that was addressed earlier in the chapter. VA groups ask a series of questions to stimulate their creative thinking. The primary output from this phase is a set of ideas, changes, and/or recommendations. Sample questions include the following:
  - Are lower cost but equally effective materials available?
  - Can any part of the design or process be simplified?
  - Is there excessive movement and handling, which is increasing costs?
  - Can any part of a process be simplified?

- Are standard components available to replace custom-designed components?
- Can features or services be added to enhance functionality more than the associated cost increase?
- Are lower cost suppliers available?
- Are material, labor, and overhead costs reasonable?
- Is there any functionality currently included that the customer does not want?
- Can packaging or logistics costs be reduced?
- Can the production process be redesigned to remove costs and time?
- Can components be ordered more efficiently?
- What else about a product or process is creating waste?

- **Analytic Phase.** A variety of tools support the detailed analysis of VA ideas, some of which were presented earlier in the chapter. The broad objective here includes assessing the reality of any proposed changes as well as the effect of any changes on internal and external customers. The VA participants also validate the improvement targets that were established earlier in the process.
- **Execution Phase.** An important part of the execution phase is to create an action plan for making any changes. Project management skills will come in quite handy here. The VA team also needs to establish a performance baseline, record when changes are made, and then evaluate the effect of the changes on the performance baseline. Establishing a baseline is an important part of verifying cause and effect and determining any performance improvements that resulted from the VA effort.
- **Conclusion Phase.** This phase involves validating and then reporting the success of any changes. This phase should also include recognizing and rewarding the participants for successful projects.

Critical to longer-term success is keeping the value analysis process alive. The way to do this is to track results, reports these results to executive management, make improvement goals a visible part of the strategic planning process, and maintain an ongoing list of VA workshops and projects. For example, managers may have a stated goal of completing three VA projects a quarter with results that are visibly reported across an organization. When one opportunity or workshop is completed, another one takes its place. Make no mistake here—VA, while not often discussed within the context of lean, may be one of the most powerful approaches for promoting lean improvements across your supply chain.

SUGGESTION PROGRAMS

How much was saved last year from suggestions received through your firm's supplier, customer, or employee suggestion programs? If your company does not have a formal program, or perhaps has an informal program but no one knows what it saves, you are certainly not alone. The time has come for most firms to put suggestion programs in place. Thanks to web-based technology the challenges surrounding suggestion programs are no longer technical. Suggestion programs can be a major tool for identifying waste and improvement opportunities.

Firms that are serious about suggestion programs must be willing to commit resources to evaluate the suggestions they receive. Often this means appointing a program manager or steering committee to lead the process. It also means making engineers, managers, and other interested employees available to evaluate the merits of a suggestion.

Progressive firms recognize the important linkage between the number of suggestions received and a willingness to share the resulting savings with those who provide the suggestions. For suppliers, rewarding supplier participation should lead to greater involvement with the program. Some firms evaluate a supplier's level of participation and include that as part of the supplier's scorecard rating. Other firms share any savings realized from the ideas, either directly as payment to suppliers, adjustments to the selling price that reflect the suppliers' share of the savings, opportunities for new business, or as credits toward future cost reduction commitments. Employees may receive cash bonuses for their suggestions, and customers that provide suggestions that remove waste and save costs may receive price discounts or, perhaps something they really want, improved quality and service.

Best-practice supply organizations track the suggestions they receive across the supply chain, respond to suggestions in an agreed-upon time frame, and report any savings achieved through the system. The suggestion system should serve as a central repository for all ideas received from suppliers, employees, or customers. Developing suggestion programs may be the most cost-effective way to identify many improvement opportunities and reduce waste across the supply chain.

Perhaps the best example of a supplier suggestion program involved Chrysler's SCORE program. SCORE stands for supplier cost reduction effort, although the suggestions that were provided involved a wide range of areas beside direct cost reductions. Chrysler executives openly acknowledge the important role this program played in improving relationships with suppliers and saving the company hundreds of millions of dollars.[15] During the late 1990s, this program become the benchmark against which other programs were compared. Unfortunately, in 2001, a new purchasing czar at Chrysler replaced the SCORE program with one that featured mandatory cost reductions for suppliers, thereby ending the cooperative environment that the previous leadership had worked so hard to create.

PERFORMANCE BENCHMARKING

Performance benchmarking should play an important role during the continuous quest for waste reduction. With the abundance of information available today, it is almost shocking how many firms remain inwardly focused. The benchmarking process helps identify new and innovative ways to work, identify objective ways to measure against the best performers, and gain valuable insights when establishing lean practices and performance targets. Formally defined, benchmarking is the *continuous process of evaluating a firm's strategies, products, processes, practices, and services against competitors or other companies recognized as industry leaders.*[16] This evaluation can be through direct visits to companies, participation in benchmarking consortiums, extensive surveys of public documents and research, or the use of third parties to collect benchmark data.

Every supply organization can benefit from benchmarking, even industry leaders. No organization can possibly be the best in all conceivable areas. Furthermore, a company that is a leader today does not have a guarantee it will be a leader tomorrow. Continuous benchmarking should help prevent complacency, arrogance, and unwelcome surprises. Lean ideas can come from many different areas, many different people, and many different industries.

The benefits of benchmarking can be profound. This process helps uncover the best lean practices from any industry. The opportunity might present itself to introduce an innovative approach that, while practiced in one industry, may not be practiced in another. This process also breaks down ingrained resistance to change. Oftentimes those responsible for managing a change are better able to implement or accept a change once they see how it works elsewhere. We know that the changes involved with transforming into a lean enterprise are perhaps as great as any changes that an organization will undergo. Any help in overcoming resistance to change should be welcome. Benchmarking also offers the opportunity to develop a network of professional contacts that can be called upon in the future. Perhaps the most desirable outcome from benchmarking is that the process can help create a culture that is externally focused and receptive to change.

Some will argue that benchmarking is overhyped and is reactive rather than proactive. After all, doesn't benchmarking study what another organization has already done? And by the time something is implemented, won't it already be out of date? While there is some merit to this argument, as there is to most arguments, it is perhaps too simplistic. The alternative to benchmarking is to not be externally

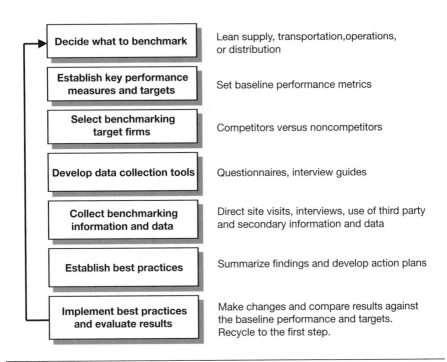

Figure 7.5 The benchmarking process

focused or ignore the opportunity to uncover some good ideas, including ideas from outside your industry. Furthermore, benchmarking offers the opportunity to come up with ideas from many sources. Quantitatively this can exceed the ideas and best practices that are in place at any one firm.

There is no shortage of areas that can be benchmarked as they relate to a lean supply chain. The most obvious areas to benchmark are those where a performance gap exists between where an organization is operating and where it should operate. One company may want help in understanding how to remove transactions costs from its supply chain, while another company may want to focus on how to rearrange a facility. Another company may need help in understanding how to transition from a make-to-stock environment to a make-to-order environment, while another company wants to understand how a kanban system works. There are always opportunities for benchmarking within the lean space.

A Benchmarking Process. Benchmarking, like many popular business terms, is overused. Years ago managers would jump in a car to visit another company. And they called it jumping in a car to visit another company. If everything went well the visit would also feature a nice lunch. We don't jump in the car and visit companies anymore. Today, we now conduct benchmarking visits.

For benchmarking to be effective it must be practiced systematically. Figure 7.5 presents a process to guide benchmarking efforts. Because lean is not unique to any one industry, firms often find that information sharing is more open between noncompetitors. It is a mistake to assume that all benchmarking involves direct site visits or face-to-face interaction. A great deal of information through secondary sources, such as databases that firms can subscribe to, is updated daily. What makes the benchmarking process systematic is the continuous loop from the last step to the first.

The differences between an internal and external perspective are profound. Lean changes demand that organizations, and this means the employees within those organizations, endorse a culture of change. Benchmarking is a great way to create a culture that endorses change.

CONCLUDING THOUGHTS

The changes associated with the transition to a lean supply chain are perhaps the most encompassing that an organization can undertake. If we want employees and managers to be excited, rather than fearful by the prospect of what lean can do for their longer-term success, then we need to provide them access to the tools, approaches, and time that will enable them to be value-added participants.

An important point is that most of the tools and approaches presented throughout this chapter are all relatively low cost. An exception to this is certainly a company-wide Six Sigma process. These approaches can be extremely effective in supporting the attainment of lean objectives if we have qualified people who know when, where, and how to apply them.

ENDNOTES

1. From http://www.isixsigma.com dictionary.
2. R. Vitalo, F. Butz, and J. Vitalo, *Kaizen Desk Reference Standard* (Hope, ME: Lowrey Press, 2003), 2.
3. See note 2, 14.
4. See note 2, 17, 68, 112, 146, and 384.
6. The author would like to thank Lily Yang, Manager of Continuous Improvement at Crayola, for sharing this example.
7. C. Dawson, "Machete Time; In a Cost-Cutting War with Nissan, Toyota Leans on Suppliers," *Business Week* 3727 (April 9, 2001): 42.
8. See note 1.

9. From the *Office Workflow Facilitator's Guide for VSM: Introduction to Value Stream Mapping*, Enna Corporation, 5.

10. See note 8, 17.

11. J. Womack and D. Jones, *Lean Thinking* (New York: Simon & Schuster, 1996), 19.

12. See note 1.

13. See note 1.

14. K. Simon, "What is DFSS?" http://www.isixsigma.com.

15. D. Drickhamer, "Six Sigma Stigma," *Industry Week* 253, no. 2 (February 2004): 61.

16. For an excellent discussion of a supplier suggestion program and how it helped improve supplier relations, see R. Rudzki et al., *Straight to the Bottom Line*, chap. 10 (Ft. Lauderdale, FL: J. Ross Publishing, 2005), 83-94.

17. R. Camp, "Benchmarking: The Search for Best Practices That Lead to Superior Performance: Part I." *Quality Progress* 22, no.1 (January 1989): 66.

PART II: LEAN CASES AND APPLICATIONS

GOING WITH THE FLOW

Imagine being part of a volunteer organization that meets just once a year. And imagine further that when this group meets, even with all its camaraderie and friendship, the experience is best described as frustrating. Many of us have probably worked at an event that was so unorganized and chaotic that it tested the pure joy of giving. This chapter presents such an event.[1]

This lean application features a holiday candle-making operation that was plagued with inefficiencies and bottlenecks. More importantly, and this may sound like a television infomercial, this analysis will show how a systematic focus on constraints, flow, and throughput can increase process output not by 10 percent, not by 50 percent, but by almost 200 percent per hour! This application will show how a focus on the bottlenecks that impede flow can transform something as basic as a once-a-year activity into a highly productive event.

BOTTLENECKS AND THE THEORY OF CONSTRAINTS

Before providing an overview of the exciting world of candle making, let's step back and discuss bottlenecks and the theory of constraints (TOC). While these topics could have appeared in various places throughout this book, its placement here will better illustrate how these ideas are applied in practice.

Central to TOC and bottlenecks is an understanding of constraints. A constraint is anything that limits higher levels of performance across a supply chain. Simply stated, constraints limit the output of a system. Eventually everything can become a constraint since capacity is always finite. Problems occur when capacity at some point along the supply chain falls below expected demand. Constraints can result from insufficient supplier capacity, inadequate internal production and equipment performance, transportation shortfalls, labor and material shortages, quality problems, inflexible work rules, or inadequate financial resources. These constraints, which can be physical or nonphysical, are the primary cause of bottlenecks. Bottlenecks are the visible result of constraints.

Central to a discussion of constraints is the many kinds of *capacity* that exist across a supply chain. We can have industry capacity, company capacity, work center capacity, individual machine capacity, employee capacity, and supplier capacity, to name just a few. It's important to know these capacities, especially for those areas that are the most likely to constrain flow across an operation or supply chain. We can view capacity in terms of maximum, effective, and actual capacity.[2]

The highest rate at which a process or operation can perform is its *maximum*, or theoretical capacity. This capacity assumes no unscheduled downtime for equipment maintenance, efficient changeovers each and every time, and no shortages of materials or labor. It is the rate that a supply chain operates at if everything happens perfectly. *Effective* capacity, which is usually lower than the theoretical capacity, is the rate that an operation is expected to operate, given the likelihood that some unplanned events will occur, such as machine repairs, scheduling delays, or delivery delays from suppliers. It is usually a lower capacity level compared with the theoretical capacity. The third level, *actual* output, is the real output of an operation or part of the supply chain over an extended time period. This figure reflects what is going on in the real world. At times the difference between theoretical, effective, and actual output can be quite large, indicating opportunities for continuous improvement. What we hope for is that the differences between the three kinds of capacity are narrow rather than large.

Given the important role that measurement plays when pursuing lean, a worthwhile exercise is to calculate the various capacities across critical parts of the supply chain. A measure that should be reviewed regularly is the *ratio of actual capacity to theoretical capacity*. A ratio closer to 1.0 indicates that a supply chain (or at least a part of the supply chain) is operating close to its theoretical levels. An organization that is serious about managing flow across a supply chain will monitor capacities closely and then compare them against expected demand. It is possible that even a theoretical capacity could fall short of what is required to satisfy market demand. Capacity (or lack of) can be a constraint that causes bottlenecks.

The lowest capacity across a supply chain is often the most likely to create a bottleneck that limits flow. Assume the demand for a finished product is 1000 units per day, but the lowest capacity supplier within the supply chain can only provide components to build 750 units per day. Whether we like it or not the supply chain capacity will not exceed 750 units, assuming there are no other suppliers for that item immediately available. Progressive managers view capacity in terms of supply chain capacity rather than the more traditionally used perspective of internal capacity.

Structural versus Transitory Bottlenecks

Bottlenecks, which are the visible result of a constraint, are an operation or part of the supply chain that has insufficient capacity. Two types of bottlenecks are typically present across a supply chain: (1) structural or (2) transitory bottlenecks. A *structural* bottleneck is one where normal capacity falls short of what is required to satisfy our goals, such as meeting product demand, because the capacity simply does not exist. We are structurally constrained. Consider some of the following examples of structural bottlenecks or constraints:

- Assume the rate at which ships can enter the locks of the Panama Canal is three per hour. If the growth in world trade has created an average demand of four ships per hour into the canal, then the lock system presents a structural constraint that becomes a bottleneck. In its current form the canal can only allow a certain number of ships to enter each hour. Furthermore, the width of the locks is a structural constraint that prohibits very large container ships from using the canal locks.

- An airport with few available gates faces a structural bottleneck or constraint if an airline wants to use that airport as a hub or expand existing operations. The number of allowable takeoffs and landings given a fixed number of runways, as regulated by FAA rules, also present a structural constraint.

- Any woman who has attended a sold-out concert or sports event faces a structural constraint that most men can't even begin to appreciate— long lines at the bathroom due to insufficient restroom capacity. It's probably safe to conclude that these stadiums and arenas were designed largely by men.

- Perhaps the granddaddy of structural bottlenecks, at least for people who live on the East Coast of the United States, is the Holland Tunnel. This tunnel connects New Jersey to Manhattan, and vice versa. The massive delays and traffic backups that result at this tunnel, regardless of the time of day, day of the week, or month of the year, are the result of trying to squeeze a whole bunch of traffic lanes into just a few.

Examples of approaches for addressing structural bottlenecks include outsourcing (perhaps not in the women's bathroom example), equipment and physical expansion, shortening the time for machine changeovers, adding a second or third shift, and process redesign. Each of these strategies is designed to add to a system's capacity. At times structural constraints may force a business to forego customer orders.

At other times there is enough capacity to satisfy normal demand but events converge to create a transitory or temporary constraint or bottleneck. Transitory bottlenecks shift from one part of an operation or supply chain to another as circumstances change. These types of bottlenecks can be tricky, if not impossible, to predict where they will occur.[2] For example, a store has four of six check-out lines open and all four, which were customer-free just a minute earlier, are now backed up as customers arrive simultaneously for check-out. And some of the customers have coupons! A machine that has enough capacity to satisfy normal demand becomes a bottleneck as three separate jobs arrive simultaneously for processing. Unanticipated spikes in demand may also cause temporary bottlenecks. Level scheduling, routing flexibility, cross-trained workers who can be reassigned from nonbottleneck areas, and overtime are examples of approaches for managing transitory bottlenecks. Flexibility is central to managing this type of constraint.

The Theory of Constraints

A discussion of constraints and bottlenecks is extremely relevant to lean. Bottlenecks impede flow, either structurally or temporarily. A consistent theme throughout this book is that flow is a central element of a lean supply chain, making TOC an important part of any discussion of supply chain flow. TOC is a body of knowledge that deals with anything that limits a supply chain's ability to achieve its goals.[3]

TOC gained popularity after Eliyahu Goldratt and Jeff Cox published a book called *The Goal*. This highly readable story chronicles the life of an operations manager who discovers how managing constraints allows his company to meet his customers' needs. This book raised awareness among managers about the importance of constraint management.

The first step when applying TOC is to *identify those constraints that restrict a system* from meeting its objectives. From personal experience and working extensively with managers, it is usually not hard to identify those areas that present the most serious constraints, particularly those that are structural. Second, after identifying the most restrictive constraint(s) the organization *exploits that constraint*. This means creating schedules that maximize the throughput of that bottleneck to the maximum extent possible in order to meet system requirements. Third, an organization must *subordinate all nonbottleneck resources to the schedule of the constraint* identified in the second step. This means not producing more than the constrained area can accommodate. Producing more will again create a bottleneck, which will further restrict system flow. Fourth, *elevate the constraint.* This means focusing efforts on reducing the effect of the constraint by adding another work shift, adding capacity through additional equipment, or perhaps through a process redesign (to name a few possible courses of action). The last step when applying TOC is to *cycle back to the first step* to identify the next constraint. Software solutions are available that support facility scheduling based on a system's constraints.

THE CANDLE-MAKING PROCESS

The preceding discussion set the groundwork for the focus of this analysis—the exciting world of volunteer candle making. Figure 8.1 diagrams a process used by a volunteer group when making holiday candles once a year in October. Each number represents a workstation that is part of the overall process, which closely resembles a work cell, a concept that was featured in Chapter 4. The following describes each workstation *before* making any process changes.

Station 1—Block Wax Chipping. Large blocks of wax are physically chipped or cut into smaller pieces. It is impractical to try and melt large blocks of wax. The chipping happens away from the main process since it involves various tools that could cause injury. Chipped wax is carried over to the wax melting station (a distance of over 30 feet) as it becomes available throughout the day.

Station 2—Wax Melting. Wax melting takes place at a large stove. Chipped wax is placed in two pots in a double boiler (pots placed in a larger pan with water) for melting. As clamped molds become available the melted wax is transferred into a watering can for pouring into the clamped molds. The distance from the melting station to the pouring station is about 8 feet.

Station 3—Mold Powdering. The inside of the candle molds are coated with baby powder so that the candles can be removed easily after the molds cool down. After applying the baby powder the molds are sent about 6 feet to the wick wrapping station.

Station 4—Wick Wrapping. Candle molds come in three pieces: a middle section and two outside sections. A slotted block of wood is placed across the top of the middle piece and a continuous wick is then wrapped around the middle section. Each mold produces 12 candles. After wrapping the wick the three sections come together to form a single mold. The wrapped molds are manually moved about 8 feet to the mold clamping station.

> *Station 5A—Mold Clamping.* Each mold is clamped tightly with four clamps (two on each side of the 12-candle molds). The molds are moved about 2 feet to the wax pouring station.
>
> *Station 5B—Wax Pouring.* The worker from Station 2 walks to the wax pouring station (about 12 feet) and pours melted wax into a clamped mold. The poured molds are moved 6 feet to the mold separation and cutting station.
>
> *Station 6—Mold Separation and Cutting.* After the molds cool down a worker separates the three-piece molds. The finished candles are separated from the center part of the mold and then placed on a holding rack to further let the candles harden. At this point the 12 candles are still connected to wax that formed at the top of the mold. The worker cuts the individual candles away from the top piece of wax and moves the candles 5 feet to the finishing and packing station. Any excess wax from this station is recycled back to the wax melting station, thereby reducing material waste.
>
> *Station 7—Finishing and Packing.* Finished candles are inspected to ensure they are formed correctly. Each candle is rolled along a hard surface to smooth the candle and to remove any excess wax. The candles are placed in a box where the rows are separated by wax paper. A group of elderly volunteers will place colorful frills on each candle at a later date. Frilling is not part of the candle-making process.
>
> *Station 8—Donut Station.* Since the candle makers are volunteers, this is perhaps the most important part of the process. The donuts are placed physically away from the main flow of work, particularly the mold powdering station. If the donuts are not placed far enough away from the mold powdering station, which was the case several years ago, they mysteriously start to taste like baby powder halfway through the day.

Historically, a crew of 10-12 people working from 9:00 a.m. to 2:00 p.m. produced 625-750 candles per day, or 125-150 per candles per hour. The first-pass yield, which represents the percent of candles moving directly from production to packing with no defects, was around 95 percent.

The Bottlenecks

From a learning perspective, the good news is that this process had a bunch of constraints that affected flow and production. For the people who make the candles, the bad news is that this process had a bunch of constraints that affected flow and production. This process provides a real-life laboratory to try out various

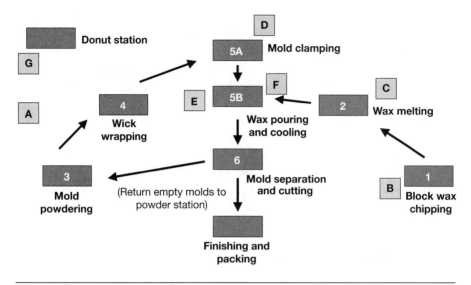

Figure 8.1 Improving flow in a candle-making operation

ideas to improve flow. Each letter designation in Figure 8.1 represents a bottleneck that impeded the candle-making flow. The past tense of the word *impede* is used here because each constraint was systematically identified, elevated, and resolved.

> ***Bottleneck A.*** On candle-making day the volunteers traditionally arrived at 9:00 a.m. to begin setting up the work cell stations. The required equipment (such as clamps, molds, wicks, holding racks, melting pots, etc.) was stored in boxes in a closet. Since setting up the process only required a few people, the other volunteers usually enjoyed coffee and donuts. Production could not begin until the process was set up.
>
> ***Bottleneck B.*** Wax can't be melted until it is chopped into smaller pieces from larger blocks. This station delayed the entire process at the start of the day as participants waited for the first batch of wax to be cut and then melted, a process that could take over half an hour. Also, it was not unusual for the entire process to be idle during the day while waiting for the individual who was chopping wax to provide more wax for melting. A lack of chopped wax at the start of the day and at times throughout the day was the most serious system constraint.
>
> ***Bottleneck C.*** This process used two pots to melt wax on a stove. Inadequate wax melting capacity sometimes caused the wax pouring station to back up with molds awaiting melted wax.
>
> ***Bottleneck D.*** Inadequate clamps sometimes caused hot wax to leak through the three-part molds. This was usually due to the type of

clamp used to secure the molds. While the volunteers could recycle any wax that leaked after it solidified, this recycling interrupted the flow of the process and resulted in wasted effort. Also, when leaks occurred the clamps had to be quickly adjusted on the molds to prevent further leaking. This created a safety concern since the molds still contained hot wax.

Bottleneck E. The three-part molds must cool down before they can be separated for candle removal. The cooling time actually becomes longer as the molds retain heat throughout the day. Some law of physics dealing with heat transfer is clearly at work here.

Bottleneck F. Hot wax solidified in the spout of the container that is used to pour melted wax into the molds. This required manually scraping wax out of the container before more melted wax could be added to the container.

Bottleneck G. The donut station seemed to attract people at the most inopportune time, causing bottlenecks as work flowed into abandoned workstations.

Overcoming the Bottlenecks

Before continuing it might be a worthwhile exercise to stop reading and consider ways to overcome each bottleneck. As Chapter 7 pointed out, lean improvements benefit greatly from the creative thinking process. It is important to remember that when employing creative thinking techniques the *quantity* of ideas is a primary objective. Assessing the *quality* of the ideas occurs during critical thinking and objective analysis.

Similar to the industrial world, not all of the constraints within this process equally affected process flow and output. Recall that the first step when applying TOC is to identify those constraints that restrict a system from meeting its objectives. Without question, a process that was not set up at the start of the day, along with a lack of chopped and melted wax were the most serious constraints faced by the group.

A number of changes were made to address the constraints presented by not having the process ready and the lack of chopped and melted wax. First, an individual now takes the large blocks of wax home and chops them into smaller pieces before the scheduled candle-making date. This requires about two or three hours of effort. Plastic bags containing the day's entire amount of wax are then placed at the wax melting station. Second, two individuals now arrive one hour early to set up the process. When the volunteers arrive at 9:00 a.m. the process is completely assembled, thereby eliminating any idle time.

The capacity of the wax melting station was also doubled from two melting pots to four. This, along with having chopped wax available throughout the day, alleviates any waiting for wax. The melting of the wax can now easily be balanced to match the flow of work through the other workstations. Finally, the individuals who set up the process at 8:00 a.m. also start melting the wax shortly thereafter. When the volunteers arrive at 9:00 a.m. melted wax is available to pour as soon as molds are ready. The workers who arrive at 8:00 a.m. have also taken it upon themselves to wrap and clamp several molds to get the process started. This demonstrates the value of workers who are cross-trained to perform multiple tasks, which is a major element of lean. *These actions resolved Bottlenecks A through C.*

The leakage of wax through the molds, while not nearly as serious as the constraints presented by Bottlenecks A through C, was nonetheless bothersome. The decision was made to purchase larger clamps that would provide more strength. It was also discovered that the larger clamps eliminated the need to use four clamps per mold. Now, two clamps instead of four are used to hold each mold together. This reduced the amount of labor required at this workstation, while still largely eliminating any leakage from the molds. *This eliminated Bottleneck D.*

The cooldown period for molds actually gets longer as more and more hot wax moves through the molds. A simple solution was to place the molds in a refrigerator for about 10 minutes before transferring them to the mold separation and cutting station. The cooling effect of the refrigerator accelerates the transfer of heat away from the molds and shortens the total cooling time required, which supports faster throughput. The group also discovered that the candles are removed more easily from the molds as they go through this cooling process. *This resolved Bottleneck E.*

The hardening of the wax in the spout of the pouring can was the least serious of the bottlenecks. As with the cooling of the molds, a very simple solution was identified. An idle burner on the stove was set to a low temperature and the pouring can was placed on the burner when it was not in use. Maintaining a small amount of heat prohibited any wax that remained along the walls of the pouring container from solidifying. *This resolved Bottleneck F.* The last bottleneck, the donut station, was not changed. The decision was made to never mess with the donuts.

Other ideas that supported further productivity improvements became part of this process. With the existing layout there is no direct line of sight between the wax melting station and the wax pouring station. When melted wax was needed someone would come over and request wax, the individual who melted the wax would wander over to see if molds were ready for pouring, or someone at the wax pouring station would yell that they needed wax. Or sometimes none of the above happened and the flow of the process slowed.

A simple solution was to ding a small bell when the wax pouring station had a clamped mold that was ready for pouring. The number of dings indicated how many molds were ready. This allowed the wax melting station to know how much wax to transfer from the melting pot to the pouring can. This nonverbal, pull signal has proven to be very effective in eliminating nonvalue-added movement and balancing the flow of melted wax through the system. Nonverbal communication is an important feature of lean operations.

Another effective idea involved measurement. The individual at the finishing and packing station is responsible for tracking the number of finished candles. This individual now announces the total candles produced in increments of 100. This allows the group, in a relatively unobtrusive way, to gauge their progress against that day's production goal. As the last molds work their way through the process, and the quantity of candles produced begins to approach the day's target, some of the workstations at the start of the process are dismantled. A concurrent approach that combines disassembly and cleanup with the end of production saves a considerable amount of time as volunteers remain productive rather than idle.

Finally, a volunteer now moves from workstation to workstation as needed to help alleviate any bottlenecks that might arise. This demonstrates the value of having a workforce that is flexible and cross-trained. Fortunately, no restrictive work rules govern these volunteers.

The modifications to this process were remarkably subtle. They did not involve radical layout changes or major modifications to the candle-making process. They did not even require any major changes in behavior. Instead, the changes promoted flow by supporting faster throughput by eliminating bottlenecks, thereby reducing the effect of each constraint.

Did a focus on bottlenecks improve output? As mentioned earlier, this group produced candles at a historical rate of 125-150 per hour. Using even slightly fewer volunteers to staff the workstations as in previous years, this group recently produced 900 candles in 2.5 hours, or 360 candles per hour! Furthermore, the first-pass yield for the candles is around 99 percent, a level that far exceeded previous years.[4] As a side note, any additional candles produced are now used as part of a fundraising event.

What can we conclude here? We can conclude that an emphasis on removing bottlenecks dramatically improves flow, reduces throughput times, and increases production capacity. And perhaps most importantly, the volunteers do not have to commit an entire Saturday to a frustrating activity.

Tried but Not Used

Not all of the ideas this group came up with became part of the candle-making process. For example, in a business setting the trend today is to rely on suppliers to provide higher levels of value-added services. A representative from the candle making group approached the beekeeper that supplies the wax and requested that he cut the blocks of wax into smaller pieces. The beekeeper, a small businessman who makes his money selling honey, showed absolutely no interest in taking on this responsibility. The bees also showed no interest in this idea as they continued doing whatever it is that bees do.

The group also investigated ways to speed up the wax melting process. In an experiment that provided very conclusive results, the candle makers found that blocks of wax do not melt well in a microwave oven. The wax tends to *pop* in a manner that one person described as a series of small explosions. Don't try that one at home.

The group also found it frustrating that molds retained heat as candles were made throughout the day, although arguing against some law of physics proved to be even more frustrating. Before finally deciding to place the candles and molds in the refrigerator for cooling, one of the members suggested that a quick blast of the molds from a fire extinguisher would provide a quick cool down. Fortunately, this idea never made it to the testing stage. Besides leaving the fire extinguishers dangerously low in the event of an actual fire, the group was concerned that a rapid cooling would crack the valuable molds.

An idea that probably had the most merit was to purchase larger candle molds. Instead of making 12 candles per mold, why not make 18 or 20 candles at a time? Here, a lot size of one refers to the physical mold rather than the candles within the mold. More candles in a mold would represent better efficiencies rather than overproduction since the group uses all the candles it produces. Besides a concern about leakage from larger molds, the group is having trouble locating a supplier that can craft these molds (the current molds are over 50 years old).

Analyzing the Process Quantitatively

While producing 360 candles per hour is impressive, it still does not represent what might be theoretically possible with existing resources. One way to approach this is to look at the throughput time and turns of the candle molds. Without question, the 12 molds that work their way through the process are critical. Let's look at some key metrics:

Production:	900 candles
Production time:	2.5 hours
Average candles made per hour:	360 per hour
Total filled molds:	(900 total candles/12 candles per mold) = 75 total molds filled

Mold turns (12 molds available):   (75 molds filled/12 molds available) = 6.25 turns for each mold during production, or 2.5 mold turns per hour (6.25 turns/2.5 hours of production)

Mold turn time: (150 total production minutes/6.25) = 24 minutes cycle time per mold

Mathematically, an increase in mold turns from 6.25 to 7.25 per mold during the day would increase production in a comparable 2.5 hour period to almost 1050 candles (7.25 turns per mold × 12 candles per mold × 12 total molds available). An increase of one additional mold turn reduces the cycle or turn time for each mold from 24 minutes (150 total minutes/6.25 turns) to 20.7 minutes (150 total minutes/7.25 turns). This simple example demonstrates how increased throughput increases capacity with a fixed amount of labor and physical assets. It assumes this faster throughput does not constrain other parts of the system. The other parts of this process have enough slack to absorb a faster throughput rate.

If over 1000 candles are not needed (and that figure does represent more candles than are required yearly), then total production time could be reduced to meet a production target of 900 candles. Instead of working 2.5 hours, our hearty volunteers would require just over two hours of total production time to make 900 candles with an additional mold turn per shift. An activity that previously required a good part of the day could potentially take only several hours.[5]

While further improvements in throughput are desirable, the question becomes how to achieve an additional mold turn. An analysis of the physical process reveals that each mold passes through powdering, wick wrapping, clamping, wax pouring, cooling, and separation. Of these steps the cooling stage has become the constraint that most affects process flow, or the constraint that should be elevated. In fact, the cooling process now consumes 50 percent of the total turn time of a mold. Since the purchase of additional molds seems unlikely (although the group raises this question every year), identifying ways to accelerate the cooling process offers the best opportunity to increase candle throughput and per-hour production. Perhaps the time has come to cool molds in the freezer instead of the refrigerator!

CONCLUDING THOUGHTS

This chapter highlights how bottlenecks restrict flow. It also shows how restricted flow adversely affects productivity. Perhaps most importantly, the chapter illustrates that the principles of lean can be applied in some interesting settings.

One lesson to take away here is to be cautious when applying production-oriented techniques outside of an industrial setting. By all means apply the techniques, but do so quietly. Some healthcare professionals have argued that management's objective when applying lean techniques is simply to cut costs and increase profits. These professionals feel this begins to focus too much attention on efficiency and less attention on the patient. College students have been vocal at times in their dissatisfaction when their institution refers to them as customers. These students argue that being viewed as a customer is to be viewed as nothing more than a revenue stream in a business setting.

In the process featured here, the 70-year-old grandmother who wraps wicks around the candle molds doesn't really care about flow (at least the way flow is defined here), first-pass yield, or productivity per hour. Becoming too serious about a volunteer activity just might take the fun out of participating.[6] As finished candles seemed to fly out of the molds one day, a group member announced loudly that "fellowship is nice, but productivity is critical." His comment was met with stares from the group and a kick from his wife.

Volunteers can exert tremendous power when they become dissatisfied—they can walk out the door and not look back. It's not like they can be fired or have their pay reduced. At best we might be able to chase them down and retrieve any uneaten donuts that were taken on the way out. Managing a lean transformation requires a solid understanding of the personal needs and wants of those who must carry out the many changes required by the transformation.

ENDNOTES

1. The author would like to thank the volunteer candle makers at the Palmer Moravian Church in Palmer Township, Pennsylvania, for sharing their time and allowing changes to be made to their process.

2. A. Raturi and J. Evans, *Principles of Operations Management* (Mason, OH: Thompson Southwestern, 2005), 142.

3. J. Heizer and B. Render, *Operations Management* (Upper Saddle River, NJ: Prentice Hall, 2006), 606.

4. The primary reasons for rejecting a candle are (1) wicks do not line up correctly in the mold and therefore do not center correctly in the candle; and (2)

broken candles that result from separating the mold incorrectly or while the mold is still too warm, a condition that prevents the candles from hardening fully.

5. The determination of two hours is arrived at as follows: 60 minutes/20.7 minutes mold turn per hour = 2.9 mold turns per hour. Next, 2.9 turns per hour × 12 candles per mold × 12 molds = 418 candles produced per hour. Next, 900 required candles/418 candles produced per hour = 2.15 hours of required production time.

6. Shortly after conducting her first meeting as PTA president, the new president was told discretely by a parent that the meeting was too efficient and serious. This parent said the new president failed to realize the meeting was part of "the girls' night out." Apparently, none of the "girls" wanted to go home after just an hour.

9

LEAN IS THE PITS

To the dedicated fan it is a choreographed thing of beauty, more precise and inspiring than a ballet performance. To the casual observer it looks like nothing more than loosely controlled chaos. And to an organizational leader who wants to pursue lean improvements it offers some important lessons. What are we talking about? We are talking about a NASCAR pit stop, of course.[1]

In a sport where only the top 12 drivers qualify to compete for the Nextel Cup championship over the last 10 races of the season, every point earned during the season is valuable. Points are awarded based on where a car finishes a race, so a driver's final track position is literally rewarding.[2] Many races, and even championships, can be won or lost in the pits.

Does a well-trained pit crew really make that much difference in where a driver places during a race? With even the smallest pit mistake, the most important thing in racing—track position—may be lost in a fraction of a second. Consider a race at Richmond International Speedway. During that race the television commentators boldly announced, and for good reason, that Kevin Harvick was the driver to beat. He had already led the race for over 100 laps and was easily fending off all challengers, including some big names like Jeff Gordon, Tony Stewart, and Jimmie Johnson (the eventual Nextel Cup champion). Unfortunately, Kevin Harvick got into an accident—during his pit stop! As he was exiting his pit area he collided with David Regan, who was entering the pit in front of Harvick's. Then, in the rush to get back on the track Harvick was penalized for speeding through the pits.

Since stock cars have no side mirrors the drivers can't see very well the traffic that is entering nearby pit stalls. The driver relies on his crew chief or a spotter who is high above the grandstands to warn him of nearby traffic. This mishap moved Harvick all the way back to 17th position. While he eventually fought his way back to finish 7th, a miscue in the pits ensured he had no chance of winning. Instead of receiving 190 points for a victory, Kevin Harvick was forced to settle for 151 points. Harvick asked his crew chief shortly after the accident, "Isn't anybody watching?"

Matt Kenseth, on the other hand, can thank his pit crew for gaining him valuable track position during that same race. Late in the race Kenseth entered the pits in 14th place and exited in 9th. He eventually finished in 10th place, receiving 139 points instead of the 121 points he would have received for a 14th place finish. At Darlington Raceway the next week he entered the pits in 9th place and exited in 4th place after a phenomenal 12-second pit stop. He eventually finished the Darlington race in 7th place. Several weeks later one of the commentators for the Speed Channel noted that Denny Hamlin, a driver they said has led as many laps as anyone over the course of the season, "keeps losing it in the pits."

This chapter presents the lessons and innovations that industry can learn from NASCAR pit crews. It also highlights how various organizations are using these lessons to reduce downtime that impedes flow across their supply chain. By the end of this chapter, even if the reader is not a NASCAR fan, he or she should appreciate that innovation and good ideas can come from the most unlikely places.[3] Leading companies pursue lean ideas no matter where they originate. The *not invented here* syndrome has no place in this chapter.

LEARNING FROM NASCAR RACING TEAMS

One way to look at a pit stop is that it is a necessary activity, like a machine changeover, that impedes continuous flow. Unfortunately, the longer the stop, or the longer the machine changeover, the longer we impede flow. At one time, and not all that long ago, an average NASCAR pit stop required 45 seconds. About 10 years ago the average time was reduced by over half to about 20 seconds. Now, teams are starting to hit 12- to 13-second pit stops. In a sport where fractions count, every tenth of a second removed from a pit stop offers the potential for a faster exit from the pits and better track position. Many companies are looking to NASCAR pit crews to make their operations more efficient, particularly as these operations relate to machine setups and equipment turnarounds.

What do the top NASCAR crews offer that is worth emulating? To name but a few features, these crews hire good people, train them until a pit stop comes as close to a predictable event as possible, search for innovative ways to improve the process, systematically plan and stage their equipment, maintain their equipment through a strong commitment to preventive maintenance, and use technology to minimize downtime. The crews are also high-performing work teams, something that most companies are trying to rely on. Let's look at these elements in a bit more detail.

Hire the Right People

The various jobs that comprise a pit crew are much more difficult than they appear in person or on television. Many of the top teams have hired former college and professional athletes for the various pit crew positions. And most teams have trainers who have the crew member lift weights and run sprints. Why would teams hire athletes instead of mechanics? Breon Klopp, the senior director of motorsports at Pit Instruction and Training explains, "When one team brings in an ex-NFL player, and that person is two steps quicker than everybody else, you've elevated the bar for everybody. And that's what's happening."[4]

On the shop floor, companies are increasingly searching for employees with higher education who have the mental ability to operate in a knowledge-based environment rather than a physical or brute force environment. Problem solving, working in a group, and the ability to make decisions are important parts of a lean environment.

A Focus on Teamwork

Anyone who has worked to transform an operation understands the importance of common goals, standard processes, and teamwork. NASCAR pit crews typify work teams at their highest level, something that most companies are trying to achieve. Table 9.1 summarizes the characteristics of teamwork observed in NASCAR racing teams that are worth duplicating.

Practice, Practice, and More Practice

The typical observer would be surprised at the extensive training a NASCAR pit crew undergoes. The best racing teams build a separate area just for practicing pit stops. The practice area will have the same size wall as a racetrack and the team will use the same tools as used during a race. A race car drives into the practice area and the teams go through an actual pit stop over and over. The practices are videotaped for detailed analysis later. A pit coach studies the videos to perfect the pit crew's footwork and hand speed.[5]

This separate area is similar to a company that performs process-proving studies to verify that a process is capable before entering actual production. The process-proving area can also be used to study machine setups and changeovers and to try new work methods and improvements. Once a process is shown to be capable it can become part of the normal production process.

Each job in a pit crew requires precise movements by individuals that are closer to athletes than to mechanics. And these movements and changeovers require practice, practice, and more practice. NASCAR rules allow seven pit crew members, each with very specific responsibilities, to jump over the wall to work

Table 9.1 Teamwork characteristics in high-performance racing teams

Characteristic	How observed
Common goals	Teams establish daily plans and schedules, weekly plans and schedules, and race objectives
Regular feedback	Teams hold daily discussions about the prior day's accomplishments; immediate feedback is received about the car and team performance during a race
Reward and recognition	Team members share in the winnings and awards; teams receive sponsor recognition; drivers congratulate the team publicly after a victory
Focused leadership	Leaders provide common focus for the group, facilitate timely feedback on individual and collective performance, provide needed resources, hold the team and individuals accountable for assigned tasks, commit to open and honest communication, and listen
Individual strengths	The specialized skills and knowledge of members is respected within the team and continually improved in multiskill job roles
Ownership	The team has a sense of collective ownership for everything they do rather than singling out an individual
Common team processes	Teams conduct daily morning meetings and a Tuesday evening postrace meeting; the team conducts practice pit sessions and maintains checklists for each car

Source: Adapted from R. Williamson, "NASCAR—A Model for Equipment Reliability and Teamwork," http://www.leanuniversity.com.

on a car during a pit stop. The over-the-wall gang includes a jackman (who jacks up the car so tires can be changed), a front tire changer, a rear tire changer, a gasman (who can also help remove old tires from the pit box), the catch can man (who holds the second gas can and uses a small gas can to catch any overflow during refueling), a front tire carrier, and a rear tire carrier. An outside observer should equate this practice with training, something that far too many companies view as an expense rather than an investment.

Planning and Staging

A tour of the pits before a race reveals careful attention to even the smallest of details. The layout of the staging area behind the wall is well thought out. Every tool, fuel can, air gun, hose, pit cart, and tire stand has a precise location to assure efficiency and accuracy. This location does not change from race to race, which aligns well with the pursuit of standardization. On race day the crew marks the exact stopping point on the pavement where the car should stop in the pit, which is an example of nonverbal communication. Everything in the pit is pre-positioned according to where the car is expected to stop.[6]

During the race the crew chief is in constant communication with the driver. When a driver enters his pit area there is no question about what will be done to the car—and the crew has everything available to perform the task at hand. For example, a driver may complain that the car is loose coming out of the corners and needs an adjustment. Or the crew chief may inform the driver that only two tires instead of four will be changed. Perhaps the car will only take on additional fuel. Constant communication helps ensure there are no surprises in the pits. Racing at 180 mph only inches from other cars usually offers enough surprises.

Even the truck that delivers the cars, parts, and equipment to each race epitomizes planning and staging. The driver that transports the cars to and from the track (each team brings two race cars—a primary and a backup) is responsible for making sure the hauler contains all the parts and pit carts that will be needed during practice, the time trial, and eventually the race. A crash cart is loaded on the truck with the kinds of parts that can be quickly switched during a race in the event of damage.[7] The planning is extensive so the right parts and equipment are readily accessible.

Using Technology to Reduce Downtime

While the cars that race around the track are relatively unsophisticated compared with their Formula One counterparts (stock cars still use carburetors and, until recently, leaded gas), the behind-the-scenes use of technology in the pits and the garage is widely endorsed by NASCAR teams. Let's see some examples that show how sophisticated the quest for time reduction and improvement has become.

Most teams actively endorse the use of technology to evaluate and improve their pit stops. The reality is they have no choice once their competitors begin to gain an advantage from technological innovation. XOS Technologies has created a digital video-editing tool to digitally record pit stop action from multiple angles, analyze real-time data, and store the footage. The XOS Pit Coach Station allows teams to measure pit crew actions using a frame-accurate stop watch to view pit stops in full-screen mode on a laptop or to feed the video to a larger plasma screen. This tool allows the user to play back and review; organize and store multiple pit stop and race videos; record time data and comments for each position; and view video in real time, slow motion, and reverse.[8] The pit coach for Richard Childress Racing commented that this tool has revolutionized pit stop breakdown and review.

Other examples of technology include many hours of design and modification so gravity driven 11-gallon fuel cans, each weighing over 80 pounds when full, empty their contents in under six seconds. Pit crews have developed modifications to the high-speed race guns used to change tires and the one-pump jacks that raise the car during a stop.[9]

Companies should follow the example of NASCAR and constantly search for new technology that will promote continuous improvements. For example, numerically controlled machines that feature rapid changeovers are usually a good investment. There's no reason that machine setups or changeovers (both terms are used interchangeably here) can't be videotaped and studied to identify improvement opportunities. And why not simulate on a computer the effects of a facility layout change before ever making the change?

Preventive or Planned Maintenance

One area that too many companies ignore is the practice of preventive or planned equipment maintenance (PM), although there always seems to be no shortage of resources to fix something that has gone wrong. Think about our personal automobiles. How many of us studiously follow the manufacturer's schedule of preventive maintenance? With NASCAR teams a focus on equipment reliability is not only important, it is an obsession. Imagine the impact on a race if the tire changer's air gun refused to work while the car was sitting in the pit box.

NASCAR teams provide some valuable lessons in the area of equipment maintenance and reliability.[10] One lesson is the importance of preparing a compelling business case for a PM program, which can be a challenge. Why focus so many resources on something that has no visible problems? Next, understand what needs to be done to prepare and maintain tools and equipment, including equipment testing. This helps when planning and scheduling the maintenance work well ahead of time. It is also important to have alternate PM plans in the event a schedule must change due to unforeseen circumstances. Another lesson is to recognize the importance of communication between operations and maintenance personnel. If possible, have operators assume ownership of some part of the PM. Finally, don't forget to coordinate the schedules of all involved to ensure maximum effort in the allotted time and to debrief after the PM to identify how to improve the process.

Performance Feedback

One advantage that NASCAR pit crews have is immediate feedback about their performance. If a driver enters the pits in 15th place and leaves in 10th place, assuming all the cars that pitted received similar service, such as receiving a full load of fuel and four new tires, then the crew knows immediately whether their performance exceeded their target or not. The feedback is nearly instantaneous, and in the case of deficiencies, corrective action can be taken before the next stop. Every pit stop is measured precisely and also videotaped for an extensive review after the race.

Don't Discount the Little Ideas

The top crews have also come up with a bunch of smaller ideas that help remove a tenth of a second here and there from the pit stop. While these ideas by themselves are not revolutionary or game changing, they do support continuous improvement. Companies that practice *kaizen* will certainly appreciate this part of the pit stop improvement process. Here's a sample of some of the ideas that crews have come up with to take time out of a pit stop:

- The lug nuts that hold the tire to the car are glued to the wheels with an adhesive before the race. This saves time as the tire is lifted, placed on the car, and then secured to the car.
- The pit crew member who changes the tires sprays the air gun that removes the lug nuts with a lubricant so the nuts come out of the gun easily. The lug nuts are also sprayed with a lubricant.
- Car races are notorious for turning a clean windshield into a greasy mess in no time, particularly as fluids hit the windshield. Tear-away sheets are placed on the windshield before each race. During pit stops a crew member quickly tears a clear sheet off the windshield, revealing a new, clean sheet and clear windshield.
- Teams coat the front grill with cooking spray to reduce the amount of rubber that sticks to the grill. A blocked grill restricts the flow of air to the radiator, which quickly causes the engine to overheat.
- Teams also spray cooking oil on the inside of the wheels to reduce the amount of brake dirt that is blown into the tire changer's face during a tire change, thereby reducing a serious distraction.
- Most pits have a practice wheel so the tire changer can remain ready during the race by practicing his motions.

What is the point here? Combining the incremental effects of even the simplest of ideas can add up to valuable time savings. And do not discount the importance that innovation plays when pursuing lean. These two concepts are not mutually exclusive.

APPLYING NASCAR LESSONS TO INDUSTRY

Industries that rely on rapid changeover or turnarounds, both large and small, are candidates for learning from NASCAR pit crews. The following highlights what some industries are doing to bring the intensity, commitment, speed, and lessons of a NASCAR pit crew to their organizations.

Rapid Maintenance at a Railroad

Increased demand for coal along with increased imports and exports have been good for the Union Pacific (UP) Railroad. Central to the UP system is its huge maintenance yard in Nebraska, which is the world's largest.[11] While the Bailey Yard is an essential part of the UP system, it can also become a bottleneck as trains back up awaiting switching and scheduled maintenance. Trains traveling from the western United States to the east funnel into this yard, as do trains moving from the eastern United States that are traveling westward. The trains enter the yard in need of fuel, engine checks, lubricants, and possibly even an engine tune-up before they proceed on the remainder of their trip. It is a pit stop on the grandest scale. But, as rail volumes have grown, this yard has experienced capacity constraints.

The traditional response from railroad managers when facing a yard crunch is to add more track. UP currently has four tracks leading into the yard from the west and four tracks leading into the yard from the east. The yard then fans out into 150 tracks. As one manger commented, "My first instinct as a yard manager (when demand increases) is always to ask for more track. Asking the railroad to postpone laying new track means the pressure is on us to deliver results." Trying to be more productive with existing workers and physical resources required a new way of doing business, including engaging employees to help drive the improvement process.

This new way of doing business involved yard workers acting like NASCAR pit crews. The idea to act more like NASCAR pit crews goes over well with the yard's blue collar workforce, many of whom are avid NASCAR fans. UP hired Pit Instruction & Training of Mooresville, North Carolina, to help its yard employees understand the intricacies of standardized processes, teamwork, improved communication, and coordination.

The railroad created five-man teams to handle the maintenance needs of the trains passing through the Bailey Yard. The teams are composed of electricians, machinists, firemen, oilers, and car inspectors. They rotate between the yard's tracks providing service to locomotives, including fueling, adding lubricants and oil, performing safety checks, and performing maintenance checks on the engine and electrical system.

A key measure at the Bailey Yard is dwell time. Dwell time is a measure of the train's downtime in the yard. From an average dwell time of 3.8 hours per train, the yard is targeting a dwell time of 2.5 hours, which gets the railroad closer to the industry benchmark. Every minute of reduced dwell time means more trains can pass through the Bailey Yard. Typically, the yard handles 55-60 run-through trains a day. (A run-through train is one that has no stops to add or remove cars.) After its NASCAR-type changes, the yard processed 72 run-through trains in a 24-hour period, setting a new record. The yard's longer-term goal is to handle 80 trains per day.

The yard is pursuing other innovations that align well with a lean philosophy. Each day hundreds of empty coal cars enter the yard on their way back to the massive coal mines of Wyoming. Traditionally, coal cars that require repairs are separated from the train and sent to a special yard for repair. Now, UP maintenance crews are increasingly trying to repair the cars without removing them from the train. The process of removing the car, moving it to a yard, and finding and hooking up a replacement car is a time-consuming one. Sensors placed along the tracks help the railroad identify those coal cars that are in need of repair.

The tremendous growth in rail demand is clearly a mixed blessing for UP. While adding track to alleviate bottlenecks will always be part of the railroad's strategic plan, progressive managers are starting to recognize that utilizing lean principles, with help from others outside the rail industry, can also be a major factor in increasing capacity and improving flow.

Faster Aircraft Turnaround

If there ever was an industry that should benefit from faster turnarounds and better asset utilization, it is the U.S. airline industry. Over the last five years it seems that most of the major U.S. carriers fall into one of three categories: (1) in bankruptcy, (2) emerging from bankruptcy, or (3) should be in bankruptcy. Like UP, some of the major airlines have begun to look to NASCAR pit crews for inspiration.

One of United Airlines' improvement strategies while sitting in bankruptcy has been to hire NASCAR pit crews to help it better orchestrate the pit stop that planes go through between flights. In particular, the planning and staging of equipment, sequencing of tasks efficiently to ensure process flow, and standardized practices working as a team are major take-aways from the NASCAR experience. United has plans to put 1200 employees through *Pit Crew U* and hopes to expand the training to customer service agents.[12]

The airline hopes to eventually reduce aircraft turnaround time by 15 percent or more. The Chief Operating Officer of United Airlines has said that improving turnaround time, which includes refueling, cleaning, stocking, and unloading and loading passengers, luggage, and freight, has added 125 more flights to United's schedule with existing planes. Let's face it—a jet sitting on the ground just doesn't generate much revenue. More flights with the same number of ground crews and planes will increase revenues and lower United's operating costs per mile, a key industry metric. Of course, all of this assumes there are customers that want to fly these additional flights. If not, adding more flights will be wasteful.

An exception to the problems faced by most U.S. airlines is Southwest Airlines, an airline that is consistently rated as one of the best, and most profitable, U.S. airline. Since its humble beginnings, Southwest has pursued a business model that focuses on operational excellence, a model that endorses lean principles as a way of life. Southwest's model is about as close to lean as anyone in the U.S. airline industry has attained. It is also a model that many new start-up airlines around the world are emulating. The airline relies on a flexible (and unionized) workforce that can perform a variety of tasks, pilots and crews that fly more hours than their counterparts, no costly hub and spoke system, and a standardized fleet that relies on a single type of aircraft, the Boeing 737. Southwest has recently noted its use of the 737 in advertisements as it seeks to assure travelers they will not be crammed into the smaller regional jets that are becoming so popular with airlines.

Southwest's pursuit of a lean business model has resulted in operating costs per mile that are almost always lower, often by a factor of more than half, than other U.S. airlines. But that still has not stopped airline executives from being inspired by their counterparts at NASCAR. Southwest wants to achieve regular turnaround times of around 14 minutes, far exceeding the industry norm of about one hour.[13]

Another airline that has a pit stop mentality is Federal Express (FedEx is classified legally as an airline). In a six-hour window starting just after 10:00 p.m., pre-positioned crews unload 150 planes at the FedEx superhub in Memphis, sort the packages and overnight letters from these planes, and then reload the planes for their outbound destination. Starting at 2:18 a.m., the first outbound freighter departs and by 4:30 a.m., the last freighter out of Memphis is on its way to its destination. Every part of the unloading and loading process, including the flight rooms where pilots prepare their flight plans for departure, is highly scripted to serve the world on time.

When Speed May Mean Life or Death

Imagine being part of a team where downtime can place the lives of your fellow teammates in jeopardy. For the U.S. military this scenario is quite real. It should come as no surprise that NASCAR thinking permeates the turnaround of vehicles, helicopters, and fighter jets. Turnaround time is critical, so pit stops have to be fast and efficient.

Kadena Air Base in Okinawa is the first U.S. military base to maintain F-22 Raptors.[14] A normal turn time for a fighter jet between missions is three hours, but the Air Force, inspired by what NASCAR pit crews accomplish, has developed a process for faster turnaround for the F-22s known as *hot pitting*. Hot pitting allows fighters to be refueled much faster than if the aircraft was shut down during a normal refueling. Using precise planning and staging techniques, as well as cross-training service personnel to support the turnaround, hot pitting can reduce the turnaround time for an F-22 to as little as 45 minutes. Tanker trucks are pre-positioned with hoses extended awaiting the arrival of the aircraft. Even a weapons technician who is responsible for placing weapons on the aircraft takes on additional duties by helping with refueling and reviewing a series of checklist items prior to sending the plane back into the skies.

The U.S. Marines have relied on NASCAR pit crews to help them streamline the process for refueling helicopters in forward battle positions. The longer helicopters sit on a battlefield or forward position, the longer these helicopters become enticing targets. Here, taking seconds out of the process has nothing to do with track position. It has everything to do with becoming less vulnerable to attack. NASCAR experts observed and analyzed forward-arming refueling points to identify ways to make them more effective and efficient. Something they noted was the need for the Marines to work together better as a coordinated team. As one participant noted, "A couple of seconds can mean the difference of life and death for the Marines on the ground."

These examples illustrate that rapid changeovers are important to any industry. Besides using capital assets more effectively, rapid changeovers allow us to serve customers or fulfill our mission faster and better through enhanced flow. Without quick changeovers the goal of producing small lot sizes will remain but a dream. Down with downtime!

CONCLUDING THOUGHTS

Any organization that needs to focus on rapid changeovers or turnarounds must endorse the same mindset as NASCAR pit crews. Running smaller lot sizes in a pull system is simply not feasible when changeover times are measured in hours rather than minutes or seconds. On a larger scale, such as rail yards and airline gates, faster turnaround can mean better asset utilization, faster flow, increased capacity, and enhanced profitability. Faster maintenance and turnaround of military equipment may mean the difference between mission success and failure, or even life and death. Perhaps the most important lesson to take away from this chapter is a recognition that good ideas can come from everywhere. Smart people are not shy about where they find their inspiration. For some, inspiration comes at a race track. Thinking outside the box means thinking outside of one's own comfort zone. Ladies and gentlemen, it's time to start…your…engines!

ENDNOTES

1. NASCAR is the acronym for the National Association of Stock Car Auto Racing.

2. Teams can earn bonus points for winning a race and leading a lap in a race.

3. Information in this case is based on conversations with various pit crew members at the Pocono 500 and Pennsylvania 500 NASCAR races over a three-year period, and from information available in the public domain.

4. V. Bernstein, "On Pit Row, It's First and Tire Change," *New York Times,* http://www.nytimes.com, August 15, 2006.

5. N. Boudette, "Racing Teams Recruit Athletes and Train Them Hard," *Wall Street Journal,* June 16, 2005, A1.

6. R. Williamson, "Lean at the Wheel: Pit Crews in Action," http://www.leanuniversity.com, from an article that originally appeared in the June/July 2005 issue of *MRO Today* magazine.

7. See note 6.

8. From http://www.xostech.com.

9. See note 6.

10. See note 6.

11. This example is adapted from N. Carey, "U.S. Railroad Seeks NASCAR Cue to Speed Up Yard," *Reuter News,* November 6, 2006.

12. S. Carey, "United Airlines Workers Go To School for Pit Crews," *Wall Street Journal,* March 25, 2006, A1.

13. "Beyond Singapore: Being Efficient the Southwest Way," *The Edge Singapore,* February 6, 2006, retrieved from Factiva database.

14. K. Nichols, "F-22's use Refueling Pit Stop," Air Force News Agency, http://www.af.mil/news/story.asp?id=123049176.

10

WHAT GOES AROUND COMES AROUND

During a trip through a distribution facility several years ago, and after seeing the amount of corrugated shipping containers in use, an acquaintance boldly predicted that the death of corrugated as we know it was near. How could anyone not reach this conclusion about such an obvious source of waste? As we now know corrugated boxes and shipping containers still remain a widely used packaging material. As Mark Twain once said, and changed slightly here for our purposes, "Reports of the death of corrugated have been greatly exaggerated."

Without question there is a time and place for using corrugated packing and shipping materials. And perhaps more importantly, there is a time and a place for not using corrugated materials. This lean application focuses on a very specific but important element within the supply chain—the use of returnable containers within a closed-loop transportation system. This chapter looks at how to calculate the number of containers to populate within a system, how to make the financial case for returnable containers, and the kind of costs and benefits that should be part of a cost-benefit analysis. The chapter concludes with the story of how one convenience store chain works with a distributor to realize all the benefits that a returnable container and closed-loop transportation system have to offer.

UNDERSTANDING CONTAINER REQUIREMENTS

As mentioned in Chapter 3, a returnable container, pallet, or tote, usually made of steel or reinforced plastic, is one that is designed for repeated use. Some sources use the terms returnable and reusable containers interchangeably. Unlike corrugated shipping containers that are intended for a one-way trip before being disposed of or recycled, returnable containers are intended to return to their point of origin over and over again. It is not unusual for a returnable container to have a five-year useful life cycle.

One question that will inevitably be asked when considering the use of returnable containers is, "How many containers are needed?" This question is important for a number of reasons. Too few containers moving through a system means that corrugated containers must compensate for any shortfalls. Too many containers will result in holding returnable containers that are not being turned over or used efficiently. What good are containers if their use is not maximized? Finally, the number of containers purchased has an effect on financial outlays.

A lean supply chain benefits greatly from an ability to plan accurately. Effective planning as it relates to returnable containers requires two important pieces of data: (1) expected container usage and (2) the cycle time for a container to make a complete journey through a closed-loop system. A pilot project that studies the time it takes for containers to make their way through a closed-loop system is necessary to validate the cost and savings estimates. Some firms may go as far as to simulate the flow of containers through a closed-loop system. The simulation software will still require estimates of demand and throughput times.

Like other supply chain areas, particularly product quality and demand forecasting, a returnable container system benefits from minimal variability. Demand variability can result in too few containers being available (demand for containers exceeds the supply of containers), and at other times there may be too many containers (the demand for containers is less than the number of available containers). The probability that the system will be in some state of disequilibrium increases as demand variability increases. While most firms have some variability in their demand patterns and container cycle times, and therefore some variability in their container requirements, excessive variability makes planning difficult.

Container cycle times need to be maintained with some consistency. Think about the difficulty in planning when a container has an average cycle time of 15 days between two locations with a possible range of 8-22 days. The turnaround time for containers, along with the standard deviation for that cycle, should be measured and compared against the cycle times that are used for planning. A returnable container system requires discipline to ensure a consistent flow of containers through the system. A downstream facility or work center should not horde containers in a corner until someone feels like loading a massive quantity on a truck or railcar for the trip back to the originating location. Returnable containers, like the materials they help move across a supply chain, benefit from continuous flow rather than holding and batching.

Table 10.1 Estimating the number of returnable containers in a system

Loads shipped from Chicago to...	Loads shipped per year	Average container cycle time in days	Container turns per year	Containers required
Atlanta	19,500	9	40.5	482
Dallas	16,900	11	32.7	517
Los Angeles	23,660	16	22.8	1038
New York	32,500	11	33.1	982
Denver	14,560	10	36.4	400
Nashville	21,320	11	33.1	644
Cleveland	12,740	8	45.5	280
Total loads	141,280			4,343 containers required

Container turns per year = 364/average container cycle time.
Required containers = loads shipped per year/container turns per year.

Let's get back to the original question of how many containers a system needs. Table 10.1 illustrates one way to approach this question. Assume a company has a national distribution center in Chicago that serves seven regional centers. This analysis examines the annual demand in loads and the expected time for a container to make a complete circuit from the national center, to the regional center, and then returned back to the national center. The container cycle time includes continuous days (i.e., weekends) since transportation companies often maintain a seven-day-a-week schedule. The cycle time ends and then starts again when the container is received back at the national facility, even if at that moment the container is not assigned to any particular outbound shipment.

It should be obvious that the number of times per year a container is used (i.e., the annual turns) is the primary determinant of the number of containers required given a certain demand level. It is estimated that this system, given the expected container turns and annual demand, requires just over 4300 containers. If the closed-loop system is inconsistent regarding the average container cycle time, then the calculations regarding how many containers are required may not be as valid.

Companies that are not sure about their container cycle times, or have too much variability in these times may be tempted to add some days to the average time. Variability is best measured by the standard deviation around the average cycle time.[1] Adding days to the average is equivalent to building in safety lead times in a material releasing or material requirements planning (MRP) system, which will increase the total number of containers across the system. Ideally, the number of containers placed in the system is based on reliable times that have minimal variability around the averages, with few excess containers factored into the system. Other factors that may affect the number of containers in a system include container damage and theft.

MAKING THE FINANCIAL CASE

Most companies find that the economic case can easily be made for using returnable containers. Duane Reade, a drugstore chain that seems to have a location on the corner of every Manhattan city block, shifted from corrugated cartons to returnable containers during a revamping of operations at its distribution center. The company ships individual items to its drugstores in 32,000 returnable totes, which measure 24 inches $\times$ 19 inches $\times$ 12 inches. Delivery trucks bring back nested, empty containers from previous deliveries as part of a closed-loop system. As the vice president of distribution and transportation explains, "We had spent over $300,000 a year on corrugated and the labor required to erect cartons. We recouped that within six months of moving to returnable containers."[2] Besides waving goodbye to corrugated costs, Duane Reade reduced the amount of damaged products that make their way from the distribution center to stores, reduced jamming of the distribution center's conveyor system, and improved the tracking of orders through its system. The containers have bar-coded plates riveted to their sides for easy scanning.

Check Printers, a Nashville-based company that manufacturers and prints millions of business envelopes a year, replaced its internal use of corrugated cartons with 7000 reusable plastic containers. The containers move from manufacturing to storage, and then to printing when it is time to customize an envelope. Besides material savings, managers say the containers are safer to use since employees no longer have to cut open boxes and, because the containers have handles, are more ergonomically friendly to use. The company calculates a return-on-investment (ROI) from a returnable container of more than 430 percent during its five-year service life.[3]

The purchase of returnable containers usually has to go through a financial analysis before the investment can proceed. After all, a single returnable container can cost as much as $150. Large companies and distribution networks will need thousands, perhaps even tens of thousands, of returnable containers before they can consistently replace corrugated containers with returnable containers. Finance involvement is expected in the investment decision to determine the payback, net present value (NPV), internal rate of return (IRR), and/or ROI of the container project.

One of the challenges when evaluating the feasibility of a returnable container project is identifying the net savings that will be realized annually from the new system. Furthermore, other data are required to understand how many containers to place throughout the system. How many loads will be shipped to a specific location each day, week, month, or year? How many days, and at what cost, will it take to complete the circuit from origin to destination and back to origin? The return of containers within a single facility is a much simpler process involving material handling rather than transportation.

Assuming that reliable cost-benefit data are available, the financial assessment of a returnable container project is usually not as complex as other financial investments or alternatives. For one thing, the project is usually not being compared against anything other than the status quo, which is the continued use of corrugated containers. Oftentimes a straightforward payback method that compares anticipated savings against expected costs will satisfy the financial requirements when analyzing a container project.

Let's provide an example of a simple financial payback. Assume a company decides to put forth a cash outlay of $500,000 to purchase returnable containers. Project planners have identified all the relevant gross savings, backed out any new costs due to the returnable containers (a closed-loop system will not be free), and concludes the project will save $300,000 annually. The payback is simply $500,000/$300,000, or 1.67 years, or 1 year and 8 months. The payback method is popular because it is relatively simple (it does not require a calculation of the NPV of future savings streams) and, for companies that are in a tight cash position, it is often of interest to know how soon they will recover the funds invested in a project.[4]

A company may require a more complex financial assessment of a proposed container project, such as the calculation of the NPV, the ROI, or the IRR from the container investment. NPV is defined as the present value of projected future cash flows or benefits discounted at an appropriate cost of capital or hurdle rate less the cost of the investment. Whenever the reader sees the word *net* in a financial indicator, he or she can safely assume something has been backed out or subtracted to arrive at a final result. More complex financial evaluations, such as NPV, require a multistep process, which the following summarizes:[5]

- **Estimate the initial cash outlay.** This includes container costs as well as any other costs to introduce the containers into the supply chain. For example, freight costs to deliver new containers, when paid by the company that is receiving the containers, should be included as part of the investment cash outlay.
- **Determine annual incremental operating cash flows.** This requires quantifying the net savings that result from the use of the containers.

One way to do this is to prepare an estimated income statement and cash flow with and without the project. The difference represents the incremental impact of returnable containers.

- **Project the terminal cash flow or expected salvage value.** Add the salvage value of the containers to the final project year's operating cash flow. Returnable containers are often analyzed using a five-year usable life.

- **Determine the present value of the future cash flows.** This represents the value in today's dollars of the benefit stream over each year of the project. Future flows are discounted by some percentage, such as a hurdle rate, that finance provides.

- **Determine the net present value of the project.** The project's NPV is the sum of the present values of the inflows (benefits received each year) less the outflows (investment cost). A positive number means the current value of the discounted future benefits exceeds the project hurdle rate.

It is not that complex to extend this analysis and estimate a figure that is analogous to a project's ROI or IRR. If the container investment costs are $1,000,000 and the present value of the inflows over the useful life of the container project is $2,750,000, then a simple way to look at the return is 2.75/1, or 275 percent. Notice that this calculation uses the present value of the future cash flows or benefit stream, not the net present value. The NPV represents the current value of the benefit streams after subtracting the Year One investment cost from the gross present value.

Each benefit and cost from a returnable system must be quantified or modeled before a financial assessment can be made. This will involve, at a minimum, the participation of finance, transportation, purchasing, operations, and industrial engineering. Each will bring some relevant information to the table to help arrive at the net savings realized from a returnable container system.[6]

IDENTIFYING COST AND BENEFIT CATEGORIES

A financial evaluation of a container project requires a detailed assessment of the individual costs and benefits associated with a returnable system. A company that extensively uses returnable shipping containers to move material from its Midwest national distribution center to its regional centers around the United States discovered that the cost savings from eliminating a portion of its corrugated usage was only a fraction of its total savings. A narrow focus on eliminating corrugated costs when performing a cost-benefit analysis for returnable containers is shortsighted.

This company ships single and mixed loads of replenishment inventory from a national distribution center to regional distribution centers. Mixed loads contain more than one part number and pass through a sort area within the regional centers where material is removed from a load, placed on a stockkeeper's cart, and then placed in an active stocking location. Single loads, which contain just one part number, move directly from an inbound truck to a reserve location where the load, including the container, is placed in a rack. If the active location is empty or requires replenishment (a computerized system will notify the employee of this condition), the full load will be taken directly to an active location for restocking.

This company maintains a hybrid system of corrugated and returnable containers when replenishing its regional centers. Returnable containers are used only for mixed loads that pass through the sorting process at the regional facility. Once an employee removes the contents from a returnable container, the container is ready to be placed on the next railcar returning to a second national center. (This closed-loop system that uses both trucks and railcars will be explained shortly.)

Since single loads are moved from an inbound truck and placed directly into a reserve location, the use of returnable containers becomes an unattractive option. Using returnable containers to ship single part number loads would require transferring the contents of the load from a returnable container to a corrugated container at the reserve location, clearly a nonvalue-added activity even after factoring in the cost of a corrugated container. And it's hard to imagine that any company would knowingly place its returnable containers in a reserve or secondary location to sit idle for an extended period. The primary objective of any returnable container system is to keep the containers moving around the system. Container velocity and flow are critical.

The question that is always present when using returnable containers is how these containers will find their way home. The regional facilities at this company also receive large replenishment parts from a second national distribution center located 60 miles from the facility that is the originating point for the returnable containers. These large parts arrive at the regional centers via dedicated railcars. After a regional facility unloads the replenishment parts, the railcars are reloaded with returnable containers, returnable racks, and other miscellaneous returns. The railcars then make their way back to the railroad's one and only rail yard.

The railcars are eventually forwarded from the rail yard to the national facility to which they are assigned. At that time the returnable containers are transferred from the railcars to company-owned trucks for the 60-mile trip to the facility that is the returnable container's originating point. Upon receipt at the national facility the containers are unloaded, scanned, and again made available

Table 10.2 Costs and benefits of a returnable container system

Costs of a returnable container system	Comments
Unit cost of returnable container	Includes the initial investment cost for the physical containers
Cost of replacement panels	Damaged side panels, such as those hit by a jitney, can be removed and easily replaced
Cost of return shipment	Includes all the costs to return the container, including handling costs, paperwork costs to ready the shipment, the physical cost of an intracompany transfer between facilities, and any receiving costs to bring containers back into the system, such as scanning the container's bar code to acknowledge receipt of a container

Benefits of a returnable container system	Comments
Elimination of corrugated container material costs	Includes all the direct material costs to use corrugated shipping containers, including the corrugated container, container lids, wooden pallet, and nails used to affix the container to the pallet
Elimination of corrugated labor costs	Includes the labor costs to assemble a corrugated shipping container
Elimination of corrugated container disposal costs	Includes the labor costs to dismantle corrugated containers and any recycling or disposal costs
Reduced damage in transit	Returnable containers rarely shift or break during movement, resulting in reduced in-transit damage
Reduced transportation costs due to better cube utilization	Returnable containers can be stacked higher in a trailer compared with corrugated shipping containers, resulting in fewer trailers being shipped to a location
Reduced receiving and handling costs	Fewer total trailers due to increased cube utilization means fewer trailers received at a regional center, which reduces the total administrative costs of receiving trailers and switching trailers in a yard

for use. The downside to this arrangement, besides additional handling and transportation, is the time it takes for the containers to make their way back to their originating location. The return transit time for a railroad is not nearly as consistent or as fast as a truck. Since this company has no trucks returning regularly from regional facilities to the national facilities, the use of the rail shipments presented the most cost-effective option for returning the containers.

Table 10.2 identifies the costs and benefit categories associated with this company's returnable container system. As this table reveals, the benefits of a returnable system go beyond simply reducing the material and labor costs involved with buying, building, and then disposing of corrugated containers.

With transportation costs on the rise, any way to reduce the total number of truck shipments across a supply chain, such as through better cube utilization, should be pursued. This company uses contract carriers to ship truckloads from its national center directly to its regional centers (refer back to Chapter 3 for a discussion of contract carriers). Better cube utilization now allows loads to be stacked three high within a 53-foot trailer rather than two high. Corrugated containers were not stacked three high because the loads shifted during transit (the loads are simply placed on top of each other with no interlocking of loads), or their weight caused them to collapse onto one another during transit.

Returnable containers are designed to be stacked three high for shipment. These containers rest securely one on top of the other, somewhat like Lego blocks being snapped together. This prevents collapsing and shifting of loads, which eliminates the cost of damaged parts as well as the labor involved with sorting through damaged loads. A trailer with damaged loads can take two to three times longer to unload than one that has no damage. And there's always the risk that a part with concealed damage will make its way undetected to the end customer.

Better cube utilization also means fewer truck shipments. The business case for using contract carriers to ship air is not real strong. It's unlikely that any (normal) person opens the back of a less-than-cubed trailer that just arrived from, say, Cleveland, inhales deeply, and exclaims, "I love Cleveland air—please send me some more!" It just doesn't work that way.

An example will show how better cube utilization can make a strong case for returnable containers. One of the regional facilities in this company's network receives from the national distribution an average of eight trailers per week, or around 400 trailers per year. After implementing the use of returnable containers with better cube utilization, this facility now receives around 10 percent fewer trailers, and the items shipped within a returnable container are rarely, if ever, damaged. Over the course of a year, transportation savings are $120,000 per year ($3000 freight cost to ship a full truckload × 40 fewer trailers per year). Imagine the savings for the larger regional facilities that receive 20 trailers per week! Reduced damage and transportation costs alone justify this company's investment in returnable containers.

RETURNABLE CONTAINERS AT QUICK CHEK

This example presents the kinds of benefits that can occur when a smaller company establishes a cooperative relationship with a progressive trading partner, including the benefits gained from a returnable container system.[7] Quick Chek, headquartered in Whitehouse Station, New Jersey, operates over 100 convenience stores across New Jersey and New York. Some of Quick Chek's stores also sell gasoline, and about a dozen stores also have pharmacies.

Central to this company's successful operation is Quick Chek's 10-year relationship with its dry goods grocery distributor, McLane of Baldwinsville, New York. While McLane is not the only supplier to deliver items to the convenience stores (the stores also receive a wide assortment of beverages and baked goods from other vendors), the deliveries from Quick Chek's grocery distributor using returnable containers represents about 75 percent of a stores total receipt volume in pieces and 65 percent of the volume in terms of dollars. These figures exclude gasoline sales that occur outside the store.

McClane makes deliveries to Quick Chek stores using returnable totes. The totes arrive at stores with security seals attached, an indication that no one has tampered with the contents since they left the grocery distributor's facility. While this is reassuring from a theft perspective, it is even more assuring from a health and safety perspective. After all, we are talking about consumable food products here. The return of containers to the third-party logistics (3PL) provider is similar technically to returning a rental car. Using a wireless scanner the delivery person acknowledges the number of containers delivered and the number of totes being returned by each store. A nominal deposit is charged for each container dropped off and a credit is issued for each container returned. The document that the delivery person prints, which is essentially a transaction receipt for the containers, clearly indicates the charges, credits, and net charges or credit to the customer. The store manager stamps the receipt as *received* and forwards it to the corporate office.

The Benefits to Quick Chek

McLane provides a variety of services besides the use of returnable containers that highlight the benefit of strong supplier relationships. The distributor meets or exceeds agreed upon fill rates for a wide range of items, eliminating the need to manage backorders or risk lost sales due to out-of-stock conditions. This also allows Quick Chek to order a significant portion of its grocery needs from a single source rather than many different individual sources.

The distributor also provides regularly scheduled delivery days and times for orders that store managers submit electronically one or two days before their scheduled delivery. Approximately half the stores in the Quick Chek network receive deliveries weekly, the other half receive deliveries twice a week. Regularly scheduled deliveries eliminate the need for time-consuming communication and scheduling of deliveries between the stores and the distributor.

The short lead time between ordering and delivery allows store managers to identify their replenishment quantities with more accuracy. The short time between order and delivery minimizes the planning window for replenishment, leading to a better understanding of what is required to replenish the store shelves. Guaranteed delivery dates and times also allow the stores to properly schedule workers to process the orders and stock the store shelves. Predictability of delivery further eliminates operating inefficiencies. While the receiving process only requires around 20 minutes, which includes reconciling any quantity errors or shortages noted from the previous delivery, it can take half a day or more for employees to replenish the store shelves.

The grocery distributor has assumed responsibility for developing and managing the returnable container system. The convenience store has had to make no financial investment in this system, yet the stores realize the benefits that a returnable container system has to offer. This illustrates a key advantage of aligning with a supply chain partner that has the capability to introduce sophisticated technology and operating systems to a relationship.

This returnable system provides some material handling benefits at the Quick Chek stores. The grocery distributor has developed a system that uses three different color totes, which is a form of nonverbal communication, to help store employees identify the general contents of each tote. Totes can be positioned or staged within a store aisle based on their color and then opened, thereby reducing the need to open the totes at the receiving location to determine their contents. The color scheme is as follows:

- **Red**—includes full boxes of candy and full case packs for replenishment
- **Blue**—includes single pick or single item groceries
- **Green**—includes general merchandise—not groceries—such as aspirin, combs, and nail clippers

Quick Chek can order single pieces from the distributor for replenishment rather than master packs, allowing the stores to better manage their inventory. This has enabled the company to reduce its inventory on slower moving items, make additional shelf space available, and stock more products for sale, particularly faster moving items. Unfortunately, items are not placed in totes at the distributor to minimize the walk time or distance traveled during the restocking of the shelves (or what the company calls pack out) at the individual Quick Chek store. The Quick Chek stores are too diverse in their size and layout to support a picking algorithm that minimizes travel distances at the stores.

This relationship also features a streamlined flow of communication, transactions, and funds between the two companies. Store managers input their orders into a handheld scanner, attach a phone to the scanner, and transmit the order electronically. McLane submits its invoices electronically to Quick Chek's corporate accounts payable system. The accounts payable staff at Quick Chek audits a portion of the invoices for accuracy, although few exceptions ever occur. At some point the company could decide to eliminate these checks since they generally create no new value. Payment is made to the distributor via an electronic funds transfer, further removing transactions costs and inefficiencies.

The grocery distributor is also willing to perform some value-added services for its customers. For a fee, McLane representatives will come to a store and write orders, clean the shelves, and pack out (i.e., replenish) the shelves. This is similar to relying on an on-site supplier to perform various operational duties, and could certainly be an attractive option if a store is located in an area where it experiences labor shortages.

The bottom line here is that a relatively small convenience store chain, through its relationship with a third-party grocery distributor, is benefiting from supply chain systems and practices that are characteristic of the most sophisticated retailers. The grocery distributor featured here offers its customer a high fill rate, ordering windows that are close to the delivery dates, scheduled and reliable deliveries featuring an efficient returnable container system, a fast delivery and receipt process, efficient communication linkages, and a high picking accuracy rate for orders. Quick Chek's relationship with a key distributor has allowed the company to enjoy the benefits of lean. Life is good.

CONCLUDING THOUGHTS

A returnable container system is certainly not for every organization or supply chain. This system requires an efficient way to return the containers to their point of origin as well as an effective way to track and measure container usage. For those companies that are candidates for using these containers, the payback is almost always worth the effort.

Companies that are considering the use of radio frequency identification (RFID) tags might discover that returnable containers are a good use for the tags. RFID tags should streamline the receiving process at the container's point of origin. Instead of scanning individual bar code labels that are affixed to a container when a container enters or exits a facility, the containers can quickly pass through a portal that captures the necessary information. Turn rates can be updated on a real-time basis while providing a timely picture of how many containers are available within a facility. As the containers begin another journey around the supply chain, the RFID tags can be read so system managers know the outbound location of the containers. Because the containers are returnable, this process occurs over, and over, and over again. And because the containers are used repeatedly, the savings realized from this system occur over, and over, and over again.

ENDNOTES

1. Standard deviation represents a measure of dispersal around an average and is one of the most important statistical tools available. Readers who are unfamiliar with standard deviation are urged to consult a basic statistics book.

2. D. Maloney, "Containers Deliver Healthy Return," *Modern Materials Handling*, retrieved from http://www.mmh.com, October 1, 2003.

3. N. Bodenburg, "Reduce, Reuse, Recycle," *Modern Materials Handling*, retrieved from http://www.mmh.com, July 1, 2006.

4. S. Weaver and F. Weston, *Strategic Financial Management: Application of Corporate Finance* (Mason, OH: Thompson Southwestern, 2007), 337.

5. See note 4, 382.

6. The author would like to thank Professor Sam Weaver for reviewing this section.

7. The author would like to thank Chuck Boyer, Controller for Quick Chek, for generously providing his time to support the development of this case example.

11

WHY PUSH WHEN YOU CAN PULL?

An important principle underlying this book is that lean applies to just about any organization and any part of the supply chain. Every organization must tailor its approaches to fit its unique requirements. This chapter highlights a lean transformation within the packaging operation of a major OEM. Over several years, this operation underwent radical changes that demonstrate how lean objectives can be applied in an environment featuring product forecasts rather than customer orders. This is a story of pursuing lean in a make-to-stock environment.

Here's the scenario. Material arrives from suppliers from around the world into a central facility. One of this facility's many responsibilities is to package items (if they require packaging) for distribution to regional distribution centers. This center supports other functions besides packaging, such as cross-docking parts to regional centers that do not require packaging; short-term storage for excess material not immediately needed at regional centers; and distributing aftermarket parts to special accounts and the U.S. government. The downstream regional centers are responsible for filling orders for spare and replacement parts from this company's dealer network. Figure 11.1 illustrates the supply chain.

Let's review what the traditional material replenishment and packaging system looked like before undergoing a massive transformation. A material planning group developed national forecasts at the stockkeeping unit (SKU) level for thousands of parts, and generated material releases to suppliers that detailed what to ship to the central facility. This is characteristic of a push environment. When material arrived, those items that required packaging were moved via automatic guided vehicles (AGVs) from the receiving dock to a short-term storage line behind the appropriate packaging equipment in the order the material arrived at

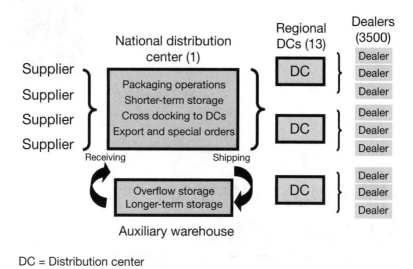

DC = Distribution center

Figure 11.1 Supply chain illustrated

the facility.[1] In other words, first-come-first-serve was the scheduling logic used to load this facility's work centers.

After items were packaged they were sent either to an outbound shipping line for forwarding to regional distribution centers, stored within the central facility awaiting future shipment to a regional center, or, when storage space was constrained or the item required longer-term storage, sent to an auxiliary warehouse located several miles away. There was no guarantee that packaged goods would flow toward the end customer. This case application chronicles the steps this facility took to shift from a purely push environment to one that began to look and act like a demand-driven supply chain.

SIMPLIFIED SCHEDULING IS NOT ALWAYS LEAN SCHEDULING

Perhaps the greatest flaw with first-come-first-serve scheduling logic is that it assumes an item's priority is simply a function of when it arrives at the central facility. Let's face it—many supply chains use first-come-first-serve logic because it is simple. While simplification is a worthwhile pursuit within the context of lean, and usually for good reasons, an adherence to this simple logic may be the single greatest factor that forced changes in this facility's scheduling, layout, and material handling systems. What are some wasteful flaws with first-come-first-serve logic?

A first-come-first-serve system provides no insight into actual demand. Presumably a material planning group considers an item's demand or need when it generates material releases. However, this does not mean that suppliers deliver in an order that considers actual demand requirements at the time of delivery. A supplier may be past due for material that is needed immediately further downstream. This sometimes happens for new parts when the OEM focuses more on obtaining production parts rather than aftermarket parts. Or stocking positions may have changed abruptly between the time a material release was generated and the eventual arrival of material into the receiving center. Perhaps a computerized inventory record of physical stock on hand was found to be in error.

The opposite occurs when a product is no longer in production. While the OEM's plants shift over to new products, the aftermarket is concerned about replacement availability over the next 7–10 years. Aftermarket buyers generally have three options for obtaining parts that are no longer in high-volume production: (1) they can try and convince the current supplier to continue to produce the part in smaller volumes (an often undesirable option for suppliers), (2) the buyer can source the part from a new supplier that specializes in smaller production runs, or (3) the buyer can commit to a forecasted all-time buy.

All-time buys are often used to ensure access to out-of-production parts. When these multiyear quantities are received they assume their rightful place in the first-come-first-serve system. Unfortunately, packaging parts is like putting rabbits together. Several bunnies turn into a bunch of bunnies in a short period of time. Here, two pallet loads of unpackaged nested or stacked parts quickly turn into 10 or more packaged loads once the parts are placed into unit containers, particularly if the containers are corrugated boxes.

Since this facility was designed to be a flow-through facility it has limited space for long-term storage. Unneeded packaged goods are transported several miles away to a longer-term warehouse to eventually be sent back to the central facility as needed. This extra transportation, material handling, labor, storage, and cycle counting is pure waste. This unnecessary packaging also consumes valuable labor and equipment resources that could be used to package more critical items.

There are also times when parts are unavailable from suppliers due to planned supply disruptions or shutdowns. This requires the material planning group to buy earlier in anticipation of the shutdown. Do you know, for example, what happens in August in France? The answer is nothing happens in August in France. If your business relies on French suppliers, as the company featured here does, then you know the importance of forward buying larger quantities to compensate for production and shipping delays. As with the all-time buys, should these larger quantities that were obtained to compensate for fun in the sun shutdowns be packaged? Like all-time buys, packaging these goods leads to waste.

WHAT ARE THE LEAN CHANGES?

Over a period of several years this facility underwent a host of changes that directly support lean principles. And while these changes were not always referred to in the context of lean, their end result demonstrated that a push environment can achieve the same kinds of benefits that a company operating in a pull environment achieves. The following explains these changes.

Replacing Transportation with Material Handling

At one point this company's packaging facility was located 30 miles from the central facility. Suppliers shipped material directly to the packaging facility where it was packaged on a first-come-first-serve basis. After packaging was completed the goods were loaded on company trailers for the trip to the central facility. At the central facility these trailers, which competed for dock space with other inbound shipments from suppliers, were unloaded with the packaged material forwarded through the distribution network as required, or stored as required.

It became obvious that maintaining two facilities with extensive intracompany transportation and facility overhead was wasteful. After almost a year of planning and preparation the packaging facility was physically moved to a location within the central facility. The packaging equipment was now only feet from the outbound shipping dock, making material handling movements to the outbound side of the operation quick and easy. On the inbound side AGVs efficiently move material from the receiving area to the packaging area. The central facility became a facility within a facility.

Locating the packaging facility within another facility creates supply chain savings that align well with lean objectives. Previously, this company relied on extensive intracompany transportation of goods from one facility to another. Now, transportation *between* facilities is replaced with material handling *within* a facility, much of it via automated equipment. Material movements that required a day or more now take minutes, and movements that cost hundreds of dollars now cost a fraction of that amount. Companies should search for ways to replace transportation with material handling wherever possible. The savings will not be disappointing.

Deferring for the Longer Term

Supply chain planners recognized that packaging all-time buys was not creating any value. Deferment logic was developed to programmatically identify those items that should be kept in a deferred or bulk status until they were needed at a later date. The quantity that is needed for replenishment is now separated at receiving from the all-time buy quantity and moved to the packaging operation (assuming it requires packaging), or transferred to the appropriate outbound shipping line. The remainder, called the *deferred quantity*, is moved to a bulk storage area that is not part of the main flow of the central facility. A planning group reviews deferment items regularly to determine when to move the remaining quantities into the normal replenishment flow within the supply chain. Deferment logic ensures the deferred items remain in a bulk state and do not become burdensome packaged items with no immediate need.

Prioritizing Work Daily

At first glance a first-come-first-serve system appears compatible with the tenets of lean. It is easy to understand, it does not require complex scheduling algorithms or systems, and material moves directly through the facility. Do you want to know what job to run next? Look down by your feet and see what items are sitting next in line. What could be easier? In this case, first-come-first-serve, even though it is part of a simplified scheduling process, often leads to waste. Simple, nonverbal systems work best in a pull environment, which this surely was not.

The heart of any scheduling system is the logic that prioritizes work. The prioritization system developed here awarded points based on various conditions of downstream demand for every item that is awaiting packaging. The more points that a job earns the greater the likelihood it will appear on the next day's packaging schedule. Each night the system considers the criticality of an item by looking at its current inventory position around the United States and its expected demand. Parts and kits that have customer backorders are naturally prioritized the highest. Next, items with the least amount of inventory available at the regional centers (or finished goods in storage at the national center) with a higher expected demand will also rank highly. This system also provides a higher priority to subassemblies that are required to support the kits that are packaged each week.

Before assigning priorities each night, the system first calculates an economic package quantity (EPQ) for each part number or kit that is eligible for scheduling. This formula, developed by a materials planning group and similar in concept to the economic order quantity (EOQ), determines if the full quantity of a receipt should be packaged. The EPQ formula considers the current packaging need as well as machine setup charges, material handling, transportation, and stockkeeping costs.

While packaging more than what is necessary to replenish regional stocking locations usually results in waste, the EPQ calculation does not allow an unpackaged load to be divided into partial loads. If the quantity in a single unpackaged load is 500, for example, and the EPQ is 395, then the schedule would round to the entire load. The decision was made to not leave partial loads in racks for future

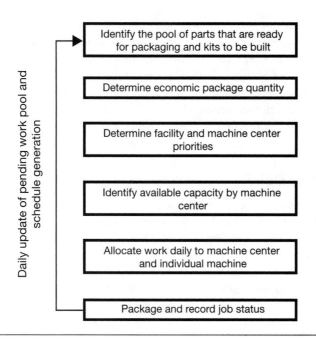

Figure 11.2 Daily scheduling sequence

scheduling. Subdividing loads would result in excessive manual handling and increase the probability of inventory errors.

After calculating the EPQ the prioritization logic takes over. Each night this system assigns a priority to every item and its EPQ that is available for packaging. The system also prioritizes the items within each machine center. This is important since the actual allocation of work through the scheduling system is not done by plant capacity. Rather, the basis for work scheduling is the capacity available within each type of packaging machine. This facility has several dozen different types of packaging equipment or centers. When employees arrive early in the morning they receive that day's schedule for each machine type.

Figure 11.2 illustrates the sequence of events when prioritizing items. A database is maintained that provides information about the total hours that each machine is available the next day. Plant personnel can add or reduce available hours as needed. If the facility plans to work a 10-hour shift instead of an eight-hour shift, for example, the database is changed to reflect the extra hours. Another database includes the per-hour rate that a part will be packaged. This determines how much machine time is required given a specific requirement.

After determining the next day's schedule the system groups items together based on their packaging material. This helps minimize machine changeovers. To illustrate, let's say there are four paper and poly machines that are available for eight hours of scheduling, or 32 total hours of available machine time. The jobs that made that day's schedule are sequenced according to the width of the paper and poly wrap used to package a part. Parts that use the same width of paper and poly are placed on the same equipment.

The system relies on clerks to input daily the status of jobs that appeared on that day's schedule. A job that is completed as scheduled is entered into the scheduling database with a "C," a job that is only partially complete, and assumed to still be on the equipment for the next shift or schedule run, is coded with a "P," with the remaining quantity noted as work in process. Partial or work-in-process jobs appear at the top of the next generated schedule. If for some reason a job was not worked even though it was scheduled, this data field remains blank. This signals to the scheduling system that this job is again available for scheduling the next day.

While parts arrive from suppliers based on a forecast of future demand (i.e., a push system), the scheduling logic only schedules those parts that are most in need at the regional distribution centers. Demand, not a forecast, pulls these parts onto the daily schedule. The daily schedule is what we call a *push/pull* boundary, a topic raised in Chapter 4.

Changing the Layout

Most organizations find that lean pursuits often involve facility layout changes, a topic that Chapter 4 covered in some detail. This case is no different. The first-come-first-serve system that characterized this facility featured side-by-side storage lines of items awaiting packaging.[2] As loads were removed for packaging, a material handler pushed the remaining loads in the line forward toward the machine. Any new loads assumed their rightful place at the back of the line. During value stream mapping (VSM), this short-term storage area is sometimes referred to as a *supermarket*.

In reality this material handling and storage system did not work nearly as well as the previous paragraph suggests. First, the storage lines were quite long, making the pushing of loads something less than an exact science. When the lines became disjointed it required some manual effort to get them back in order. At other times loads were damaged during the line movement. This manual effort and damage increased waste.

The lines were also located near specific work centers, and several of these centers contained different types of equipment. Frequently the storage lines included work for a variety of machine types, forcing some wasteful rearrangement to retrieve the next job for a particular machine. Finally, the constant moving of lines made it difficult and even dangerous to stack loads. While square footage was maximized, cubic footage was not. This facility paid for a great deal of air above the loads on the floor. Most observers would categorize this inefficient use of cube as waste.

Facility planners recognized early that a physical layout that allowed easy access to work was necessary once the first-come-first-serve priority logic went away. Horizontal storage lines along the floor were replaced with vertical racks that allowed the convenient stocking of pallet loads. Bar code scanning was used to record each item's location into an information technology system. Once an item was put away and recorded it was available for scheduling. As part numbers qualified for placement on a day's schedule, material handlers easily retrieved the parts and placed them at the appropriate packaging machine. This new layout and rack system allowed the staging of work in a convenient way and eliminated the wasted handling required with the storage lines.

Knowing What Comes Next

The daily schedule by machine center provides a quick and easy way to identify each day's work. This schedule enables the planning and staging of work to help minimize downtime. The importance of planning and staging was presented in Chapter 4. Let's illustrate how planning and staging works here.

Each work center has assigned material handlers. These individuals set up the packaging equipment as well as retrieve material from the racks to stage by each machine. These employees also stage any required packaging materials. Under the previous system time was lost staging work at the start of each shift. Under the revised system the material handlers begin work earlier than the normal shift.

With the daily schedule in hand, the material handler can ensure that each machine is ready for work at the start of each shift. Some machines will have partial jobs remaining from the day before. Other equipment will need jobs from the holding racks. The material handlers try to have at least a half day's worth of work staged by each piece of equipment. The availability of a daily schedule based on a logical prioritization scheme ensures that the material handlers stage the right items based on downstream demand. The staging process also minimizes downtime as machine operators begin their day with parts ready for packaging. Planning and staging is essential for supporting the flow of jobs through this facility.

Managing Nonproductive Inventory

The development of the scheduling system prompted a parallel project that is one of the more innovative changes at this facility. Historically, most firms classify packaging items as maintenance, repair, and operating (MRO) items, and this company is no different. This facility spends millions of dollars on packaging goods—stretch wrap, shrink wrap, bubble wrap, poly wrap, corrugated wrap, cartons, tri-wall shipping containers, pallets, labels, instruction sheets, and so on. As with so-called real inventory, poor management of these items results in some serious physical and financial waste.

A simple, yet eloquent, low-cost approach for managing corrugated cartons was identified. A decision was made to assign every carton used for packaging its own component part number. Carton 5501, for example, became KC005501. This change required working with the engineering group that manages aftermarket part numbers. In this system K means the item is a component and C designates it as a carton. A new part numbering scheme was born. So, what is the big deal here?

The information technology system, specifically the master production schedule (MPS), material requirements planning (MRP) system, and material releasing modules, now recognized cartons as components. Every part number that required a carton for packaging now had a carton component number attached to its bill of material. With the precision that MPS and MRP systems provide, the group responsible for managing nonproductive inventory now knows the quantity of dependent demand cartons required, given the independent demand parts that were scheduled to arrive for packaging. Guesstimates regarding how many cartons to order were replaced with precise numbers.

While these changes made a dramatic impact on how this facility managed its packaging inventory, the effort to make these changes was relatively insignificant. Treating nonproductive items as productive part numbers tapped into systems that already existed. Carton requirements for each part already appeared on a database, so it was a simple task to write a program to make seamless additions to thousands of bill of materials. After these changes were complete, the other programs that use the bill of material database as a source of input managed the carton part numbers like any other component number.

Carton suppliers received material releases and cartons were received the same as production components. The receiving system generated bar-coded move tickets upon receipt, the cartons were placed in racks with the location noted on a database, and cartons were now eligible for cycle counts. The space required for storing cartons decreased by about 50 percent, space that was used to expand a productive work area. Life was good for the person who managed the cartons.

What about items that are packaged in material that comes in rolls? Some parts are packaged using a corrugated wrap, for example, that is purchased in 2000-foot roles. A lack of a one-to-one packaging relationship made these items more difficult to forecast and buy. While a bit trickier to forecast than unit containers, a solution was also identified for managing materials that are purchased in rolls.

A computer program was developed that tapped into the database that contained dimensional data for each part that required packaging. In this case the length of a part was of primary interest. Here's the flow of logic when managing the inventory for material that is purchased in rolls:

1. Identify how many units of an individual part will be required each month using a packaging material that comes in a continuous roll. This company's system forecast part requirements out to 18 months with three months representing a firm releasing window. Months 4-18 were provided to suppliers for planning purposes.
2. Multiply the units required for a part by its length in inches to arrive at the total packaging material required to package a part.
3. Convert total inches into total feet. Add 5 percent to compensate for the empty package space at the ends within a package. This is not waste—parts are placed on packaging material and each machine has to have some space for sealing and cutting the package.
4. Add the total feet required for a part number using a particular type of role and divide by the number of feet in a role (usually 2000 feet) to arrive at the required number of rolls each month.
5. The logic to identify the number of roles required each month was external to the MPS, MRP, and material releasing system.

Table 11.1 provides a simple illustration of how the requirements for rolled packaging goods are identified each month. This example assumes the four part numbers in the table are the only ones that require that package roll. In reality there are hundreds, if not thousands, of part numbers that use the same packaging material. While this approach requires an additional set of calculations compared with cartons, a material planner could now order with better precision. A net quantity is determined after considering the number of rolls currently in stock and the amount of work awaiting packaging.

Managing Subassemblies

This facility packages thousands of kits, and many of these kits require subassemblies that are put together prior to the building of the final kit. A kit may require several screws, for example, that have to be sealed in a poly bag. The poly bag with the screws is called a subassembly. Some of the more complex kits require four or five subassemblies that require scheduling and assembly ahead of the final kit assembly. Unfortunately, the traditional method for managing subassemblies involved maintaining a manual file of subassembly instructions that were pulled out each time a kit was scheduled for building.

Table 11.1 Identifying monthly requirements for 6-inch-wide paper and poly rolls

Part number	January shipments from suppliers	Length of part in inches	Total feet required ((Demand x Length)/12) x 1.05	Total rolls required (Total Feet/2000)
04377892	23,223 units	17.5 inches	35,560 feet	17.8 rolls
05699323	9,500 units	24 inches	19,950 feet	9.98 rolls
04366745	3,556 units	14 inches	16,606 feet	8.3 rolls
04388222	25,000 units	30 inches	65,625 feet	32.8 rolls
Total			**137,741 total feet**	**69 rolls**

Each part number listed uses 6-inch-rolled material for packaging.

This process was cumbersome and prone to errors. An engineering change to a component that would appear on a kit's bill of material might not make its way to the manual subassembly sheet in a timely fashion, if at all. This would cause confusion when a kit was released to be built and its contents did not match the manually maintained subassembly directions. The packaging engineering group at the packaging facility, not the corporate engineering group that establishes new parts and kits, identifies and maintains subassemblies. Subassemblies are strictly a packaging issue.

The new scheduling system simply did not recognize the existence of subassemblies because they did not appear on any bill of material. While all the components in a subassembly appeared on a kit's bill of material, to the scheduling system this appeared simply as a kit with a list of components. The manual control of subassemblies meant that the new scheduling system did not know that subassemblies existed, and therefore could not schedule subassemblies before scheduling the final kit. After all, we don't know what we don't know.

This created a serious dilemma—the building of subassemblies required machine capacity that may have been allocated on a certain day to scheduling other jobs. Or, worse yet, the system might schedule kits before the subassemblies were available. On the list of issues, this one was near the top of the list.

As with the cartons, the solution to this problem was straightforward. Each subassembly identified by packaging engineers was assigned a part number that now appeared on a kit's bill of material. The system recognizes these subassemblies and schedules them prior to the scheduling of the final kit. Ensuring that subassemblies are identified and bills of material are adjusted with new numbers is a continuous process since new parts and kits are introduced throughout a year.

CONCLUDING THOUGHTS

Changes as significant as those presented here will always bring their own set of challenges. The next chapter provides an objective assessment of the lessons learned from transforming a pure push system into one that incorporates lean principles. Given the system as it is presented in this chapter, what could be done to move this system forward?

Perhaps the most obvious improvement involves the manual effort that is required to record into a database the status of every job that appears on a day's schedule. Not only is this process labor intensive (which in itself makes it a prime candidate for attention), it is also the source of errors. Failing to note that a job has been completed, for example, means that job will likely appear on the next day's schedule. Inputting the correct status for each scheduled job, and hundreds of jobs are scheduled each day, requires extensive data collection. A system that streamlines the collection of status data, such as using bar codes (or perhaps radio frequency identification (RFID) tags as that technology evolves further) to transmit data from the packaging equipment to the database would be more timely, accurate, and efficient.

A second enhancement involves the timeliness of the schedule. When this system was developed the daily schedule was printed at approximately 4:00 a.m. With the technology that is available today there is no reason to even print schedules. Schedules can simply appear on a computer screen. Also, why can't schedule updates occur every few minutes to reflect up-to-the-minute status of jobs that are awaiting packaging? Currently, an inbound receipt that enters this facility and is forwarded to the packaging group will not be eligible to appear on a schedule until the next day (which is still far better than the first-come-first-serve system). Why not go one step further and update the schedule in real time whenever a new item enters the packaging facility? A job that enters the facility in midmorning may be so critical that it could appear on that day's schedule. It is theoretically possible to schedule and package items within hours of receipt from suppliers. A move toward real-time data availability and schedule updates moves even closer toward the ideals of a lean supply chain.

ENDNOTES

1. Parts with customer backorders are separated from the main flow of material at the receiving dock of the national center. Backorders are sent to a UPS pack line for direct shipment to dealers. While this expedites backorders it does increase shipping costs. This is a classic example of a supply chain trade-off.

2. In a perfect world inbound receipts would be placed immediately by the required equipment for packaging. This facility always has multiple days, if not weeks, of work awaiting scheduling, making short-term storage a necessity.

12

WHY PUSH WHEN YOU CAN PULL? THE LESSONS LEARNED

Part of any major initiative should be taking the time to assess what went right and what went wrong. Identifying *lessons learned* is highly consistent with lean thinking. It is also a primary characteristic of a learning organization. If performed correctly, future initiatives should be better off by not repeating the same kinds of mistakes.

This chapter examines the lessons learned from the development and launch of the scheduling system presented in Chapter 11. It features those areas where the project did not progress as planned. It does not discuss the positive benefits associated with the project, although that is also an important part of the learning process. The following sections relate to important lessons learned from the scheduling project. Most of these lessons will apply to any lean initiative.

DO NOT FORGET TRAINING

Several years ago a consumer products company introduced a successful new razor blade for men. Prior to full-scale launch the development team made a troublesome discovery. The process to produce the new three-blade cartridge was significantly more complex than the one used to produce a two-blade cartridge. This complexity was not what was troubling. The new process and its technology proved to be highly capable of producing the new blades. Unfortunately, process engineers, not production employees, had demonstrated that capability. As the product ramped up toward full-scale production, it became evident that the employees who would operate the physical process were not prepared for this higher complexity level. While engineers understood the process, production employees did not. The company had to quickly commit to a training program before ramping up production.

The launch of the packaging system is similar to the razor blade example. The development team had no trouble understanding the prioritization logic, why cartons now had part numbers, or how manually controlled subassemblies were now system-controlled subassemblies. And let's not forget about the absolute discipline required to input a part's status into a database. Surely everyone understood the importance of inputs that have zero defects.

Inadequate training ensured that supervisors, material handlers, machine operators, and clerks were not as familiar with the system as were its developers. To internal users the priority logic was a black box that magically presented a sequenced list of work each day. A lack of training on the new system had an obvious effect on the system's launch and, perhaps more importantly, its acceptance. As with many systems, development is *pushed* from above onto those who have to make the system work.

Lessons Learned. Identify and involve those operational groups during system development that are an integral part of making a new system work. Develop a training schedule that maps the general and specific training required to support a new system. Do not view training as an expense that needs to be minimized. Instead, view training as an investment that will generate a positive return. Never assume that what appears obvious to system developers will appear obvious to employees.

ALIGN PERFORMANCE MEASURES WITH SYSTEM OBJECTIVES

Measurement systems are often a source of conflict and waste, an idea that Chapter 6 brought forth. A problem in the packaging facility was that the work centers historically focused on pieces packaged per hour, even if that resulted in packaging some inventory that downstream supply chain members did not need. The supervisors knew how they were measured and they behaved accordingly. Productivity was king.

This new system stressed an entirely different set of *system* rather than individual machine or work center objectives, an important one being the elimination of downstream waste. Long production runs were now replaced, at times, by shorter runs as defined by the economic package quantity (EPQ). This meant running more part numbers, which meant more machine setups, which meant more downtime, which meant the packaged pieces-per-hour rate was likely to decline, which meant the supervisors would not look quite so good on their performance budgets and evaluation, which meant they might not get a raise.

The chain of events that caused some unintended consequences here is fairly clear. Unfortunately, the performance measurement system did not change with the introduction of the new packaging system. While the development team was surprised to find the machine centers running quantities that were larger than what the daily schedules assigned, and thereby distorting that day's schedule, in retrospect the resulting behavior is not that hard to understand.

Lessons Learned. Perform a detailed assessment of the performance measurement system before changing any process. Measures that are in conflict with the objectives of a new system or process need to be eliminated or modified. In this situation a better measure to assess work center performance is *conformance to schedule* rather than *pieces per hour*.

DO NOT IGNORE EQUIPMENT SETUP TIME

The use of an EPQ created a conflict between system and operational objectives. While the EPQ logic resulted in more part numbers scheduled with shorter packaging runs, which directly conflicted with the current measurement system, most work centers were used to packaging the entire quantity of a receipt. The root cause of why supervisors want long production runs is due to the effect lengthy machine setup times have on productivity. The more part numbers that are scheduled the more machine changeovers, and in some work centers these changeovers can be lengthy. Although the scheduling system groups items that require the same package together in a sequence, the overall schedule still featured more part numbers and changeovers than previously was the case. The importance of reducing machine changeovers was not stressed during system design.

Lessons Learned. Changes that involve setup times must be reduced to the point that changeovers become a nonevent. Development teams should also include representatives from internal operations who might have stressed the importance of this issue. Here, a staff person represented the voice of internal customers, an arrangement that clearly left something to be desired.

MINIMIZE SYSTEM OVERRIDES

Have you ever encountered a problem that was so surprising that you wondered how it could have been overlooked? This project was blessed with such a problem.

In this company, a materials planning group manages a forecasting system that quantitatively determines what parts to order from suppliers. Unfortunately, the group that developed the new scheduling system and the materials planning group did not communicate all that well during system design.

Here's the problem. The only determinant about whether a part is scheduled for packaging on a given day is an unbiased assessment of that part's system-wide priority. If the part has a high enough priority it makes that day's schedule; if it does not make the cut, well, there's always tomorrow. However, the materials planning group is comprised of people who are responsible for managing different groups of parts all the way through to the regional distribution centers. These individuals are measured by how effectively (i.e., how fast) they get their parts through the supply chain. Let's be realistic here. To these planners the only parts that matter are their own parts. It quickly became obvious that when their parts did not make the daily schedule, these planners became "cranky."

An example will illustrate this issue. For simplicity let's assume there are three planners who manage 200 part numbers each, or 600 part numbers in total. Furthermore, assume that all 600 parts are in the packaging facility waiting scheduling and packaging. Assume even further that only 50 part numbers can be scheduled for packaging on a certain day, and that almost all the scheduled parts for that day are from a single planner's list. In other words, the other two planners have to sit back contentedly and watch their parts not get packaged. Remember, these planners are measured on their ability to move parts through the system, which is not happening for two of them. It's easy to see why the old crank-o-meter got revved up.

It was not long after system launch that the complaints started arriving about parts not being scheduled that were at the top of a planner's list. To appease these irate planners, the development team modified the system logic to allow *selective* overrides to a part's priority. As we will see, oftentimes the easy solution is not the best solution.

What problem was so surprising? The material planners apparently skipped the day in school when the word *selective* was taught. These planners spent a progressively larger part of their day inputting manual overrides to the scheduling system to ensure their parts would appear on the next day's schedule. The situation became so out of control it (almost) became comical. Some planners would wait until late in the day so they could override someone else's override that was input earlier—ha, ha, my override is bigger than your override! This system started to place individual planners in competition with each other. Besides being wasteful (not to mention somewhat ugly), these overrides undermined the very integrity of the scheduling system. This is an example of where the fix, the so-called selective use of overrides, did not even begin to address the root cause of the problem.

Manual overrides usually indicate a deeper issue with a system. If your firm has an automated system with an unusually large number of overrides to that system's output, such as a forecasting system, then you have a problem that needs addressing. What is the point of having an automated system if a good part of the day is spent policing and then overriding the output from that system? Is the output from an automated system only a suggestion, like the 55 mph speed limit?

Lessons Learned. Involve any project stakeholders when developing a system that affects other groups. It is also important to convey the system's benefits rather than focusing on "how this affects me." Secure executive management support when conflict between groups becomes an issue because of a change or new system. And again, it may be necessary to change the measurement and reward system so it aligns better with the new system. Avoid manual overrides to systems whenever possible, and only use overrides in special situations. Be sure to track the number of system overrides that are occurring, research the root causes of system overrides, and pursue corrective action. Also avoid the temptation of easy fixes.

BE CAREFUL WHEN USING AVERAGES

The sophistication of the scheduling logic allowed this system to load an amount of work onto a piece of equipment that represented a day's work. To do this the system developers had to rely on an industrial engineer, an ad hoc team member, to provide the per-hour rates at which to schedule each machine. For automated machines this was fairly straightforward since all parts on these machines are packaged at a fairly consistent per-hour rate.

The methodology to determine the per-hour rate was derived from production records. Histories were available that provided average production rates for each piece of equipment for parts and for kits. And for most equipment the standard deviation or spread around each average was not that large. These averages became part of the algorithm when developing the daily schedule.

In several work centers the use of averages proved to be problematic. In these work centers the rate at which jobs are packaged is often highly variable due to the length of the part being packaged, particularly when the packaging material comes in a roll. Longer parts consume more machine time than shorter parts. Two parts may require the same eight-inch wide packaging material, for example, but if one part is 24 inches long while the other is 50 inches long it is easy to see that the per-hour packaging rates will vary dramatically. The wide variability of part lengths makes the daily schedule unreliable.

Once the decision was made to develop a finite scheduling system, the need for accurate per-hour production rates for each part number became critical. A finite system schedules a fixed amount of work given the available capacity for a particular time period. Here, the system scheduled a day's worth of work for each piece of equipment. An infinite scheduling system does not consider capacity constraints. This type of system generates a schedule by machine center starting with the most critical item and then moving down in priority until all potential jobs are scheduled. The scheduling issues for these problematic work centers were eventually resolved by creating scheduling algorithms that considered factors such as part length.

Lessons Learned. At times an operation may be so complex that it becomes difficult to factor every possible condition with precision. The scheduling system can actually create new sources of waste. Facilities that are extremely complex might benefit from an infinite loading system that prioritizes potential jobs in their sequence of importance, at least in those areas where determining reliable rates is difficult. Production work groups will then determine how to load work throughout the day using each part's priority as a guide.

Work center input is highly consistent with the notion of an empowered workforce and localized scheduling, which are important elements of lean operations. Another lesson is that a phased system launch should uncover scheduling problems in a more controlled manner as compared to a big bang launch.

ESTABLISH THE BASELINE FOR MEASURING PERFORMANCE IMPROVEMENT

Setting the baseline means identifying performance levels prior to making a change or launching a new system. This particular lesson has been echoed by numerous managers who were responsible for lean projects at their organization. How else can we objectively tell the impact of a change? Because the system featured here was so volume-oriented it was difficult to quantify the systemwide storage, labor, and handling waste that resulted from overproduction. These types of measures simply did not exist. A lack of performance measures made it difficult to quantify the true impact the traditional system was having on total supply chain costs and customer service. This also makes selling the system to other supply chain members who are affected by the system that much harder. Baseline measures that focus on narrow output measures do not help when assessing the benefit of any changes from a total system or total cost perspective.

An example of a baseline measure here is the percent of parts moving directly from a packaging machine to an outbound shipping line. What percent of packaged parts move immediately to the shipping dock for replenishing downstream needs versus the percentage of parts being stored upstream awaiting future demand? An objective of the scheduling system is to package those parts and quantities that are needed right now, while reducing the wasteful handling and stocking of unneeded packaged material. Getting the right goods to the right location faster should also reduce customer backorders, another important performance indicator. Having the right material flow through the supply chain faster and in a sequence based on need should affect customer service levels.

Lessons Learned. Identify performance levels in key areas before making a major change. Use these levels to establish a baseline against which to gauge the effect of changes. Be sure the baseline indicators align with system objectives. Also, develop new baseline measures as required. Some examples of baseline measures that align with the objectives of the new system include the following:

- The percent of parts moving downstream toward the end customer rather than upstream storage
- The change in total system backorders for items that require packaging
- The reduction in transportation and labor costs as fewer loads move to auxiliary storage
- Total system fill rate for items that require packaging

Never underestimate the value of an effective performance measurement system.

LAUNCH THE SYSTEM IN PHASES

This facility consists of four work centers with over 70 total pieces of equipment. These diverse work centers each presented their own unique challenges when developing and launching a daily schedule. Instead of launching the system simultaneously across all four centers, in retrospect most participants recognize that a phased approach to system launch, such as a pilot program, would have been more manageable. Two of the four work centers have many different machine codes or types, making a phased launch by machine code within those work centers a possible option. Because system programming took longer than projected (there's a surprise), the development team felt pressure to introduce the system as soon as possible. Unfortunately, this approach did not work as well as anticipated due to a lack of internal training, misaligned performance measures that promoted longer-than-scheduled packaging runs, and excessive manual priority overrides.

Lessons Learned. A phased approach to system launch should help identify and minimize any issues or system weaknesses that will affect the entire system.

Issues that are common to the entire facility can be managed across a smaller scale with fewer negative effects if problems arise. Issues that are unique to a work center should also receive more attention in a phased system launch.

INVOLVE STAKEHOLDERS DURING SYSTEM DESIGN

Ownership of any project must extend beyond the team that is responsible for that project. Most organizations would benefit from more careful planning when forming teams. This includes not only conveying the team's purpose across an organization but also making available any resources that are necessary, including human resources.

The development team for this system was quite small. It included three full-time members: one member who was responsible for addressing operational issues in the packaging facility and two full-time systems resources. While the IT team members were highly qualified, they lacked operational experience. To software developers and programmers a new software program or technology can handle most any issue, which far too often leads to system complexity. As an old saying goes, "When you're a hammer everything looks like a nail."

It's not who was on the team but rather who was not on the team that is important here. Many other groups had a stake in this system but were only consulted informally, if at all. There was no formal declaration or charter that identified as-needed group members.

Certain groups should have been more engaged, formally and informally, during system design. Many of the lessons learned involved these groups in one way or another:

- **Packaging facility supervisors.** This group has a major effect on the success of the new system. Since an important part of a supervisor's job is to direct the workforce, a system that identifies what sequence of jobs to run throughout the day could be seen as a threat to the supervisors. This involvement will also help with understanding the system.
- **Packaging employees.** This facility is unionized, making communications important. Certain employees, such as clerks and material handlers, play a major role in the operational success of the daily schedule. Time spent by the development team to gain insights and support from this group would have been beneficial.
- **Materials planning.** This group manages the forecasting system that generates material releases to suppliers. The earlier lesson learned

regarding manual system overrides illustrates why this group's involvement is critical.

- **Industrial engineering.** This group identifies the packaging rates for each machine code. The earlier cited problems with using averages when scheduling production for certain machines highlight the importance of involving a qualified industrial engineering representative during system design.
- **Packaging engineering.** This group's responsibility for specifying subassemblies and ensuring that all incoming parts have correct packaging material specifications and dimensions makes the involvement of packaging engineers critical.
- **Operations planning.** This group is responsible for developing the EPQ algorithm. This group also included some of the best operating minds in the aftermarket division.

Lessons Learned. Identify all key stakeholders during the project planning phase. Project development teams rarely succeed without support from others external to the team. Formally identify the individuals who need to be assigned as formal or ad hoc team members. Conduct regular coordination meetings to update stakeholders during development. Take advantage of all opportunities to communicate informally with stakeholders about the system and its progress, perhaps through electronic mail or a project web page.

CONCLUDING THOUGHTS

Becoming a learning organization means taking the time to learn from experience, summarizing that learning, and applying it to subsequent projects across an organization. Just because there are areas here where the transformation from a push environment to a pull environment encountered some hurdles does not mean this system was unsuccessful. In many areas, particularly getting the right products scheduled at the right time, this system was right on. The logic of turning cartons into components was about as low cost and effective as an idea can get. The new storage system that resulted in less material handling was a major improvement over the previous system. And eliminating the paper-based system for managing subassemblies could not happen soon enough.

The lessons learned process is completely supportive of the lean philosophy. Applying these lessons helps avoid waste during subsequent projects by preventing the same kinds of mistakes from happening again. Instead of referring to this as "lessons learned," a more apt description might be "wisdom gained."

13

LEAN TAKES TO
THE SKIES

This chapter showcases a company that, at first glance, may not appear to be as likely a candidate for lean as those in high volume industries.[1] As we will soon see, nothing could be further from the truth. Boeing, as much as any company in the world, has benefited from the application of lean principles and techniques. It has demonstrated that lean can be applied in the unlikeliest of settings, and it would not come as a surprise if automotive companies, the original pioneers of lean, started benchmarking Boeing's capabilities.

This chapter looks at many different dimensions of lean at Boeing, including the market challenges the company faces, a summary of the company's lean journey, the extraordinary achievements in the 737 program, and how the company promotes lean innovation. We will also look at the defense side of Boeing's business, the radically new 787 Dreamliner program, and the relationship between suppliers and lean success.

BOEING'S MARKET CHALLENGES

Boeing Commercial Airplanes is one of two major aircraft producers of large commercial aircraft in the world (the other producer is Airbus). While there are several producers of regional jets such as Embraer and Bombardier, these companies, at least for now, are not direct competitors. Although the aircraft industry experienced a significant downturn during the early 2000s, there is no question that both Boeing and Airbus now face a marketplace, at least for now, where the demand for jets far outstrips the ability to produce jets. Starting in 2005, the

Table 13.1 When supply and demand don't agree at Boeing

Year	Orders	Deliveries
2000	589	492
2001	314	527
2002	257	381
2003	249	281
2004	277	285
2005	1022	290
2006	1058	398
2007	1423	441

Total unfilled commercial aiplane orders: 3645 (737 model-2222; 747 model-119; 767 model-48; 777 model-360; 787 model-896).

Source: http://www.boeing.com, June 2008.

floodgates opened and demand for planes from around the world, including many start-up airlines, resulted in aircraft orders that were almost four times the levels of previous years. To say that Boeing is facing some market challenges would be an understatement.

Table 13.1 shows the imbalance between aircraft orders and deliveries at Boeing over the last several years. From 2000 to 2004, Boeing's commercial business showed some general semblance of equilibrium between deliveries and orders. The company received orders for almost 1700 planes and delivered over 1900 planes (aircraft producers always have a backlog and lag between orders and deliveries). Today, any semblance of equilibrium between the demand for planes and the supply of planes is gone. Boeing has a backlog of aircraft orders for every model it sells, and the backlog is much larger for some models than others. If you are thinking about ordering a 787 Dreamliner, for example, be sure to act quickly. Dreamliners ordered today won't even be available for delivery until 2015. The strength of Boeing's order book guarantees it will remain the largest exporter in the United States for some time to come.

To address this imbalance between demand and supply, why doesn't the company simply make more planes? It is not as simple as it sounds. Boeing has been hesitant to ramp up production volumes quickly or add physical production space for a number of reasons. During the late 1990s, the company tried to grab as much market share as possible from Airbus. More orders meant the company had to quickly ramp up production, and the resulting production, supply, and quality problems forced Boeing to shut down its production while the company got a handle on its problems. With the memories of that debacle still painfully fresh in management's mind, the company has pursued a more methodical ramp up of production. Boeing has endorsed lean probably as strong as any U.S. manufacturer as a way to achieve faster throughput and to better utilize corporate resources. The company has no plans of building anytime soon a 2-million-square-foot assembly facility. Even if Boeing did plan a massive expansion, it would be many years before that capacity were available.

Internal constraints are only part of Boeing's market challenges. The supply base supporting the aerospace industry is proving to be a major concern. The downturn of the early 2000s forced many suppliers out of business or away from the aerospace industry. The dramatic upturn in aircraft orders over the last several years is placing a severe strain on many of the remaining suppliers. Some suppliers simply cannot ramp up fast enough to meet the surging demand for new aircraft. A Boeing executive noted that "smaller subcontractor suppliers always cause you more time and attention. There's always some little shop out there that doesn't hack it."[2]

A particular concern is a bottleneck in the process of converting raw materials into aerospace-grade metals such as titanium and aluminum.[3] Many metal processors closed down or sold off a significant portion of their capacity after the post-2001 downturn. When airplane orders recovered with a vengeance, a lag in regaining this metal capacity has clearly strained the aerospace industry. It does not matter if Boeing has the internal capacity to produce 500 planes a month. Without the required parts and systems that suppliers and subtier suppliers are asked to provide, Boeing's planes aren't flying anywhere.

BOEING'S LEAN JOURNEY

Lean is a journey, and Boeing did not simply wake up one day and decide to transform suddenly into a lean enterprise. The company experienced some important milestones as it began its lean transformation. It is important to step back and recognize that the Boeing of yesterday practiced a massive batch-and-queue production system rather than a lean system focused on flow.[4] Production units made parts on large machines by the thousands, which were then stacked, stored in buildings, warehouses, or even parking lots, and then moved between buildings as they awaited their next step in a prolonged journey. While individual managers met their production quotas, astute observers soon realized this probably was not the best way to coordinate a massive production effort.

Units that were physically disconnected from the assembly process, communication failures between groups, and a lack of efficiency eventually lead to an ironic situation. Even though Boeing was awash in inventory, the company was not meeting its customer commitments. These problems left the door open for customers to check out a relatively new kid on the block called Airbus. The rest, as they say, is history.

Boeing can trace its lean roots back to 1991 when the company sent teams of executives to Japan to study that country's quality processes. That simple step started Boeing's lean journey, which will always be a work in process. Noteworthy milestones in lean for Boeing's commercial aircraft group include the following:[5]

- 1990-1991—A team of Boeing executives arrive in Japan to further their understanding of the Japanese quality management process.
- 1993—Boeing begins to apply the lessons learned from the Japanese visits.
- 1992-1994—Boeing employees attend workshops designed to enhance their skills and the competitiveness of the company.
- 1993—Boeing's first production cell was created to build an escape hatch for the 737.
- 1994—Boeing starts a 5S program.
- 1995—Boeing initiates the use of *kaizen* events.
- 1996—Boeing charters its lean Manufacturing Office, formerly Boeing's Quality Improvement Council; the company hires the Shingijutsu Consulting Company of Japan to provide guidance on lean manufacturing issues.
- By 1998, around 1500 employees have traveled to Japan to study the Toyota Production System firsthand.[6]
- 1999—A pulse assembly line is put in place to support the 717 program
- 2001—The moving assembly line for the 737 is instituted.
- 2006-2007—Boeing begins to build tail sections and wings for the 737 on a moving line; the 777 begins its transition to a moving assembly line.

Lean is a never-ending journey of continuous improvement.

THE 737 STORY

The crown jewel in Boeing's stable of lean accomplishments is unquestionably its hugely successful 737 program. The twin-engine, single-aisle 737, first introduced in the late 1960s, is now the best selling plane in the history of commercial aviation. With over 7000 of the planes ordered since its debut, the plane introduced much of the world to lower-cost flying, even though at the time of its introduction many people had never even seen a commercial jet. Today, the plane is used by airlines in 115 countries. To put this in perspective, the planet earth has 194 countries.

A major constraint that Boeing has faced when it assembles any type of aircraft is the production process that it used. The traditional process for assembling commercial airplanes is described as being similar to a parking lot.[7] Planes remain stationary in angled stalls as workers move in and out to retrieve parts and install them on the plane. With this type of process the workers, tools, parts, and equipment move in and out as needed to a product that remains stationary. At night, crews use material handling equipment or cranes to perform the time-consuming task of moving partially finished planes from one stall to the next. The only flow that occurs is the flowing in and out of the workers, tools, parts, and equipment needed to assemble the product. Unfortunately, that is not the type of flow we have been promoting throughout this book. The plane cannot be worked on during its physical movement, a movement that is nonvalue adding and likely even wasteful.

One Boeing executive summed up the issues with the traditional methods of building the 737, or any plane for that matter, as centering around six primary issues that lean clearly addresses. These issues include: (1) excess inventory; (2) time loss during airplane line moves; (3) production and support groups working to different schedules and priorities; (4) tools, parts, and drawings not readily available to assemblers; (5) a lack of visibility to the production status of the factory; and (6) flow time not correlated to customer demand.

Boeing decided that a shift from a stationary layout to a line flow process was critical if the company was to increase its productive capacity and drive out waste. Without question, the major innovation here is that Boeing has successfully created a moving assembly line that supports the production of around 30 737s a month. Normally, line flow processes are associated with very large volume applications, which Boeing has proven does not have to be the case. Truly radical innovations usually require truly radical changes that may alter the way an industry operates.

The most visible part of Boeing's lean system is the company's 737 continuous-flow assembly line. The first part of the assembly process involves receiving a fuselage in Washington from a supplier in Kansas, a supplier that used to be part of Boeing. Upon receipt of the fuselage, employees install wiring and ventilation systems. Next, the wings and landing gear are attached to the body of the plane. At this point the moving assembly line takes over and proceeds to move the body of the 737 from one workstation to the next at a blistering rate of 2 inches per minute. During assembly a 737 is attached to a winch, cable, and aluminum platform created internally by the assembly plant's moonshine shop (moonshine shops are explained shortly). The platform rides along a magnetic strip track embedded in the factory floor. At any given time, four fuselages are being prepped for assembly and five planes are working their way down the assembly line.

As planes are assembled they progress toward their next workstation, rather than the workstation moving to the plane, and the line is calibrated to allow employee teams to complete their tasks as planes progress from one workstation to the next.[8] As the planes make their way down the assembly line they pass carefully defined workstations, the locations of which are painted on the floor. The planes also pass hundreds of portable, color-coded work kits. Blue kit boxes contain tools, green boxes have chemicals, and gray boxes contain parts.[9] The tools and parts arrive when and where they are needed to support installation on the plane.

The main assembly line is supported by 35 feeder lines that bring people and assemblies to the right place at the right time.[10] This is a key part of the level build concept discussed in Chapter 4. These feeder lines are responsible for performing subassembly work that was previously performed during the main assembly of the aircraft. Under the previous process, for example, a shop floor employee (which Boeing calls a mechanic) would spend eight hours installing flight deck components while working within the stationary cockpit. Now, a half hour or so of prep work performed on a feeder line helps reduce the final cockpit assembly time to less than three hours.[11] A host of other subassembly work has been moved to the feeder lines, with some impressive assembly time reductions achieved.

It isn't only the assembly of the plane that benefits from a moving line approach. Recently Boeing has started to build the vertical fin and horizontal stabilizers for the tail section, called the *empennage*, on a moving line.[12] Through the increased use of planning and staging, as well as changes to the physical flow of the tail section, Boeing has reduced the time and the number of tools required to build this important assembly. These changes have removed one day out of a six-day cycle time, with further reductions expected, and have supported higher production rates without additional people. This first phase of the transformation for building the empennage featured the following changes:[13]

- **Make the product flow.** Instead of workers moving to fixed tools, the large tools required to build the tail assembly have been placed on wheels and move in a line to the employees. Tools and parts are staged next to their point of use on the production line. This reduces waste and improves flow by eliminating unnecessary movement.
- **Improve layout and appearance.** The floors are now painted white to better reflect light and improve visibility. An overhead utility rack with swing arms now feeds power and cords to each workstation, thereby eliminating floor cables. Floor cables restrict the flow of material around the shop floor and present workplace safety hazards such as tripping.
- **Work with suppliers.** Employees are working with certain suppliers to develop packaging that allows parts to be delivered and unloaded

directly into the production area. Suppliers were early participants here as Boeing moves ever closer to a just-in-time (JIT) delivery system for the tail section.

These changes are part of a well-defined plan to build the tail section of the 737 on a continuously moving production line. The transformation from stationary positions to moving lines required about eight months. And where does this transformation in the 737 process evolve to next? Boeing plans to apply the same kind of lean techniques and thinking to the wing assembly area.[14]

Besides the creative use of moving assembly lines, other lean techniques employed within the 737 program include JIT parts deliveries from suppliers, point-of-use staging of tools and parts (this relates to the planning and staging concept presented in Chapter 4), standard work processes, and visual control systems. During aircraft assembly, employees know exactly where a plane should be in the assembly process. The shop floor includes markings that represent times, and these times are visible reminders to workers regarding the assembly progress throughout their shift. The moving line creates a sense of urgency all the way up the supply chain.[15]

Visual signals, or what the Japanese call *andon*, are used to rapidly respond to production floor problems. Flashing yellow lights on the assembly floor indicate that line employees need help. If a problem is not resolved in 30 minutes the light changes to purple and the assembly line stops.[16] In a clever use of a lean signal, problem support teams are also alerted to problems by popular songs. Songs such as "Help" by the Beatles and "Rescue Me" correspond to different support teams that rush to the factory floor when that team's song is played.[16] If you are having problems you might as well have some fun.

The transformation of the 737 assembly followed a sequence or process that Boeing calls the 9 *Tactics*. These tactics can be used by any company that is looking for a methodical approach for rolling out lean. The reader may notice that these tactics correspond closely to the features of Lean Operations presented in Chapter 4. Table 13.2 presents these tactics.

Has all this really worked? In the end analysis, the metrics have to show in no uncertain terms that lean is worth the effort. And in no uncertain terms, at least at Boeing, lean is worth the effort. Lean innovations have helped Boeing reduce the cycle or throughput time for the assembly of a 737 from 22 to 11 days, which is now the shortest assembly time for any commercial aircraft. Boeing has demonstrated that increased throughput leads directly to increased flow, and increased flow leads directly to increased production capacity with a fixed amount of assets and square footage. With an order backlog of several thousand planes, any improvement in throughput means faster service to customers and top line revenue growth.

Table 13.2 Boeing's roadmap to continuous flow—the 9 tactics

Tactic	Description
Tactic 1: *Value stream mapping and analysis*	Create the current state map before lean implementation and the future state map that reflects lean changes
Tactic 2: *Balance the line*	Distribute work evenly by position, day, and shift
Tactic 3: *Standardize the work*	Identify the fastest way to perform each task at the lowest total cost with the highest quality
Tactic 4: *Put visuals in place*	Make visual notification board visible from the work floor and from support cells; create audible sounds to notify support groups of production problems or line stoppages; color code part boxes; diagram kit placement areas; outline pitch marks on assembly line floor to gauge assembly process
Tactic 5: *Point-of-use staging*	Stage production parts, tools, hazardous materials, and consumables in appropriate work cell or next to the airplane where they are needed
Tactic 6: *Establish feeder and supply chain lines*	Match the flow of parts and subassemblies internally and externally with suppliers to the flow of the airplane; perform some assembly work concurrently on feeder lines to minimize main line assembly
Tactic 7: *Break-through process redesign along main line*	Change the production layout from a stationary layout to a moving flow line; install line transporter and other equipment needed to support the new process
Tactic 8: *Convert line to a pulse line*	Begin to move airplane along the main line at periodic intervals
Tactic 9: *Convert to moving line*	Move the airplane at a continuous rate during assembly

Source: Public Domain Company Records

The benefits of lean are not only about speed. In addition to faster assembly, work-in-process inventories for the 737 program are down by over 50 percent and stored inventories are lower by almost 60 percent.[17] This has freed tens of thousands of square feet of floor space that can now be put to more productive uses. Production time for individual parts and components has, in some cases, been reduced by up to 95 percent. And improved flow and a better layout have reduced overtime and shop floor injuries.[18] The same approach that is used to build the 737 is now being applied to the popular 777, a twin-aisle plane that is larger, more expensive, and more profitable than the 737.

MOONSHINE, ANYONE?

Chapter 7 addressed the importance of pursuing lean improvements by tapping into the creative skills of employees. At Boeing most of the tangible changes to support lean have been developed by teams of home-grown employees who are part of something called *moonshine shops*. These shops invent new equipment and methods that are essential to the company's lean vision.

According to Boeing managers, the Japanese first coined the term moonshine shop. During their visits to the United States after World War II, the Japanese noticed that people in the Appalachian region could make alcohol from stills made out of spare items such as refrigerator coils and old steel drums. These ingenious stills made a product with very little, if any, investment. In Japanese plants the term has come to mean low cost, right size, innovative, and requires no money.[19]

Boeing's moonshine shops include design engineers, maintenance technicians, electricians, machinists, and operators. Team members are known for their problem-solving skills and ability to think outside the box. They work to create new innovations, such as scaling down massive pieces of machinery and material handling equipment to improve the fabrication and assembly process.

Innovations developed by these shops include the equipment that powers the moving assembly line and an array of lower cost, smaller machines, such as drill machines and portable routers that support smaller lot sizes. Not only does this modified equipment support faster setups and smaller production runs, the smaller equipment also alters the financial investment structure underlying aircraft assembly. Another innovation is the development of a conveyor loader that carries seats up into the fuselage for installation. This loader is similar to a conveyor that moves baled hay into a farm barn. A job that previously required hours to perform now only requires 25 minutes.[20] This attention to even the smallest innovation is no doubt a contributing factor behind Boeing's lean success.

THE DEFENSE SIDE OF THE BUSINESS

Boeing is a company that is made up of different business units, the two largest of which are the commercial airplane group and integrated defense systems (IDS). While the commercial group has received the most publicity about its lean efforts, this does not mean the defense side has been sitting idly. This side of Boeing tends to be a bit lower key regarding its activities.[21] The following highlights some success stories on the defense side of the business.

Since 1998, the plant that assembles the AH-64D Apache combat helicopter has used a pulse assembly line to help realize over a 50 percent reduction in the hours required to build a helicopter. A pulse line is one that moves forward at regular intervals rather than at a constant rate. By relying on lean tactics, the area required to support construction of a Delta IV rocket shrank from a planned 4 million square feet to 1.5 million square feet, and multiple assembly areas were replaced with a single moving line.

One of Boeing's most impressive lean accomplishments involves improvements in the F/A-18 Super Hornet program. Process improvements that focused on lean resulted in a lower cycle time for engineering changes from 35 days to 6 days, lower rework costs by 60 percent, and 75-90 percent fewer defects per plane. Deliveries are always on or ahead of contract delivery dates, and the price of each plane has actually declined! The latest version of the Super Hornet has fewer parts than previous models. Fewer parts mean fewer suppliers, lower costs, higher reliability, less movement and handling, less inventory, less internal and external supply chain complexity, and, of course, less waste.

THE NEXT GENERATION OF LEAN

Each initiative just described, while impressive in its own right, will pale in comparison to one of the most significant revolutions in the design, sourcing, and assembly of commercial aircraft—the Boeing 787 Dreamliner. One thing the Dreamliner project will never be called is *evolutionary*. This revolutionary new plane, which will likely be in production for the next 30 years, is already changing the way that aerospace companies design, source, and assemble airplanes. It is also going through its fair share of development pains.

Anyone who has followed the Dreamliner story is probably familiar with the features that make this plane revolutionary. The 787 will feature a fuselage made of lighterweight composites, entire systems designed and built by suppliers, a new generation of efficient engines, enhanced climate control systems, interiors that are designed, at long last, with the comfort of the passenger in mind, a platform design that will support a short-, medium-, and long-range version of the plane, and advanced avionics that will push technology boundaries.

Perhaps just as revolutionary is the way that Boeing plans to receive materials and systems from its worldwide suppliers, as well as the way the company plans to assemble the 787. Specially modified 747s are already available that pick up major systems and assemblies from around the world, such as fuselage sections in Japan or wing assemblies from South Carolina, and deliver them directly to Boeing's production facility in Everett, Washington, on a JIT basis.

Upon receipt of these systems or modules, one of the most ambitious parts of the 787 program takes over. Instead of assembling a plane with millions of components and assemblies over multiple weeks, the plan is to piece together giant modules, sections, and systems in three days. If this assembly time is achieved, it will result in the most aggressive build schedule of any twin-aisle plane in aviation history.

Boeing's extensive use of suppliers for designing and building entire modules or systems, while new to the aerospace industry, has been practiced in other industries for some time (admittedly on a less complex product). Chrysler has a number of vehicles that are composed of large-scale modules or systems that are designed and provided by suppliers. General Electric relies on various systems when designing and building locomotives. This illustrates once again that most principles that align with lean are transferable across industries.

While the Dreamliner remains a challenging work in process, and at the time of this writing Boeing has announced several slippages from its original launch date and production schedule, there is no question that this plane is pushing not only the boundaries of design and assembly, but also the boundaries of how global supply chains are managed in the aerospace industry. Compared with other major industries, there is not much going on that displays such a bold disregard for the restraints imposed by industry convention and practice as the Dreamliner program.

SUPPLIERS ARE PART OF THE LEAN VISION

A lean supply chain means that companies must move beyond simply pursuing lean within internal operations. As with most companies, Boeing began its lean journey with a keen eye on its own operations. But how the times have changed! Boeing now relies on suppliers for increasing amounts of value add like never before in its history. Like most companies, Boeing has taken a close look at where it sees its greatest contribution and, in more cases than not, company executives have concluded that contribution no longer includes fabricating parts or even complex assemblies such as fuselages. In the words of one aviation expert, both Airbus and Boeing are evolving into giant global, concurrent engineering task forces that also manage final assembly lines while subassembly manufacturing, the development of metal or composite materials, and systems design become the responsibility of risk-sharing partners.[22] The bottom line is that suppliers are a major contributor to Boeing's success.

Boeing knows that the capacity of its business is a function of the capacity and capability of its suppliers. The company now works closer than ever before with suppliers it calls *global partners,* even going so far as to create the executive position of Vice President of Global Partners. Boeing has also committed significant resources to improving supplier performance by sending cadres of lean specialists to work with suppliers to improve their lean capabilities, many of whom are assigned to the Dreamliner program. And in a major investment in trying to develop a common set of best practices, Boeing has created its intensive Supplier Management University program. This program is designed to create a learning environment where those personnel who work with suppliers become familiar with a set of best supplier management practices, understand how to apply those practices, and share experiences with others from around the company.

CONCLUDING THOUGHTS

If we really think about it, it should not come as a surprise that Boeing is a leader in the application of lean techniques. Given this company's rich history in extending the boundaries of air and space, pushing some boundaries closer to earth should not be out of reach. Something that continues to evolve during Boeing's lean journey is management's realization that the company will never be truly lean until its supply chain is truly lean. We will hear a great deal more about Boeing's lean pursuits over the next 10 years.

ENDNOTES

1. This case is the result of conversations over the past five years with Boeing managers and from information extensively available in the public domain.

2. A. Karp, "Supply Chain Growing Pains Hit 787," *Airline Procurement* (October 2007): 3-4.

3. J. Anselmo, A. Velocci, and R. Wall, "Supply and Demand," *Aviation Week & Space Technology* 163, no. 23 (December 12, 2005): 28.

4. P. Arnold, "Boeing Knows Lean," *MRO Today*, http://www.mrotoday.com/mro/archives/Cover%20stories/BoeingFM2002.htm.

5. See note 4.

6. A. Cort, "Toeing the Line: To Survive in an Increasingly Competitive Market, Boeing has Completely Revamped the Way it Builds 737 Aircraft," *Assembly* 48 no. 9 (August 1, 2005), retrieved from http://global.factiva.com.

7. See note 4.

8. M. Jenkins, "Getting Lean," *Boeing Frontiers* 01, no. 4 (August 2002), retrieved from http://www.boeing.com/news/frontiers/archive/2002/autgust/cover.html.

9. See note 6.

10. See note 4.

11. See note 6.

12. S. Angers, "A Lean Tail Tale," *Boeing Frontiers* 5, no. 4 (August 2006): 26-27, retrieved from http://www. Boeing.com.

13. See note 12, 27.

14. See note 6.

15. See note 6.

16. See note 8.

17. From http://www.boeing.com.

18. See note 6.

19. Arnold, "Boeing Knows Lean." *MRO Today,* See note 4.

20. See note 6.

21. The defense examples presented here are reported in note 6.

22. P. Sparaco, "Two Way Street," *Aviation Week & Space Technology* 165, no. 21 (November 27, 2006): 68.

BEAM ME UP, SCOTTY

This lean application features a company that has developed sophisticated processes to separate air into its component elements, primarily nitrogen, oxygen, and argon. It is also a story of a company that has mastered how to manage inventory remotely at thousands of customer locations. Air Products, a global producer of industrial gases and chemicals, serves customers in the technology, energy, healthcare, and industrial markets. With operations in over 30 countries and annual revenues exceeding $8 billion, the company promotes a culture of innovation, operational excellence, and commitment to safety and environmental awareness. This application will present lean innovation at its finest.[1]

The gases that Air Products produces pass through a sophisticated cryogenic (i.e., very low temperature) process to create liquid gas. These gases are then delivered in bulk truck carriers to on-site storage tanks at customer facilities. A major innovation at Air Products is the development and wide-scale use of a remote telemetry system to collect, store, and manage data about customer inventory levels and usage patterns. Data from customers are transmitted to the company on a regular basis, thereby allowing Air Products to manage remotely the gas levels at each customer's tank. This technology allows the company to provide an uninterrupted flow of gas to customer facilities.

The following describes how remote telemetry improves customer service and removes waste from the Air Products channel of distribution. It also shows how a company that essentially provides pure commodity products differentiates itself through value-added services.

LET'S LEARN MORE ABOUT TELEMETRY

Air Products has developed, and now markets a technology product called TELALERT, a telemetry system that supports efficient inventory management at customer locations. This system allows the company to monitor nitrogen, argon, and oxygen levels remotely at customer tanks. Hydrogen can also be monitored remotely, although it is a much more complex element to manage. While all the gases that Air Products sells are specialized cryogenic gases in a liquid state, perhaps the fact that hydrogen must be maintained at –423°F has something to do with the challenge of managing this unusual element.

Telemetry systems have existed for quite a while. Generally speaking, telemetry is the science or process of transmitting data using a telemeter, which is an electrical apparatus for measuring quantities and transmitting data to a distant station. At Air Products, telemetry units are physically attached to customer tanks to track liquid gas levels. Air Products has installed telemetry units at over 4800 tanks at 4000 U.S. customer locations. Some customers use more than one type of gas so they have multiple tanks, each requiring a telemetry device.

Besides improving customer service and removing the transactions costs associated with ordering and replenishing gases, the remote telemetry system allows Air Products to develop daily delivery schedules that employ advanced algorithms to optimize the company's distribution network. Anyone who understands the term *optimize* knows that an optimized system contains minimal, if any, waste. Chapter 1 argued that optimization should be a key objective of any lean supply chain.

The system featured here is primarily U.S.-based, although telemetry growth is now occurring in Western Europe. Air Products also has a fledgling remote telemetry operation in Asia. In Europe over 1000 tanks are centrally managed at Air Product's European headquarters, and this system is shifting from a technical perspective toward the U.S. system. This should provide further benefit as the company realizes the advantages of global standardization, another important objective of a lean supply chain. Inconsistent land-line capabilities, wireless communication that is not yet practical for transmitting remote telemetry data, and the need to complete a companywide enterprise resource planning (ERP) installation before taking on additional capital projects have slowed the use of sensing technology within Asia.

The remote sensing system at Air Products is conceptually straightforward. A telemetry communications server (TCS) regularly dials and polls the telemetry units at each customer for current inventory readings. Should the sensor detect levels at or below the target-refill level, which generally indicates a day or two of supply remaining based on predetermined usage patterns, the remote telemetry unit (RTU) sends out an alarm.[2] At this point a signal is sent to a scheduling group

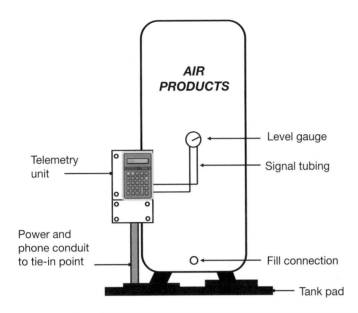

Figure 14.1 Air Products telemetry system

at Air Products and a replenishment delivery is automatically scheduled. Data provided by these units allow Air Products to offer vendor managed inventory services with a pledge of no gas interruptions to customer facilities. This system also allows Air Products to optimize its gas delivery network. Figure 14.1 illustrates the tank and telemetry unit.

Telemetry units only measure tank levels and not operating performance. At one time Air Products collected performance information but determined that since the tanks are relatively simple in design with high reliability, the data were of minimal value. Continuing to collect unnecessary performance data contributed to digital waste.

The customers that benefit from remote telemetry are the middle segment of the U.S. gas market. Some customers purchase gas in canisters (a segment that Air Products has exited), some have on-site tanks with telemetry units attached (the focus of this chapter), and some larger customers have their own on-site Air Products plant that feeds gas directly into their operations (such as the steel industry). This middle segment relies on storage tanks with variable sizes and capacity that are meant to match the customer's usage requirements. Numerical models are used to identify the optimal tank size that a customer requires. The largest available tank stores 11,000 gallons.

Air Products estimates that it installs 50 new storage tanks a month within the United States while 35 a month become inactive, usually because a customer exits a business or no longer requires the gas. Air Products has assembled a team that is responsible for designing, installing, calibrating, and maintaining the telemetry system. Another group is responsible for maintaining and repairing the equipment at customer locations. These services further simplify the buying process for customers by making it seamless and transparent.

Turnover from one gas provider to another is low, and customers usually rely on a single supplier for their requirements. It is customary to sign five-year supply agreements when installing a tank and telemetry unit. The company that wins the customer's heart usually remains that customer's single source indefinitely. In the customer's mind the physical gas is a commodity, and winning customers results more from factors such as total cost, ease of ordering and product use, delivery reliability, service, and product availability.

Remote telemetry is not a stand-alone system, meaning that a successful telemetry system supports other groups that are integral to the Air Products supply chain. Two such groups include delivery scheduling and field service. While only 10 percent of a field service technician's time is committed to telemetry systems, customer response rates when field services are required is an essential part of the company's total product package. Part of the telemetry manager's job is to predict field maintenance needs and then work with technicians to ensure that a proper mix of telemetry items are available on a service truck.

A dedicated group is assigned responsibility for managing the telemetry system. This group, which is not the same one that schedules daily gas deliveries, manages the costs associated with operating the system. These costs fall primarily into one of four buckets, including (1) the telemetry group's overhead costs, (2) field hardware costs and depreciation, (3) hardware maintenance at the customers' tanks, and (4) communications expenses. Customers pay the fixed cost of a telephone landline while Air Products pays for incoming calls. Air Products also assumes the charges for the 600 customers who transmit their telemetry data via a wireless system.

The telemetry group also assumes responsibility for some aspects of customer service. The group receives a regular report, for example, about any remote units that are not forwarding data. This helps the telemetry group follow up with customers to determine if there are issues the customer can resolve before dispatching a field technician.

THE AIR PRODUCTS DELIVERY SYSTEM

Air Products has established 34 coast-to-coast terminals where gases are produced and tanker trucks fill up. The terminals, called *Independent Business Units* (IBUs), are regional businesses with very different economics that are a function of competition, operations, and distribution. Determining where to place the IBUs has historically been a function of two major considerations: (1) energy costs and (2) geographic proximity to customers. While beyond the scope of this discussion, the determination of how many IBUs to maintain and where to place them greatly affects operations and distribution. Tanker trucks will cross their geographic IBU lines to ensure access to supply or to make needed deliveries if necessary, but that often results in increased distribution costs. Like many firms, a shortage of qualified drivers and hours of service regulations remain a concern.

Gas companies will also buy products from each other, an arrangement that helps ensure supply in periods of unusual demand or when supply issues occur internally. This also points out the commodity nature of gas products and the importance of taking steps to ensure that the promise of uninterrupted supplies to customers is more than marketing hype. Joint plants between gas providers have also been built when it makes economic sense.

At customer sites, inventory levels are managed by what the company calls a dynamic target-refill system. This is a computer-generated inventory target that considers parameters such as the type of gas, a customer's distance from a terminal, customer usage, and the size of the storage tanks. If a customer has multiple tanks for the same gas, each tank has a separate reader. A software program combines the inventory volumes to provide an overall view of the customer's stocking level. This reduces the effort of manually combining quantities for the same gas.

Air Products relies on a centralized logistics operation to manage the gas replenishment process on a day-to-day basis. This group evaluates itself against two primary objectives: (1) how well it optimizes payloads and (2) its performance at not interrupting operations at customer sites. Optimizing payload is especially critical since freight charges are embedded in the gas price. These twin objectives, optimizing payload and noninterrupted supply, underlie the business model behind the remote telemetry system.

A scheduling group at corporate headquarters has responsibility for developing a daily delivery schedule. An automated system generates a delivery list for the next 12 hours, a route optimizer tweaks the schedule, and drivers work the schedule after it is made available electronically. Drivers from around the U.S. log in daily to a computer network to view their scheduled trips, and then download this information to a handheld computer. The driver then plugs the handheld computer into an onboard truck computer, a process that establishes communications with corporate systems. As the drivers make their deliveries various data are forwarded to the corporate systems, including the amount of gas delivered and each driver's hours of service data. Data from tens of thousand deliveries each month are forwarded seamlessly to a central system. The drivers appreciate this system because it has eliminated paperwork. As data are received at the corporate server the forecast error rate for each customer is calculated. This calculation compares the actual tank level to the predicted level that was built into the system parameters.

The corporate system is updated at the end of each day. During the update the process identifies each driver's status as an available resource for the next schedule, forwards delivery information to a corporate group for billing and other updates, and reinitiates the system with the most current inventory data. The daily cycle then starts over again. Forecasts are updated whenever new data arrive and at least one full shift has occurred at the customer's location.

Continuous improvement is an important part of the company's philosophy, and this philosophy carries over to the telemetry and scheduling system. Every Friday the manager of North American logistics, an equipment manager, a global supply chain manager, the manager of remote telemetry, and other business representatives as required meet to review the performance of the telemetry and scheduling system. This group reviews problems that may have occurred during the week, such as system interruptions, attempts to identify the root causes for any problems, and determines what can be done to prevent problems from occurring in the future. These managers know that the relentless pursuit of perfection is essential to a lean supply chain.

REMOTE TELEMETRY SYSTEM DEVELOPMENT

In its earliest days of telemetry Air Products manufactured its own electronics. Its original telemetry system relied on landline communications with each individual terminal receiving data over teletype machines. Each business unit had responsibility for developing manual schedules. Today, the company is much more focused on its core businesses with suppliers supporting its electronic needs. In other words, Air Products is no longer in the business of manufacturing electronic components.

The early 1990s began the transformation toward the current remote telemetry system. At that time senior management commissioned a reengineering project of the telemetry system. The new telemetry model was to provide a radically different set of applications compared with the previous system. It would create forecasts, collect data, and schedule delivery trips for each customer from a central corporate location.

Part of this reengineering effort was to get customers to commit to the telemetry and automated inventory management system. Corporate policy is that all new customers are part of the telemetry system. The customer is responsible for providing power and a phone line, which can be an issue in remote areas. A small percentage of customers still operate on a manual reordering system.

This reengineering project brought the current technology to bear. Air Products closed all the regional/terminal scheduling operations over a several-year period. As mentioned, 100 people working out of a central corporate location perform work that previously required 200 people. The new system required a capital outlay of $6.5 million, and a financial assessment of the system by the telemetry group validated the business model for remote telemetry.

The system that resulted from this reengineering effort contains two major pieces: (1) hardware and (2) software. During the move to telemetry in the mid-1990s, the company used a supplier called Clover System, which is now called Data Online, to provide the remote telemetry units (RTUs). Since the completion of its telemetry reengineering project, Air Products has market tested its hardware requirements, which essentially involves checking what is available on the market. This market test resulted in a 40 percent cost reduction per unit from its current hardware supplier. The software that supports the system was developed by a Canadian company called TCS. This software has been customized to meet some unique requirements at Air Products.

Interestingly, during the company's effort to determine if better hardware prices were available, Air Products was able to eliminate a fair amount of technical complexity without any negative performance effects. This supports an important lean objective called *simplification*. Preparations for the market test revealed that the team that launched the reengineered telemetry system erred on the side of complexity during system design.

Since Air Products sells the system as having uninterrupted data polling availability, designers knew that some redundancy had to be built into the system. The system is configured as a fault-tolerant, hot-backup arrangement with dual systems continually monitoring each other 24 hours a day, 365 days per year. If the designated primary system fails, the secondary system takes over the primary role and carries out the necessary actions for reading the customer's tank. This part of the process is seamless to the customer.

Even though the telemetry technology is relatively mature, Air Products continually tries to improve the system or expand its reach. The design of the telemetry system is robust in that it can use hardware from different providers, making hardware switching costs relatively low. Recently, a Swiss company developed a lower cost ($300) measurement device for tanks that now has become the industry standard. Several years ago Air Products implemented a better way to identify customer demand changes, thereby allowing the inventory management system to become more sensitive to changes at the customer level. This has resulted in a large decrease in customers running out of inventory, which means more satisfied customers due to better gas availability.

NOW THE GOOD STUFF—REMOTE TELEMETRY BENEFITS

One way to appreciate how remote telemetry improves supply chain performance is to think about the system from two perspectives: (1) the provider's perspective and (2) the customer's perspective. Air Products separates the telemetry benefits that accrue to the provider and the customer into four major categories:

1. Operational benefits resulting from the elimination of emergency production and shipments, better management of daily deliveries, and the ability of Air Products customers to better serve their customers

2. Balance sheet benefits resulting from lower working capital requirements due to reduced average inventory, and improved customer asset return, such as return on assets (ROA), due to a lower capital asset base from leasing rather than owning tanks

3. Increased revenue benefits resulting from increased customer retention, an increase in single source contracts, and providing a differentiating service to customers

4. Intangible benefits resulting from the creation of integrated linkages with customers and the ability to analyze vast amounts of customer usage data

Another way to appreciate the value of a remote telemetry system is to think about what the world looked like under pretelemetry days. In the good old days every terminal was an independent entity with a large, decentralized staff that relied on large spreadsheets and predictive models that were not backed up by any field hardware or timely data. In the mid- to late 1980s, Air Products relied on a mainframe system called *Leader* that required manual inputs of data to predict usage and need. Furthermore, the workforce that managed delivery requirements was spread around the country. Today, the scheduling group resides in a centralized location in eastern Pennsylvania and about 100 people now perform work that previously required over 200 people. These 100 people also do a better job at scheduling and optimizing the delivery network compared with a decentralized approach.

The scheduling system that pulls in the telemetry data only replenishes a storage tank when a pull signal is received from a customer's tank. Corporate managers believe that relying on a system that results in drastically reduced product interruptions is a differentiating factor that separates Air Products from other providers. The capabilities that a telemetry system provides help win customer accounts.

Another benefit of reliable data is that Air Products can now allow its customers' gas levels to move lower before scheduling a delivery. This is similar to a company that can reduce its minimum stocking levels due to better forecasting and usage data. The net result is a need to fill a customer's tank less frequently, which leads to delivery savings and lower average inventory levels for the customer.

A simple example will illustrate the benefit of lower average inventory levels. Let's assume a customer has a 3000-gallon tank for storing liquid gas. Because of incomplete data about actual inventory levels and usage, refilling is scheduled whenever the tank is forecasted to be at 600 gallons. Inventory planners assume this level will provide an adequate margin of safety to compensate for the lack of actual data. The average inventory level for the customer is estimated to be 1800 gallons ((3000 + 600)/2) over each replenishment cycle. Now, let's say that due to real-time data about inventory levels the tank is now scheduled for replenishment when it actually has 250 gallons remaining, a level that represents several days' worth of demand. The average inventory level at the customer's tank is now 1625 ((3000 + 250)/2). Air Products estimates that reductions in average inventory levels resulting from the telemetry system can be anywhere from 10 to 60 percent. Unnecessarily high inventory levels have always been one of the most visible results of supply chain waste.

The benefits from lower tank levels also accrue to Air Products. Assume that on average each time the delivery truck arrives it delivers 2400 gallons (3000 − 600). Let's further assume that the truck makes two such deliveries a month. Over the course of a year the truck will make 24 deliveries involving 57,600 total gallons. As minimum tank levels decrease to 250 gallons, each delivery now consists of 2750 gallons. If we continue to use 57,600 gallons as the total amount of gas delivered over the year, Air Products now must only make 21 deliveries. Surely the costs savings that result from making three or four fewer deliveries a year across 4000 customer locations is significant.

The telemetry manager is accountable for some operational measures. Two such measures include the mean time between gross failures (at a customer tank) and the mean time between unplanned service calls. Also, the telemetry manager also tracks the mean time between repairs, run outs (customer running out of gas), on-time delivery to customers, and the percent of time that Air Products gets at least one data read from each tank in a 21-hour period. All performance measures have shown consistent improvement since the launch of the telemetry system.

Customers also experience benefits that clearly reflect the value of remote telemetry. In exchange for being the customer's exclusive supplier, Air Products leases the customer station (i.e., equipment) to the customer. This allows customers to reduce their capital equipment costs and asset base, a financial arrangement that has the likely effect of improving the customer's return on net assets (RONA). Finance managers must surely be feeling the love here.

Customers also benefit from having a third-party assume responsibility for managing their inventory investment. Replenishments are seamless, and removing transactions costs further enhances the benefits from telemetry. As mentioned, improvements to working capital are also being realized as actual data allows tank levels to become lower before scheduling replenishment. And, of course, the peace of mind that comes from an uninterrupted supply of gas should not be discounted. While customers viewed this system as a radical innovation at the time of its introduction, they now take comfort in how routine it has become.

WHAT'S NEXT?

Air Products managers readily admit that, in general, remote telemetry is a mature technology. As one Air Products manager maintains, "This always raises the question of what the next radical development will be in this area." While this is a legitimate concern, the current system still offers new possibilities and opportunities for growth.

For companies that have never seen remote sensing technology in action, this technology will still have the wow factor. Air Products is leveraging its knowledge of telemetry to new industries. These new segments include helium fill services, remote monitoring of food freezers, and inventory management within the chemical business. A seemingly mature technology may still have a few tricks up its sleeve.

A shift from landline to wireless communications should become more common as wireless networks improve. Wireless technology offers an opportunity to install telemetry units at customer locations that lack practical landline capabilities. The telemetry group at Air Products has been disappointed in the cost and lack of flexibility of wireless communication.

Many Air Products customers around the world are not yet part of a telemetry system. The opportunity to expand telemetry from primarily a regional model to a worldwide model offers attractive possibilities, particularly as the infrastructures of some of these regions become more established (think about China).

The knowledge gained from vendor managed inventory and telemetry has resulted in a joint venture between Air Products and nPhase. This joint venture, called Skychain (http://www.skychain.com), addresses the need to optimize supply chain performance in the chemicals, fuels, and other related industries. An internal system that started out as a way to capture real-time data remotely has evolved into an exciting opportunity to provide a fully integrated, automatic product replenishment system across a wide range of industries.

Air Products and nPhase expect to offer a way to seamlessly integrate into a full-service package all the components of an automatic replenishment program. These components include the tank, telemetry hardware, wireless communications, the back-end server and systems, vendor managed inventory software that works with existing ERP systems, and professional services based on years of internal experience. We don't often hear about lean initiatives leading directly to new business opportunities.

CONCLUDING THOUGHTS

The bottom line here is that remote telemetry helps ensure that a leading provider of industrial gases continues to provide exceptional customer service while removing costly waste from its supply chain. The end result of a delivery system built around remote telemetry is the timely replenishment of gases in a process that is transparent to the customer. This allows customers to focus on what they do best without worrying about supply disruptions. Remote telemetry also helps customers better manage their working capital and asset requirements while Air Products optimizes its distribution costs.

When your end product is a pure commodity, you better be good at differentiating yourself through services or else face a future at the lower end of the industrial food chain. In this case, vendor managed inventory that is supported by remote telemetry is helping to make a difference between winning and losing customer orders.

ENDNOTES

1. The author would like to thank David Burgess, Remote Telemetry Manager at Air Products, and his staff for their generous support during the writing of this case.

2. K. Chin, "Automate Inventory Management: This Telemetry System Reduces Chances of Failure When Tackling Tank Level Data," *Chemical Engineering*, 104, no. 11 (November 1997): 173.

15

LEAN IS ELECTRIFYING

This lean application features PPL Electric Utilities (PPL EU), a regulated electricity utility that serves 1.4 million customers in central and eastern Pennsylvania. While at first glance this utility might not appear all that different from other utilities, PPL EU does something that no one else in the United States can do. It is this uniqueness that motivates groups from around the country to venture to Pennsylvania to see the light.

What is so unique here? PPL EU is the only regulated utility in the United States to have installed automated meter readers (AMRs) on *100 percent of its commercial and residential accounts.* Besides the obvious savings associated with eliminating manual meter reading, every day the utility becomes better at leveraging the data provided by this system to remove costs and waste from its electrical delivery system while improving customer service. The Utility Planning Network, an association of energy company professionals, recently awarded PPL EU with its *Best Metering Data Integration Initiative* award, an award that recognizes the best use of electric meter data for the benefit of consumers. Let's learn more about automated meter reading and how it contributes to lean distribution.[1]

AUTOMATED METER READING

In 2001, PPL EU's executive management took an unprecedented step and approved the largest nonpower generating project in the company's history. The automated meter reading system, a capital project with a $163 million budget, had the lofty goal of capturing electrical usage data remotely at 100 percent of the utility's customers.

Company executives quickly established a cross-functional team, staffed with 13 full-time, co-located team members to develop and roll out the AMR system. The team included representatives from customer service, field service, rate making, market research, and information technology. Oversight of the project was handled at the highest level with the team leader reporting directly to an executive steering committee chaired by PPL EU's president.

Three objectives underlie the automated meter reading system:

1. The system is a way for the utility to reduce costs and eliminate waste. For a company that needs permission from regulators to raise rates, any system that eliminates waste and reduces costs enhances the bottom line.
2. The system is a primary catalyst for improving customer service, a subject that is discussed later.
3. The system will help position the company to better support its customers when the state of Pennsylvania removes rate caps in 2010. At that time utilities will have rate-making flexibility, and it is expected that customers will need data to better manage their electricity usage as electric rates increase.

When looking at PPL EU's automated meter reading it is important to recognize that two separate systems are at work here: one system for residential customers and one for industrial customers. During project design the development team forwarded Requests for Information (RFIs) to 10 suppliers, and after detailed analysis six suppliers were invited to submit formal proposals through a Request for Proposal (RFP) process. The project eventually selected Comverge and Distribution Control Systems, Inc. (DCSI), a St. Louis-based company, to provide the software and hardware that would make 100 percent meter reading a reality.

Over 99 percent of the automated meters at PPL EU use a two-way automated communication system (TWACS) developed by DCSI. The supplier worked with PPL EU to develop the software and hardware systems required to transmit data from residential customers over power lines to a utility substation, and then to a phone line that forwards the data to a PPL EU server where the data are processed to render a monthly bill for each customer. The utility, working with its supply partners, established a telecommunications system that works in an urban, suburban, and rural setting. Figure 15.1 illustrates the AMR system that PPL EU uses to read and transmit data from residential customers.

While supporting some smaller scale applications, DCSI had never undertaken a make or break project like this one—a project that pushed the technology boundaries at DCSI and at PPL EU. Remote meter reading has been in use for some time at smaller electricity co-ops that cannot justify manual meter reading

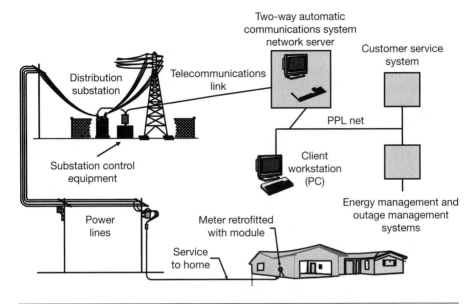

Figure 15.1 PPL EU automated meter reading system for residential customers. *Source:* PPL (used with company permission)

or were too rural to allow easy access to meter reading. PPL EU's AMR system was the first time this technology was applied on such a large scale.

Comverge, a software company based in New Jersey, supports the AMR system used for commercial customers that receive electric service at 480 volts and higher. The communication technology that PPL EU applies to commercial customers relies on cellular communication rather than landline communication. Comverge's AMR solution features cellular digital packet data (CDPD) with each meter at a commercial customer being equipped with cellular radios that tie into cellular transmitting towers. Cellular towers transmit data directly back and forth using a technology called PowerCAMP, which is Comverge's version of the AMR system. As with the TWACS used to collect data from residential customers, the data collected by PowerCamp are then processed to produce monthly bills for commercial customers.

The complexity of the AMR project demanded that the two suppliers work closely with PPL EU during development. DCSI located five people on-site to work directly with the PPL EU team, and Comverge, which is located not far from the utility's headquarters, also provided extensive personnel support as needed. This interaction between the suppliers and the customer, something that more firms must pursue if they expect to develop truly lean supply chains, was critical to project success.

At the heart of the AMR system is extensive two-way communication between the utility and its customers. Two-way communication means PPL EU can send inquiries to residential and industrial meters and receive information back from the meters. On a monthly basis PPL EU's Customer Information System requests a reading of 100 percent of the utility's meters, sends out a read signal, and receives back the reading on the meter (similar to an odometer reading on a vehicle). The data are then forwarded directly to the company's billing system as well as to a host of other systems that use these data. A manually intensive process that required days to complete, and was far from totally accurate, is now performed quickly and seamlessly with near-perfect accuracy.

PPL EU relied on the field infrastructure it already had in place to support the AMR system for residential customers, including the 313 substations where electrical and telecommunications lines converge to transfer and move data. As Figure 15.1 indicates, upon receipt at a corporate server the data are shared with many other PPL EU systems.

Prior to the full-scale launch PPL EU conducted an extensive pilot test. This test was conceptually similar to a manufacturer that conducts a process proving study using the same equipment, procedures, and employees that are used during actual production. The objective was to determine if the AMR system, including the software, hardware, and infrastructure, was capable of performing as expected. PPL EU's pilot program involved 10,000 customers and four (out of 313) utility substations. The pilot program proved conclusively that the newly installed meters and system were ready for widespread rollout.

An important part of the project was the rollout plan that would minimize the impact of meter exchanges on customers. It would be a mistake to downplay the amount of work involved with exchanging every meter in PPL EU's system. Over a three-year period the utility switched almost 1.4 million meters using a third-party contractor (Sargent Electric), and at a steady state replaced 60,000 meters a month. While customers were formally notified that a conversion was going to take place, few customers experienced any disruption to their service. The process of removing old meters and installing an automated meter was transparent. Table 15.1 highlights the daily process followed when exchanging meters.

Most old meters were returned to the third-party contractor and retrofitted at $25 per unit, an activity that helped reduce project costs. Retrofitting involves transforming standard PPL EU meters to AMR meters by installing a module under the meter's glass that reads and stores meter data. To ensure the retrofitted meters performed as required, these meters were only reinstalled at residential locations following rigorous testing to verify their accuracy.

The following highlights some of the actions taken by the utility to manage the transition to AMRs:

Table 15.1 PPL's mass meter exchange process

Step 1	PPL EU sends a data file of meters that need to be changed daily to third-party contractor, Sargent Electric
Step 2	Sargent Electric schedules meter exchanges and loads the work schedule into handheld scanners
Step 3	The meter exchanger reports to a PPL EU service center each morning to pick up a handheld with that day's work schedule and AMR meters
Step 4	Meter exchangers complete the meter exchanges and bring removed meters back to the PPL EU service center
Step 5	The service center scraps or retrofits meters and uploads the meter exchange completion information from handhelds
Step 6	Sargent Electric sends meter exchange information from the previous day to PPL EU by 10:00 a.m.
Step 7	Change Meter Orders are automatically created by PPL EU between 10:00 a.m. and 3:00 p.m. for all successful meter exchanges

Source: Used with permission of PPL-EU.

- Customers received periodic notifications in their monthly bill insert indicating the scheduled areas for meter exchange as well as the purpose of the new system.
- Customer inquiries about AMR were directed to a specially established 1-888 number staffed by a separate group of customer service representatives.
- Answers for the most frequently asked questions were prepared to ensure consistency of responses from customer service representatives.
- A message was placed on each customer's door after a PPL EU contractor exchanged a meter. Green tags indicated that PPL EU was able to successfully exchange the meter, yellow tags indicated that PPL EU was unable to exchange the meter (with the reason why the exchange was unsuccessful noted on the tag), and red tags notified the customer that some property damage occurred while exchanging the meter along with what steps the customer should take.

It is difficult to envision a successful change that does not consider those who are most affected by the change. PPL EU engaged its union throughout the project to help manage the human side of this transformation. After all, the most obvious outcome from the new system was the 100 percent elimination of meter reading jobs along with reductions in field service and customer contact personnel. Affected employees (about 220 in total) were guaranteed early retirement packages or given assignments elsewhere within the company. Most of the displaced workers who remained with PPL EU, including displaced meter readers, servicemen, and customer contact representatives, received higher-paying jobs. Management established early on a memorandum of agreement with the local branch of the International Brotherhood of Electrical Workers (IBEW) that defined the outplacement process.

Upon project completion in October 2004, the full-time project team formally disbanded. At that time responsibility for managing the system was handed over to a group headed by a manager of AMR operations. This group is now responsible for working with PPL EU's internal IT group to explore new ways to enhance this system's capabilities.

THE ROLE OF THE INFORMATION TECHNOLOGY GROUP

It should be obvious by now that the AMR system would not have become a reality without extensive IT support internally and from suppliers. PPL EU has strong IT capabilities, and this was certainly called upon during project development. PPL EU's IT group, besides playing an integral part in evaluating the technical capabilities of the suppliers that responded to the RFIs and RFPs, was responsible for creating the many software interfaces between PPL EU's systems and the software provided by the suppliers, thereby acting as a systems integrator. The IT group also had to manage two meter reading systems during the three-year rollout.

The architecture of the AMR information system, including its linkages to other PPL EU databases and systems is beyond the scope of this chapter. During systems development the project team, with the IT representatives taking a lead role, reviewed 200 separate processes and systems to identify those that would be impacted by the AMR system. In the end almost 70 areas were affected by the new system. It would be hard to exaggerate the importance of the IT group's efforts to project success.

AUTOMATED METER READING BENEFITS

The benefits from this system go far beyond a reduction in the meter reader head count. PPL EU has discovered, sometimes to its surprise that the AMR system provides a robust platform for supporting an expanding array of data applications. Interestingly, this system did not show a positive net return when first conceived since it considered only the elimination of manual meter readers as the primary costs savings.

Once the financial analysis factored in other benefits, the cash flow benefits from the AMR system became readily apparent. Almost all system benefits fall into one of four categories: (1) enhanced profitability from lower field service costs, (2) operational benefits from improved billing processes and results, (3) better outage management, or (4) benefits from using the system as a strategic data management platform. The following highlights some areas where PPL EU is reaping the benefit from its automated meter reading system.

For a variety of reasons (employee absences, inclement weather, blocked access, and less-than-cuddly dogs) humans read only about 94 percent of all meters each month. Meters that are not read manually result in estimated bills, a subject that often confuses customers when they receive their billing statement. At PPL EU, estimated bills equated to over 80,000 bills per month. The AMR system generates bills that are based almost entirely on actual readings.

A second issue is that humans have a meter reading accuracy level that is less than 100 percent, something that also creates waste for the utility. Depending on which digit of the meter is misread, this can lead to some interesting looking electrical bills. Both estimated and erroneous bills result in some portion of customers calling to ask about something that "does not look right." Customer service representatives must then take the time to research and resolve these issues. We also cannot discount the intangible cost of irate and confused customers.

The AMR system reads virtually 100 percent of PPL EU's customer meters each month, on the first try, with near-perfect accuracy. If a customer now inquires about a bill, a customer service representative can request and receive a meter reading while the customer is on the phone, answer any questions, and make adjustments to the customer's account. Since the launch of the system the decline in after-bill service calls and an increase in customer satisfaction have been quite welcome. AMR helps prevent problems rather than react to problems.

The AMR system also provides a monthly cash flow benefit. Previously, a four-day window existed for manually collecting meter data. Now, PPL EU is getting a first-day read for 95 percent of its meters instead of collecting data throughout the reading cycle. This allows PPL EU to bill customers sooner and shorten the bill-to-cash cycle time. The utility also encourages its customer to pay on-line, which further streamlines the billing and payment process.

PPL EU has also seen a dramatic reduction in the number of work orders generated by its work flow manager system. Many automated work orders generated by this system, which are referred to internally as WFMs (pronounced *woof-ums*), relate to billing issues identified by the system. PPL EU's Customer Contact Center is then responsible for resolving these WFMs, which can consume some serious staff time. In 2003, PPL EU was the lucky recipient of 41,000 WFMs. The system now generates around 17,000 WFMs annually. An impressive amount of customer service staff time is no longer spent investigating *woof-ums*.

The AMR system can also issue a work order for nonresponding meters. If a *ping* to a meter does not generate a response, a service technician, working from a system-generated work order, will investigate the problem with the meter. Technicians can resolve problems even before a customer becomes aware that a problem might exist.

Another tangible benefit is better utilization of expensive field service technicians. Previously, any time electrical service was disconnected or reconnected, which is a common occurrence as people move in and out of residences, a service technician visited the location to read the meter. On the list of value-adding activities for service technicians this one does not rate too highly, if at all. The automated meter reading system has eliminated the need to make thousands of these service calls annually.

The creative minds at PPL EU use system data in ways that are far removed from generating accurate and timely electric bills. The AMR system can determine, for example, if a meter has been physically tampered with, a feature that helps deter electricity theft and addresses an ongoing challenge faced by utilities. PPL EU also receives information about momentary electrical outages to a meter that last less than a second. These momentary outages can be an indication of a larger problem looming.

This system can also determine if a specific location has electrical power. Starting in 2007, the IT group linked the AMR system to PPL EU's outage management system. PPL EU can now analyze data to see if a pattern emerges to help service crews identify more quickly the location of electrical problems. This often leads to a faster service restoration. The system can also tell if customers have power after repairs have been made, thereby eliminating the need to manually inquire by phone about a customer's service status. PPL EU eventually plans to install computer terminals in its service vehicles that link directly to the company's outage management system.

A visible outcome due partly to this system is a reduction in the number of customer complaints about PPL EU received by the Pennsylvania Public Utilities Commission (PPUC). In 2003, the PPUC recorded 1983 complaints about the utility, and by 2006 that number had dropped to 875. Managers attribute a large part of this drop to better customer service supported by the AMR system. While hard to quantify, who can argue against the benefit of fewer customers complaining to the regulatory commission that oversees your operations?

THE LESSONS LEARNED

It would be a shame to undertake a project of this magnitude and not walk away with some valuable lessons learned. The following presents these lessons, which can easily apply to any lean transformation project.

The first lesson involves managing all aspects of the project. Development teams should use rigorous project management tools to manage the project from conception to completion. Furthermore, even when relying on third parties to support a project, it is essential to maintain appropriate control over their activities.

A second lesson is to ensure the project is adequately staffed. This means ensuring that team members have the necessary skills and time to commit to the project. It also means identifying the support resources that the team can call upon as required.

Third, it is essential the project team establishes metrics to verify that the benefits promised by the project are being realized. This was especially important here since the initial capital investment business case for this project did not indicate a positive net present value. Furthermore, a change of this magnitude will always have detractors that resist the change.

A fourth lesson is to develop contingency plans for those employees affected by outsourced or displaced work. Meter readers were invited to be part of the meter exchange program, and then were reassigned to other areas after the project was completed.

Fifth, project leaders learned it is a good practice to engage business owners early and often. This involves regular communication with executive management, affected functional groups, and union representatives.

Finally, the experience of this project reinforced the view in the minds of PPL EU's leaders that pursuing lean initiatives often yields benefits not readily seen (much less quantified) at the outset. In this case, the strategy of deploying AMRs was aimed primarily at improving the accuracy of the meter reading function while simultaneously reducing its costs—in keeping with lean principles. But a longer-range benefit of enabling broader business capabilities soon emerged—a benefit that now seems poised to more than justify the project in terms of return on investment. And this newfound benefit would never have been realized if lean was not a driving principle at PPL EU.

WHERE TO NEXT?

PPL EU managers estimate that on a scale of 1 to 10, the utility scores around a "4" in terms of fully exploiting its AMR data. Managers expect to leverage the data obtained from the automated system in ways that are far removed from the original vision of reading a meter for billing. In fact, the term automated meter reading and its system has been replaced by the term advanced metering infrastructure (AMI) at PPL EU.

As program managers look toward the future they increasingly think about something called meter data management (MDM), a process that uses data from the automated system to support two broad application areas: (1) operational efficiency solutions designed to improve the utility's overall performance and (2) multichannel customer solutions designed to allow individual customers to better manage their energy use. Within the operational efficiency arena, PPL EU expects to improve its visibility in four key areas: (1) demand, to support forecasting; (2) wire, to support distribution planning and operations; (3) bill, to support complex retail and wholesale billing; and (4) revenue, to support revenue projections. Within the customer solution arena, leveraging archived data will allow customers to access their service history on-line, obtain service usage detail, analyze their bills, and develop personalized energy consumption strategies that best meet their needs.

The AMR system can now collect meter readings every 15 minutes. These data help customers understand their usage patterns and will eventually identify the most cost-effective time-of-use rates. This information is now available on PPL EU's website through software developed by a company called Nexus. Customers will be able to identify the rate that is most advantageous given their demand profile—a capability that should become more popular after rate caps are removed in 2010. PPL EU also envisions that someday customers will use a web browser to turn power on and off to individual parts of their home.

CONCLUDING THOUGHTS

Automated meter reading has changed dramatically the way that PPL EU manages it network for delivering electricity. Perhaps more importantly, however, the system provides an ideal platform for creating innovative ways to use IT to reduce waste, improve service, and ensure the utility remains a leader in the electrical power generation industry. In reality, it won't be long before most electric utilities begin their own transformation to automated meter reading systems. We could make the argument that PPL EU's AMR project was a giant pilot test for the rest of the electric utility industry. PPL EU has proven the system's viability, and executive managers at other utilities would have to be oblivious not to recognize the advantages that an AMR system offers. Furthermore, the supply base that supports the AMR technology has also evolved to a higher capability level because of this project.

The linkage between automated meter reading and lean distribution—in this case PPL EU's ability to deliver electricity and improve customer service—is not escaping the notice of others. In fact, Forbes magazine recently named PPL, the parent company of PPL Electric Utilities, the best-managed electricity company in the United States.

ENDNOTE

1. The author would like to thank Michael Godorov, Manager—AMI Operations and Michael Weed, Lead Integrator—Information Solutions at PPL for their generous sharing of time and information when crafting this case, particularly during numerous requests for follow-up information.

16

YOU'RE CHOKING ME![1]

Barax Corporation, a producer of OEM equipment used in the transportation industry, maintains an inventory of several hundred thousand part numbers to support the spare parts requirements of its dealer network.[2] The company faces a challenge that is a mixed blessing—its business has grown to the point where it is having difficulty managing the flow of material from suppliers into its central distribution facility. While most of the facility can handle the increased volumes, the receiving process is proving to be a serious bottleneck that is impeding the flow of parts through the supply chain.

This lean application reveals how a choke point at a critical supply chain location can adversely affect a company's operations. The chapter first presents an overview of the receiving process, followed by a discussion of why this process is not lean. The chapter concludes with innovative ideas that should make this process more effective.

THE CURRENT RECEIVING PROCESS

The national facility featured here is a central part of Barax's supply chain—it manages the forwarding of spare parts to an entire network of regional distribution facilities, which are then responsible for shipping orders to dealers. When the receiving area backs up it begins to choke the flow of material to all downstream work centers and facilities, eventually affecting product availability to customers.

The receiving area has eight inbound lines that are used to process full truckloads of material received from suppliers. The facility currently receives an average of 24 full truckloads per day. Less-than-truckload (LTL) shipments are received in another area and are not part of this analysis. The LTL receiving area is usually not a constraint. Because of brick and mortar constraints, the facility's receiving area cannot be expanded and new dock doors cannot be added. Also, material handling and outbound volume constraints prohibit the unloading of inbound trucks through the outbound shipping doors.

The average receipt of 24 trailers a day is somewhat misleading. The beginning of each month usually features higher levels of material receipts, which taper off as the month progresses. At times the facility receives well more than the average number of trailers. At other times the facility may only receive 12 or 15 trailers a day. The flow of work into this facility is not at all balanced across a normal month. This directly counters the concept of level scheduling presented in Chapter 4.

Management is considering two options to better manage the processing of inbound truckloads, at least in the short term. The first option, and the one that is usually the first to come to mind when capacity is constrained, is to work overtime and add a second shift. The second option is to redesign the current receiving process and not add a second shift, except as a last resort. Some managers believe quite strongly that the current receiving process is too specialized and inefficient. They also feel it is a classic push environment since a material planning group located in another building orders material with minimal coordination with the central facility staff. As one manager commented, "Trucks just show up at the distribution center. Whether we can handle the workload or not doesn't seem to mean a thing. It's like ready or not here it comes. Besides the impact on customer service from not moving these trailers through our system quickly, at times we also face financial penalties for holding trailers too long."

Certain managers have been quite vocal about not wanting to add a second shift. Instead, they want to improve the material and processing flow before hiring new employees. These managers, some of whom are relatively new to the company, are willing to try some new ideas instead of holding on to the same set of processes and methods used to operate the central facility. In their view, why perpetuate inefficient practices across a second shift? And, if the downstream work centers in the central facility are not working a second shift, then what is the point of pushing material on them when they are not there to process it? This will simply shift the bottleneck(s) further downstream.

An internal study revealed the following sequential events and average times when physically receiving and processing an inbound trailer. Unfortunately, minimum and maximum times or the standard deviation for each step are not available, although that information would be valuable during an analysis of supply chain capacity and flow.

The following times apply to full truckloads only, and all times are averages per trailer. As mentioned, LTL shipments are handled within a separate process and are not part of this discussion.

- Common carrier trucks pass through a central entrance where a security guard logs in the trailer and directs the driver to a holding yard. The driver physically drops off the trailer in the holding yard, brings any documentation to the receiving office located next to the inbound docks, and then leaves the premises (20 minutes).

- Employee 1 (called the switcher) enters the receiving office to find out the next trailer to place in an open dock door. The switcher removes an empty trailer from a dock bay, takes it to the yard, retrieves the next full trailer from the yard, and places that trailer at a specific door (20 minutes).

- Employee 2 unloads the trailer with material handling equipment. The material is placed in a processing line directly behind the trailer (30 minutes).

- Employee 3 physically checks the load quantities against the shipping documents for accuracy and then takes the paperwork to the office for processing (30 minutes).

- Employee 4, working in the receiving office, acknowledges the receipt of material on a computer, which changes the material status from in-transit to received, and prints bar-coded control tickets to move the material to the required facility location (45 minutes). It is a corporate policy that any material entering the facility must have a move document or ticket attached to each load before it can be moved through the facility. This is done for control purposes.

- Employee 5 attaches bar-coded control tickets to individual loads. These tickets identify where to forward the material (30 minutes).

- Employee 6 performs a 100 percent inspection of inbound material for quality defects (30 minutes).

- Employee 7 transfers material from the inbound line to the automatic guided vehicle (AGV) station where the material is forwarded to the required facility location by a jitney or an AGV (30 minutes). On occasion the employee that unloaded the trailer will help move material from the inbound line. This line is now available to process another trailer.

- Employee 4 files the shipping documents and forwards copies to Accounts Payable (15 minutes).

These employees, except for the office worker, rotate across the inbound lines as needed. The average times include any time that is spent waiting for an employee to arrive at a line when needed.

If this lean application is being used as a learning exercise, then the following should be discussed:

1. Identify the specific reasons why the receiving process is not lean.
2. Calculate the *takt time* for receiving and unloading trailers given a daily demand of 24 trailers per day. Next, calculate the actual time to receive and process a trailer given the data provided.
3. Think about the current receiving process and generate a set of ideas that will improve the receiving and processing of inbound trailers.
4. Identify a set of metrics that management can use to evaluate the receiving process.
5. Redesign the process so it will increase the flow of material through receiving. Estimate the new receiving capacity.

WHY THIS PROCESS IS NOT LEAN

Determining exactly why this process is not lean might be a good place to start. Recommendations can then be made to redesign the process so it more closely resembles what we would expect from a supply chain that supports continuous material flow. At this point in the book it should be relatively easy to see why this facility is not even close to resembling a lean system.

It is evident this supply chain, at least the upstream portion of it, is a push environment. A material planning group that is disconnected from the receiving facility, physically, organizationally, and electronically, relies on forecasts to determine what and when to order. A lack of coordination and communication exists between the group that orders the material (the information side) and the group that receives the material (the physical side). One group makes decisions and pushes the consequences of those decisions onto another group.

The receiving process features each load being checked, and then checked again, usually with very little to show for all this activity. How much labor and time is wasted on inspection? A lean system focuses on the prevention of defects further upstream from the central facility.

An imbalance of incoming trailers throughout a typical month should also grab our attention. Overtime and undertime characterize this operation, resulting in waste as this facility fails to benefit from level scheduling. As a side note, this imbalance of shipments works its way downstream to the regional facilities. The regional facilities complain about receiving many trailers from the national center early in the month with a decrease as the month progresses.

The astute observer will also notice this process is far too sequential. Every task occurs one after another, thereby foregoing any benefits that might be realized from performing some tasks concurrently. The sequential nature of work is extending the time required to process a trailer, which affects throughput and capacity. Finally, the employees are far too specialized in their work. A lean supply chain features flexibility in all dimensions, including labor flexibility. Inflexibility constrains this process.

MAKING THE RECEIVING PROCESS LEAN

An important step in improving the receiving process is to understand its actual capacity. For many companies capacity is not thought about too much until there is not enough to meet normal demand. In this case business has grown to the point where the eight receiving lines, at least as the process is currently managed, are incapable of meeting expected receipt volumes. For simplicity we will use 24 trailers per day as our demand figure, although this number fluctuates throughout the month.

Because the steps in the receiving process are largely sequential, the throughput time per trailer will be a function of adding together each step's required time. The 20 minutes that are required for switching trailers could be done concurrently after a trailer is empty and the receiving line is processing the inbound loads. In reality, the trailer is often moved after the line is clear and ready for more material. Therefore, the 20 minute switching time will be included in the total processing time per receiving line. Recall that the times for each step are as follows:

Task	Average Time
Remove trailer from a dock bay and place a full trailer at a dock door	20 minutes
Unload the trailer with material handling equipment and place material in a processing line	30 minutes
Physically check the load quantities against the shipping documents for accuracy and take the paperwork to the office for processing	30 minutes
Acknowledge the receipt of material on a computer and print bar-coded control tickets	45 minutes
Attach bar-coded control tickets to individual loads	30 minutes
Perform a 100 percent inspection of inbound material for quality defects	30 minutes
Transfer material from the inbound line to the automatic guided vehicle (AGV) station	30 minutes
Total processing time per trailer	**215 minutes**

Eight inbound receiving lines are available for 7.5 hours of work a day, or a total of 3600 minutes of total processing time available (8 lines × 7.5 hours per line × 60 minutes per hour). Next, 3600 minutes divided by 215 minutes processing time per trailer means this facility can process about 17 trailers per day, on average. Unfortunately, this facility receives 24 trailers per day, on average, which explains why it works so much overtime and weekends. As mentioned, the situation is even worse early in the month but lessens later in the month, creating workforce inefficiencies.

The *takt* time calculation is also revealing. Recall from Chapter 4 that *takt* is a German word for the baton an orchestra leader uses to establish speed or flow. Lean uses the concept of *takt* to establish the steady rate at which a completed product needs to be finished. The customer buying rate, or demand, establishes the *takt* time given some level of resources.

Takt time is a function of demand and available time. The *takt* time for the receiving process is 150 minutes, or 3600 available minutes for work divided by 24 trailers per day. This means a trailer should flow into a receiving line every 150 minutes, or 2.5 hours. *Takt* time must be adjusted as available time (such as with overtime) and/or trailers (demand) fluctuates. Whenever *takt* time is less than processing time, bottlenecks are the likely result. It is impractical to bring a trailer in for processing when the *takt* time is shorter than the processing time (150 minutes takt time versus 215 minutes processing time).

The listed times for each activity within the receiving process include some nonvalue-added time or outright waste. A portion of the switcher's time to remove and then spot a new trailer, for example, is spent going into the office to find out what trailer to move from the dock and retrieve from the yard. The switcher is also a friendly guy who likes to talk with the office personnel. Part of the 45 minutes, on average, to receive and print move tickets is spent waiting for a clerk or a printer to become available (think of an in-basket). Each activity can be further broken down into its discrete elements for further analysis. Recall that this issue was raised in Chapter 7 when discussing process modeling and redesign.

The following are some ideas that support a redesigned receiving process. Some of these recommendations are relatively short term and lower cost. Some are clearly longer term and may require a commitment of financial resources. Others may not stand a chance of ever being implemented. While the actual throughput rate of this facility is only 17 trailers per day (without overtime and weekends), the theoretical rate is likely 50 or more trailers per day.

Strive for Worker Flexibility

The first thing we should notice about this process is the narrow scope of work each employee performs. Even though the employees, except for the inspector, are the same job classification, this facility has allowed itself to become too specialized and inflexible. Is there any reason that every employee can't perform every task? At times there may be five trailers at the dock waiting to be unloaded. Unfortunately, only two people operate the material handling equipment that is used to unload the trailers. Other employees sit idle or perform busy work as they wait for a trailer to be unloaded.

A radical change would be to assign an employee to each inbound line. Each employee will perform all the duties required to unload and process a trailer (a later suggestion will discuss eliminating the inspection process). Of course, the employees will likely object to these changes, which is to be expected. One conclusion is clear, however; this workforce is too highly specialized and inflexible, which is not a characteristic of a lean supply chain.

It is possible the facility will have to purchase more material handling equipment to accommodate each line if employee duties are expanded.[3] Additional charging stations might also be needed. At times capital investment is needed to achieve our lean objectives. A return-on-investment (ROI) analysis will determine if this is a viable option.

Streamline the IT Process

The processing of incoming trailers is far too manual and paper driven. A logical action is to require suppliers and carriers to provide advance notices of all incoming shipments. Advance shipment notices (ASNs) from suppliers are essentially an electronic bill of lading that a customer receives in advance of a supplier's shipment. ASNs allow a receiving operation to see what is on an incoming trailer and to receive that trailer's content list before it physically arrives. By the time the trailer arrives, all necessary documents, such as move tickets, can be available. This supports the lean practice of planning and staging.

Using electronic documents will eliminate the need to handle multiple copies of shipping documents. Seamless linkages with the accounts payable system along with the electronic transfer of funds to suppliers will further remove waste from the receiving and payment system.

The receiving office could also consider faster printers, which would further streamline the processing time per trailer. Managers could also investigate the purchase of extra printers to increase printing capacity. Of course, the ultimate scenario is for suppliers to attach any move tickets to the load before they are sent to the distribution center. While this may work well in a manufacturing environment, this work center presents some challenges. Loads received at this facility can be broken down for several dozen different downstream locations. Furthermore, the receiving process benefits from up-to-the-minute information concerning how much material to send or allocate to the downstream centers.

Another system enhancement should be the development of an efficient way to record any quality problems with suppliers. This information is needed to target improvement efforts and to identify those suppliers that are exempt from incoming inspection.

Pursue Nonverbal Communication

Nonverbal communication is highly consistent with a lean philosophy. At this facility the switcher's physical presence in the office is not only inefficient, it is a distraction to other employees. There are a number of creative and low cost ways to make this employee more productive. An obvious improvement is to communicate with the switcher via a walkie-talkie phone. The receiving office simply relays to the switcher the next truck to take out or bring to a receiving dock.

If ASNs are available, an even more sophisticated system would prioritize the trucks in the yard to ensure the most critical material is placed at the dock. A nonverbal communication system might feature a message board placed in a location where the switcher can easily see it. The board would display the order of trailers to retrieve for unloading. Or, the switching truck could have a laptop computer that displays the sequence of trailers to bring to a receiving dock. This system could even be available for the attendant or guard at the gate when he or she acknowledges the arrival of a trailer. If the contents of a trailer are critical, the gate attendant can direct the driver to a spot that is close to the receiving dock. Once the receiving system becomes more efficient, the guard could direct the driver to place the trailer at an open dock door.

A kanban system can also be used to communicate when a trailer should be removed from the dock. A red and green light can be placed by each dock door. A green light means that an empty trailer is ready to be safely removed and a full trailer needs to be retrieved. While other nonverbal communication opportunities are available, you get the idea.

Reduce Nonvalue-Added Activities

A number of activities in this process are not providing much of a payback given the resources they consume. In particular, (1) checking the load quantities before generating move tickets and then (2) inspecting 100 percent of incoming material before moving it downstream are candidates for elimination. These two activities consume almost 30 percent of the 215 minutes of total processing time.

Perhaps the largest nonvalue-added activity is the matching of shipping documents to the load quantities before printing move tickets. In reality few quantity discrepancies occur in this system. Furthermore, if a discrepancy exists the employee that attaches the physical move ticket should discover the discrepancy.

Any discrepancies that are discovered should be tracked and their root cause identified and eliminated.

An absence of adding any value also holds true for physical inspection. Inspecting 100 percent of incoming material for damage and defects is not at all consistent with the lean objective of striving for excellence. Companies that practice Total Quality Management believe in preventing defects rather than inspecting for defects. Inspection is a drag on flow.

There are a number of ways to exit the inspection business. One way is to certify a supplier's quality performance, either through site visits or through historical performance. Suppliers that are exempt from inspection can be noted in a database. Unfortunately, in this system no data are collected during the inspection process, which limits the use of historical performance information.

Inspection, if performed at all, should be by exception rather than by rule. The employee that hangs the move tickets could perform a cursory material check. Or, a database of historical supplier performance can be developed that places suppliers into one of three categories: (1) green, (2) yellow, or (3) red. Green suppliers are the highest performers and require no incoming inspection, except perhaps for a cursory damage check. Yellow suppliers are marginal and require some degree of inspection, perhaps through random sampling. Red suppliers require 100 percent inspection based on historical performance. If these yellow and red suppliers do not improve their performance they become candidates for elimination.

Perform Some Tasks Concurrently Rather than Sequentially

The idea of concurrency does not receive enough attention during lean discussions. During product development, for example, the overlapping of various design activities is well understood as a way to reduce product and process development time. This same logic of concurrent or overlapping activities applies in this receiving process.

Think about the printing of move tickets. While some may argue the wastefulness of paper tickets, anyone who has worked in a complex distribution center knows that moving material without some type of control document is asking for trouble. Actually, these tickets are quite compatible with lean. These programmatically generated tickets are a form of nonverbal communication that efficiently tells employees what to do with each item. How much material should go to the export line? How much should be cross docked for immediate shipment to the regional centers? Does the material require packaging?

The processing of paperwork in the receiving office requires, on average, about 20 percent of the total processing time per trailer. While this processing occurs, inbound material sits in a receiving line, which ties up valuable dock space and severely limits throughput and capacity. A better approach would be to print all move tickets before the trailer is even spotted at a receiving dock. Any quantity discrepancies that are discovered between the move tickets and the physical loads can be handled later with a simple receiving discrepancy transaction. This approach should become the normal operating procedure if we are doing business with reliable suppliers. Preprinting any move tickets should reduce the total processing time by 45 minutes.

Expand Less-than-Truckload Shipments

It is not unreasonable to put forth the idea of more frequent deliveries of smaller quantities from suppliers, a component of lean supply presented in Chapter 2. Care will have to be taken to ensure that expanding LTL shipments does not shift the constraint from the full trailer receiving lines to the LTL receiving lines. This company might even want to consider working with a third-party logistics (3PL) provider to develop a closed-loop delivery system featuring returnable containers.

Balance and Schedule Full Truckload Deliveries

The imbalance of shipments throughout a month is a serious issue. Recall from Chapter 4 that level scheduling is an important element of lean operations. At times this facility is paying huge amounts of overtime; at other times it has huge amounts of idletime.

This company should form a high-powered team and charge it with leveling the flow of inbound material over the course of a month. Participants should include operations managers, who are responsible for running the central facility; material planners, who are responsible for forecasting and generating material releases to suppliers; IT personnel, who will be important if information system changes are made; and procurement and transportation managers, who will have to manage any issues with suppliers and carriers. Smart people who know how to develop scheduling algorithms should also be part of this effort. Level scheduling must become a major objective.

Improve the Organizational Design

A possible consequence from an improved receiving process is that inbound material moves so fast through receiving that downstream work centers are unable to handle the work flow. This would shift the bottleneck from receiving to a point(s) elsewhere in the central facility. This would reinforce the notion that this is a giant push facility.

Executive managers should form an operations group that meets every morning to evaluate the sequence of trailers to bring into the facility. This assumes this group has visibility to what is on each trailer. Furthermore, the operations group should have visibility to trailers expected to arrive throughout the next several days. Besides receiving personnel, this group should include representatives from other work centers within the central facility.

This group should develop priority logic that programmatically sequences the unloading of trailers. Trailers with the most critical material, such as customer backorders, should be unloaded first. Trailers that have material for work centers that are short of work might be next. The last trailers to be brought in for unloading might be those that have material destined for work centers that are currently backlogged. The system can also consider the age of trailers and factor in possible demurrage charges. Because this approach considers the needs of downstream work centers, it begins to move the central facility toward pull rather than push on the push/pull continuum.

Measure Receiving Performance

An important theme presented in Chapter 6 is that measurement is critical to lean success. This facility needs a set of measures that will provide insight into the receiving process. Some possible inbound processing measures include the following:

- **Days workload pending in yard.** This measure reflects the number of receiving days that the trailers in the yard represent. For example, 55 trailers in the yard waiting to be unloaded represent 3.23 days worth of work at the receiving dock (assuming a capacity of 17 trailers per day with the existing system).
- **Percent of material or trailers received via ASNs.** This type of measure reflects how well this facility is removing paperwork and transactions from the receiving process.
- **Percent of material bypassing inspection.** This reflects the amount of inbound material that is not subject to inbound inspection, a major impediment to supply chain flow.
- **On-time arrivals.** This includes a comparison of on-time material deliveries from suppliers and carriers compared to a promised delivery time.
- **Supplier quality discrepancies.** This measure reflects any defects other than late arrivals received from suppliers. Ideally this metric is reported in parts-per-million opportunities (ppmo). Defects may include incorrect quantities, labeling or documentation errors, and damaged or faulty goods.

- **Average total system time per trailer.** This represents the total elapsed time for trailers from receipt into the yard through completed processing at receiving.
- **Average processing time per trailer.** This represents the total elapsed time from placing a trailer at an inbound line through processing.
- **Direct labor hours per trailer.** This measure tracks the direct labor hours required to process an inbound trailer.
- **Percent of trailers moving directly to the receiving dock.** A future ideal is to manage a balanced receiving system that no longer requires holding trailers in a yard. This measure reflects the percent of trailers entering the central facility's property and moving directly to an empty receiving dock.

Bypass Material Receiving Lines

At some point someone should ask why material is staged in receipt lines. Why can't an employee transport the material from an inbound trailer directly to the AGV area that forwards the material further downstream? Any move tickets could potentially be affixed at a location away from the inbound receiving lines, such as in the AGV area. Material that is not moved via an AGV could be moved by material handling equipment to its next destination within the facility. Each material stopping point detracts from flow and material throughput.

Ship Some Items Directly from Suppliers to Regional Centers

An idea that could reduce incoming volume is to investigate if opportunities exist to ship some items directly from suppliers to the regional facilities, thereby bypassing the national center. One outcome of this would be a greater use of LTL shipments as material moves in smaller quantities from suppliers to regional centers. A total cost analysis would have to support the business case for not using the cross-docking capabilities at the national center. Supply chain planners would also have to determine the capacity of regional centers to manage additional LTL shipments. The willingness of suppliers to make LTL shipments to regional facilities instead of a single truckload shipment to a central facility will also be an issue. This might be a realistic option for bulkier items that consume valuable floor space and handling time in the central facility. Total system throughput might also be faster for items that are shipped directly to regional centers.

Evaluate RFID Applicability

New paperless technologies, such as radio frequency identification (RFID) tags should be explored to determine their applicability. An inbound load or trailer could pass through an RFID portal, which would trigger the receipt of an item and start the printing of move tickets. This would eliminate the need for office staff to manually receive trailers as well as the travel time to and from the receiving office. As one employee removes a load from a trailer a second employee can immediately affix a move ticket. At some point all the moves within the facility might be controlled with RFID tags rather than bar-coded move tickets.

CONCLUDING THOUGHTS

This process requires a realistic plan to increase the flow of inbound material through the receiving process. Eliminating the checking of physical quantities, eliminating, or at least sharply reducing inspections, and preprinting move tickets before placing the trailer at the dock offer the most immediate opportunities. These three changes will remove as much as 105 minutes from the process. The new processing time would be 110 minutes per trailer, on average. This makes the new receiving dock capacity to be almost 33 trailers per day (3600 total available minutes divided by 105 process minutes per trailer). After the lower cost/higher impact ideas are addressed, supply chain planners can begin to pursue the longer-term or resource intensive changes.

The recommendations presented here are certainly not a complete set. Those who are familiar with receiving operations could identify dozens of other potential ideas, many of which have not been discussed here. The challenge is to tap into the creative thinking that is too often bottled up inside employees or is constrained by existing ways of doing business. Methodologies that promote outside the box thinking, such as brainstorming sessions, may be the most powerful tools that exist today. Innovative thinking should be a major part of lean.

ENDNOTES

1. The lean application presented here is somewhat different from those presented earlier. This application can be used for training or as a teaching exercise. While recommendations are provided with this analysis, they can be omitted for the purpose of group discussion.

2. While this lean application is based on the operations of an actual company, the company name has been changed.

3. To view different kinds of material handling equipment visit http://www.crown.com, www.raymond.com, or northamerica.yale.com.

EPILOGUE

It would be incomplete to end this book without some closing thoughts. After everything is said and done, a handful of important ideas or themes capture the reality of lean management as it should be practiced today. While these themes are simple, their message is so powerful that they should guide lean efforts at the corporate level. They reflect the need to shift our thinking about lean from a focus on techniques endorsed by manufacturing firms to a broad-based philosophy endorsed by any organization.

With that said, an appropriate starting theme is that lean is a *philosophy rather than a set of techniques*. This philosophy, which must become an ingrained part of an organization's culture, states that an organization will relentlessly pursue and attack sources of waste wherever they exist. While the early days of lean focused extensively on techniques, and applying these techniques can deliver some tangible performance benefits, never lose sight of the need to view lean as a philosophy that executive leaders must endorse and convey. This philosophy includes an inherent belief that lean is a worthwhile pursuit, and that we can and we will become better because of this pursuit. This belief is one that executive leaders must communicate in no uncertain terms within an organization as well as across the supply chain.

It's also important to remember that *the pursuit of lean management is an end-to-end undertaking*, a second important theme. Chapter 1 revealed how some parts of the supply chain don't receive much, if any, attention in terms of lean management. Since the next generation of lean performance improvements will likely be outside of internal operations, the time has come to expand our lean horizons. Unfortunately, previous research and writing, consulting, and other forms of business development support (such as state-supported manufacturing resource centers) still present a narrow and often disconnected view of lean. To many observers lean is about what happens within our own four walls. While what happens internally is important, today's version of lean management demands an end-to-end view that includes supply, transportation, and distribution.

A third theme recognizes the universal application of lean. Organizations must *pursue a lean model that best fits their unique requirements*. Not every organization has to follow the Toyota model, and not every organization is a manufacturer. This book presented dozens of examples that featured nonmanufacturing firms or examples that focused on some part of the supply chain other than internal manufacturing operations. The need to reduce waste is universal, and every organization has waste somewhere within its supply chain. Take the time to understand lean principles, create the model that works best for you, and relentlessly pursue lean improvements.

Fourth, *lean is everyone's concern*. It's tempting to create a new position such as a lean czar or champion and charge that individual with the daunting task of making lean a reality. Unfortunately, the success record for such positions, whether these individuals are placed in charge of total quality or identified as the organizational guru for the theory of constraints, is not all that great. While attractive in theory, these positions usually lack the resources and authority to make meaningful changes across well-protected functional turfs. Most internal observers are content letting someone else carry the lean banner, and conversely, suffer the consequences when long-lasting success proves elusive. Lean is organizational, which implies that participants at all levels and locations must have a vested interest in its success.

Perhaps the most important theme, and one that will be expanded here, is that *lean management is a continuous journey*. A fitting comparison is between lean and Total Quality Management. During an interview several years ago an executive was asked to discuss the quality initiatives his company had put forth to ensure customers receive defect-free products. He responded quickly that his company had "this quality thing licked." This executive wanted to talk about the more current and exciting initiatives his firm was pursuing. Talking about quality was so 1980s and 1990s. But does an organization ever achieve total quality, or for that matter, lean? If so, why did *Industry Week* recently feel the need to present a cover story titled "Whatever Happened to Quality"?[1] And why did Toyota recall more models in the United States than it sold in the United States during a recent year? High-profile lapses in product and service quality are not hard to find. Simply open the newspaper.

---

1. See B. Kenney, "Whatever Happened to Quality?," *Industry Week* (April 2008).

If we think continuous improvement is not that important, consider the following example. In 2003, consumers responding to the JD Powers automotive quality survey bestowed upon Kia the dubious honor of being the lowest-ranked automotive brand in terms of defects per 100 vehicles (and from Chapter 1 we know that defects are a prime source of waste). By 2007, consumers reported that Kia had reduced its defects per 100 vehicles by 40 percent, an impressive achievement when looking at this statistic in isolation. But, guess what? Even with a 40 percent improvement Kia still found itself as one of the lowest rated automotive brands in the JD Power survey. It seems the other 35 or so brands that consumers can choose from were not content with simply maintaining the status quo in terms of their quality performance.

The moral of this story is that only a fool doubts the need for continuous improvement. While the scale of improvements should diminish over time as the most obvious opportunities are worked, the inherent need for improvement never goes away. Imagine the quality gap if Kia chose not to pursue continuous improvement while its competitors kept charging along!

The danger that an organization faces when it believes it has achieved something as important as lean (or Total Quality, for that matter) is that the organization begins to divert its resources to other endeavors. Employees become lax, perhaps even complacent, when thinking about lean. And while these other endeavors are likely worthwhile, this diversion initiates something called *entropy*. Entropy means that any process or system left unattended, and make no mistake that lean management is a process, reverts toward disorganization and chaos. It is easy to predict that when resources are diverted away from critical initiatives such as lean, an organization begins its performance journey backward. Will we be asking in the next few years what happened to lean?

Most organizational leaders would benefit from a healthy dose of paranoia as they scan their competitive landscape. Just because you are paranoid doesn't mean they really aren't out to get you. Make no mistake about it—other companies covet your customers and market share as much as you do. Global business is as tough as it has ever been, and rest assured they are out to get you. Lean management will help ensure your organization does not succumb to the wrath of angry customers or become a victim of aggressive competitors. Today's realities demand that lean management not be a halfhearted pursuit. It is a strategic necessity that warrants the full attention and resources of executive leaders, today and tomorrow.

INDEX